Free, Equal and Mutual

Rebalancing Society for the Common Good

Martin Large & Steve Briault, editors

Hawthorn Press

CONTENTS

FOREWORD — Nicanor Perlas — 6
INTRODUCTION — Steve Briault and Martin Large — 12

PART ONE — PERSPECTIVES ON SOCIETAL THREEFOLDING

CHAPTER 1 **Rudolf Steiner's Threefold Image of a Healthy Society**
Steve Briault — 23

CHAPTER 2 **Images of the Human Being and Their Effect on Humanity's Relationship to Power**
Andrew Scott — 34

CHAPTER 3 **Nine Propositions in Search of a Threefold Social Order**
Christopher Schaefer — 44

CHAPTER 4 **Threefold Development at Work in Organizations**
Steve Briault — 59

CHAPTER 5 **A Primary Approach to Threefold Thinking – or Red and Blue, and the Lost Primary**
John Bloom — 67

CHAPTER 6 **Rudolf Steiner and Social Threefolding during and after the First World War**
Edward Udell — 75

PART TWO — THE CHALLENGES

CHAPTER 7 **Rebalancing Society for the Common Good**
Martin Large — 99

CHAPTER 8 **The Dance of Shadows in America: Reflections on the US Presidential Election of 2016**
Christopher Schaefer — 117

CHAPTER 9 **Great Again? Thoughts about the World Situation**
Gerald Häfner — 127

PART THREE   INSPIRED INITIATIVES

CHAPTER 10   SEKEM – A Model for Holistic Sustainable Development in Egypt
Christine Arlt   139

CHAPTER 11   A New American Revolution? Associative Economics and the Future of the Food Movement
Robert Karp   153

CHAPTER 12   Land for People, Homes, Farms and Communities
Martin Large   168

CHAPTER 13   Toxic Excess: Income Inequalities and the Fundamental Social Law
Christopher Schaefer   182

CHAPTER 14   Education beyond Capital and the Neoliberal State: Challenging the 'Academizing' of England's Schools
Richard House   194

CHAPTER 15   Money and the Threefold Social Order Movement
Glen Saunders   211

PART FOUR   OPENINGS FOR CO-CREATING OUR SOCIAL FUTURE

CHAPTER 16   Three Conversations: Human Encounter in Threefold Society
Steve Briault   223

CHAPTER 17   How Threefolding Fits – or Not – with Current Political Ideologies, and Dialogue in Threefolding Developments: An Interview
Christoph Strawe with Martin Large   235

CONCLUSION Telling a New Free, Equal, Mutual and Earth-caring Story
Martin Large   250

ABOUT THE CONTRIBUTORS   258

INDEX   263

FOREWORD

Nicanor Perlas

The world today is in chaos. Serious problems plague humanity. Challenges abound, including climate change, massive species extinction, terrorism, poverty, a massive disparity between the rich and the poor, unstable economic systems, and irresponsible governance – to name just a few.

And newly arisen on the horizon is the unprecedented and wide-ranging disruption stemming from the rapid deployment of artificial intelligence in all walks of life. The obvious extensive benefits of this technology are accompanied by negative consequences. These include the intentional manipulation by tech giants of billions of human beings towards addictive behaviour, especially by Apple, Google and Facebook; deep intrusion into the privacy of humans all over the planet; the threat of massive unemployment levels in the tens of millions – a threat that is already starting to manifest; and the extinction of humanity itself in the event of a single mistake in the deployment of artificial super intelligence (ASI) (on which, see below).

All of these problems arise from the inaccurate and downgraded image of the human being, society and nature that millions have internalized and made a crucial part of their belief systems and behaviour. In addition, millions, knowingly or unknowingly, have created and are creating, or participating in, the creation of societal structures that reinforce this inaccurate and degraded version of reality. Furthermore, a tiny privileged and powerful minority make practically all key decisions that animate these worldviews, values and structures that bring so much suffering to the world. Several contributors to *Free, equal and mutual* also point these questions out very clearly in their chapters in this book.

One systemic solution exists that, given the opportunity, can creatively address all these challenges. That solution is societal threefolding and the worldview and values that are implicit within it.

What societal threefolding consists in – its nature, history, present practices, challenges, achievements and future prospects – is the subject of this groundbreaking book. It is nothing less than an inspiring and wide-ranging articulation of societal threefolding in the context of the challenges and possibilities of the twenty-first century.

The book is full of concrete and exciting examples of threefolding at the organizational and sub-sectoral levels. Examples of the latter involve education initiatives, community supported agriculture (CSA) towards an associative economics, community land trusts, ethical banking, finance, philanthropy, and Sekem – a far-more comprehensive manifestation in the attempt to achieve sustainable development in the deserts of Egypt.

It is also clear from this book that the threefolding paradigm has the power to bring insight into current world events, such as the Trump phenomenon, global developments from a European perspective, a deeper understanding of money and blockchain technology, as a number of contributors have shown in this book. And it is also clear that the pioneers of organizational, meso-level and sub-sectoral threefolding have provided fertile grounds for the rapid adoption of similar-level threefolding approaches in many other areas of life. Robust working models, properly adapted to fit differing contexts, are ready and available.

The remaining frontier of societal threefolding is its application at the macro or societal level involving diverse groups of sectors, and involving much larger numbers of people. That would be the next step towards ultimately threefolding an entire country.

The threefolding approach, at the macro or societal level, encourages and harnesses the participation of all key actors in the functional subsystems of society – businesses in the realm of the economic, governments in the realm of polity, and civil society in the realm of culture.

The key ingredient of making societal threefolding work is the activation and engagement of civil society – the relatively undeveloped, under-financed, unstable and volatile sector of society. Despite these hindrances, civil society has demonstrated in many settings around the world its capacity to constructively and partially address the many challenges of our time. Without an organized, cohesive and engaged civil society, there can be no effective societal threefolding process, and the world's challenges will not only remain, but will worsen.

Nonetheless, key individuals, groups and movements have planted the seeds for on-the-ground, macro societal threefolding. Possibly the most advanced of these efforts at macro-level societal threefolding as inspired by Rudolf Steiner is taking place in the Philippines. In this country, macro societal threefolding initiatives have started to take root in towns and cities, collectively numbering over 200,000 residents.

The most advanced of these efforts in conscious threefolding is taking place in Bayawan City, Negros Oriental, with over 120,000 residents. The city has just allocated over P1 billion pesos ($20 million) of its budget to fund programmes and projects identified in a societal threefolding process involving key sectors of business, government and civil society. The top leadership of the government itself convened and facilitated the threefolding initiative, including the City Mayor and his top aides, assisted by a formal, legally mandated threefold council.

This initiative is by no means perfect, but it is a very promising beginning. Already, dozens of mayors of towns and cities have expressed their interest in undertaking societal threefolding processes in order to craft their sustainable integrated area development (SIAD) plans. The Philippine Development Plan (2017–2022), the official medium-term strategic plan of the entire government, explicitly mentions threefolding and SIAD. And an entire government agency of the Philippine government, the Department of Environment and Natural Resources (DENR), has adopted SIAD and threefolding as its strategy for achieving environmental protection and sustainable development.

There are other threefolding-like initiatives sprouting up in many parts of the world and at different scales and levels, including at the macro level. These initiatives are commonly referred to by other names. Some of these are trisectoral partnerships (academe), solutions revolution (journalism), innovation ecosystems (Silicon Valley), public policy network (UN), collective impact (Stanford University), solution ecosystems (Philippines), impact investing (US State Department), creative capitalism (business, Bill Gates), convergence (government) and collective intelligence (civil society).

Whatever the proponents call them and the nomenclature used, all of these attempts have an explicit recognition of the importance of bringing together the collective wisdom of the three key sectors of civil society, business and government for developing constructive and creative solutions to the issues and challenges of the times. For example, they may begin from the business side, but then move on to constructively engage government and civil society – this is impact investing. Or they may start from government that then engages business and civil society. This is the UN's public policy network paradigm. Or it may begin from civil society that then acts as a backbone organization towards the meaningful participation of governments and civil society. This is the solution the ecosystems framework.

These efforts have arisen because more and more key leaders in business, government and civil society are recognizing that we are living in a 'VUCA' world, where VUCA stands for a world that is Volatile, Uncertain (also Unpredictable), Complex, and Ambiguous. No single sector of society has the answer to a VUCA issue: not government, not business, not civil society. Instead, leaders and societal innovators are realizing that comprehensive tri-sectoral conversations and deep engagements are critical to emerging collective human intelligence (CHI) that has the power to address the massive and potentially disastrous challenges facing humanity, including climate change and artificial super intelligence (ASI).

Societal threefolding will be critical in addressing the deep and complex problems of our time. This is going to be particularly significant in the field of ASI. Already, AI experts are calling for worldwide, cross-sectoral consultations, involving the most diverse societal identities, in order to find a creative solution to the so-called 'alignment' challenge in deploying ASI. If humanity does not solve this problem in a 10–20 year window of time (the average estimate), then humanity faces the danger of all-out extinction.

No one in the world currently knows how to solve the challenge of making sure that AI goals are aligned with human values and goals. AI has reached a point where smarter versions of AI can change their own programming in a non-transparent manner (genetic or evolutionary algorithms), a reprogramming that may not be aligned to the original programmes that humans have given to the AI. Facebook had to shut down its AI when it faced a version of this problem. But the more advanced versions of AI in the future will not be able to be shut down as easily as the Facebook example.

There is one final comment that needs to be made. A unique value of this book is that it gives a rare picture of Rudolf Steiner, the founder and articulator of the threefolding approach, as a societal activist. He dared to step out of his comfort zone of immense cultural and spiritual creativity in order to advocate deep and strategic policy initiatives, in the sphere of polity, to the top leaders of the Austrian and German empires. He did this while remaining clearly and consciously within the cultural sphere. He thus gave an early example of how to engage in politics while remaining solidly within the cultural sphere.

As a guide to helping civil society activists avoid being infected with RUST (or the 'residue of unresolved statism'), I have elaborated on this important point in an earlier book, *Shaping globalization: Civil society, cultural power and threefolding*. RUST is the mistaken belief that power to change societies lies only in the state. In this book, I point out that civil society wields cultural power in contradistinction to the economic power of business and the coercive power of government. In addition, if there is a conflict between *organized* civil society and the government/business tandem, civil society often wins out in the end. There is no need for civil society actors to crave for state or economic power.

This is the basis for the earlier statement that an organized civil society is crucial and necessary in order to realize macro-level societal threefolding processes and substance.

Steiner thus demonstrated the powerful creative impact of an organized cultural civil society force in the societal agenda of his times. He did this with his books, memoranda, lectures, articles, and an Appeal memorandum, which latter was signed by thousands of prominent German citizens, among them many prominent people. This signed Appeal memorandum had a significant impact on his society during his time even if it did not result in the societal threefolding of Germany in his time. Even *The New York Times* has picked up the uniqueness and importance of its threefolding innovation, in January 1923 reviewing Rudolf Steiner's book *Towards social renewal* (publ. 1917), remarking on its '…novelty and bigness as a contribution to sociological literature – the most original contribution in a generation'.

In conclusion, Steiner developed societal threefolding in the war-torn Germany of 1917–19 as a non-ideological alternative to Bolshevism, state socialism, capitalism, imperialism and nationalism. He saw the dangerous potential of toxic nationalism for more war in President Wilson's 'national self determination' which became enshrined by the 1919 Treaty of Versailles. *Free, equal and mutual* shows how today, societal threefolding can build the conditions for lasting peace through untangling the current muddle of economics, politics and culture. This will in turn enable the business or the private sector, the state or public sector and the civil society or plural sector to contribute their strengths to rebalancing society for the common good.

We are living in a crisis-ridden, 'Brexit and Trump' time, with the rise again of toxic nationalism and populism, and with both Britain and the USA and also countries of the EU exploring their social futures. This affords a golden opportunity for re-imagining a Europe – and a world – with distinct but connected vibrant narratives of cultural flourishing, of respecting fundamental human rights, of thriving social businesses, and of care for the planet which is our common home.

Nicanor Perlas
Holder of a Right Livelihood Award 2003 (Alternative Nobel Prize) and UNEP's Global 500 Award

Manila, Philippines
2 March 2018

INTRODUCTION

Steve Briault and Martin Large

Justice is what love looks like in public.
Cornel West

Neoliberalism is what lovelessness looks like as policy.
Naomi Klein

The election of Donald Trump in 2016 was the culmination of a decade and a half of renewed assertiveness on the part of the neoliberal agenda. Neoliberalism is predatory capitalism, the doctrine that 'the market is always right, regulation is always wrong, private is good and public is bad, and taxes that support public services are worst of all'.[1] Central to this ideology is protecting the interests of corporations against those of governments, workers and citizens, and denial of anthropogenic climate change. But rescuing the environment from its current precarious situation on the verge of large-scale collapse cannot be left to the market. It requires far-reaching multinational agreements that would inevitably limit the ability of corporations to marketize natural resources – thus threatening the trillions of profits to be obtained from ecocidal practices around the globe.

The dissatisfaction and anti-establishment feeling that enabled 'a kleptocratic thug to grab the world's most powerful job as if it were a hostess at a strip club'[2] – and which at least partly underlay the Brexit referendum result – also led to a surprise resurgence in the popularity of socialist politicians such as Bernie Sanders in the USA and Jeremy Corbyn in Britain, who offered what looked like a real alternative to mainstream 'business as usual'. However, it is all too easy to ridicule and undermine the track record of the state management of national economies and to highlight the threat of tax rises which a left-wing agenda may invoke. The pro-business social-democratic consensus maintained in the 1990s by Bill Clinton and Tony Blair – in hindsight, always a precarious compromise – has been superseded by the increasing polarization and fragmentation which have been effectively exploited by the far right in the USA and, to a lesser but still significant extent, in the UK and Europe.

As argued throughout this book, our society is out of balance: the two-legged stool of business and state cannot create stability or security without the inclusion of an independent cultural or plural sector and a realignment of the relationships between these three pillars.

In this context, the image of a threefold organization of society described in this book takes on a new relevance and urgency. Neither the left nor the right wings of contemporary politics – nor, indeed, the hopelessly compromised 'centrist' politicians – can offer a compelling and credible alternative to the perilous situation which the world now faces. Unlike the notions of previous UK prime ministers – Tony Blair's illusory 'third way' or David Cameron's ineffective 'big society' – social threefolding is not a mixture of, or a compromise between, capitalism and state control; it is a radical realignment of the fundamental elements of social life to allow each of them – culture, politics and economy – to express itself in a healthy and humane way. Although inevitably still untested on the macro-social scale, the thinking behind Rudolf Steiner's proposals has proved fruitful in many innovative social initiatives – such as in education, banking and farming – several of which are described in this volume, alongside more general articulations of the key concepts. The editors and authors hope that the book will provoke both thought and action towards the rebalancing of society for the common good that is so urgently needed.

The publication of *Free, equal and mutual* marks the centenary of Rudolf Steiner's articulation of societal threefolding in 1917, in war-torn Germany. We asked a variety of people who are working with these ideas to write a contribution drawing on Rudolf Steiner's vision for a free, equal, fraternal/mutual society. Our burning question was, 'How can Steiner's social thinking help us now in practical terms?'.

So why this book now? Whilst humanity faces a perfect storm of challenges such as global warming, the 'war on terror' which has had such disastrous consequences, and massive inequality, we also see everywhere signs of hope, of social, cultural and economic renewal. People are waking up and becoming active in a global 'blessed unrest' of serving the common good for planet and people.[3] For example, the record-breaking round-the-world yachtswoman Ellen MacArthur's transformation

> started on a trip to South Georgia, a desolate island in the south Atlantic, where she helped with an albatross survey. 'It made me stop and think. It gave me space and time to see things differently; to realise things I hadn't let into my head before.' The sight of so many abandoned whaling stations, an industry destroyed by exploitation and greed, struck her as a warning. 'It seemed as though we had just taken what we wanted and moved on. That's what we do.'[4]

MacArthur created a Foundation for researching, re-thinking, re-designing and building a positive future through developing a circular, regenerative economy.

Rudolf Steiner (1863–1925) was an Austrian philosopher and spiritual thinker who founded Waldorf education, biodynamic agriculture and anthroposophic medicine, and who inspired ethical banking and encouraged social business. However, Steiner was also an activist who proposed to the Chancellor of the German government in 1917 a 'threefold social order' to address the growing social breakdown, and to build a more peaceful, prosperous, inclusive and just society. This was intended as a human-centred alternative to the bureaucratic despotism of the imperial German state, to Bolshevik communism, and to US President Wilson's proposal for 'national self-determination' which Steiner saw as an invitation to backward-looking, toxic nationalism and, thus, further war.

Figure I.1: President Wilson; Lenin; Hitler; Rudolf Steiner

This war was not inevitable

Steiner saw that the 'nation state' structure constricted the movement towards more human freedom and individuation. States were too big for the small problems, and too small for the big challenges. He saw the need for a growing differentiation between an associative, fraternal world economy for business, a human rights-led politics for states, and cultural freedom 'without borders' for education, arts, religion and health. People could engage as citizens in politics and the rights life, as producers and/or consumers in the economy, and as individuals in cultural life. This 'threefold social order', or dynamic societal threefolding, emerges from the interaction of business, government and cultural life. This would enable each sector – public (state), private (business) and plural (cultural) – to flourish in its own right; a free, equal and mutual society. Such tri-sectoral thinking resurfaced from 1989 when the Eastern European communist countries were rebalanced by a resurgent plural, civil society, and then when the toxic World Trade Organization treaty which threatened to embed the secretive corporate capture of governments was overturned by plural, civil society at the 1999 Battle of Seattle.

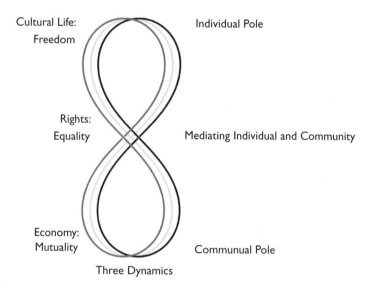

FIGURE I.2: SOCIAL THREEFOLDING: CULTURE, RIGHTS AND ECONOMY

Steiner's innovative approach to the optimal developmental conditions for cultural, political and economic life was based on his profound understanding of the human being. He rejected the competitive, greed is good, 'rational economic man' image in favour of a creative, spiritual, ethical, social, anti-social, enterprising and mutual image. He drew upon the ideals of the French Revolution, of *liberté* (freedom), *égalité* (equality), and *fraternité* (brotherhood) – yet applied them in a new way.

In order to develop and maintain a dynamic and just life across all of society, Steiner indicated that freedom is the key principle in the domain of culture and spirit, equality in the domain of rights and agreements, and brotherhood in economics. This threesome of practice is the foundation for organizing an empowered, self-governing citizenry that would find its authority, responsibility and accountability through active civic engagement. Further, such a threefold practice would assure that every person matters, and that what matters to each person matters to the whole. Where individuals sought to develop and maintain their creative potential in cultural life, Steiner saw the tendency to individualism, to selfish behaviour. However, the antidote to this is our work in the modern economy where the complex division of labour means that we have to learn how to collaborate in serving the needs of others.

In January 1923, the *New York Times* reviewed Rudolf Steiner's book *Towards social renewal* (1917), remarking on its '…novelty and bigness as a contribution to sociological literature – the most original contribution in a generation'. But how relevant is societal threefolding today? The maps, ideas and examples in this book offer stimulus and inspiration for people engaged with social, cultural, ecological and economic change.

Overview: How to Use This Book

This anthology is designed as a handy reference to be dipped into, sparked by readers' questions and interests. Students taking courses and study groups can read a particular chapter to prepare for a session. Many of the contributions include follow-up references. Ideas such as these often need testing out through action research and practice in order to be really understood. For example, it took our UK-based Community Land Trust National Demonstration Projects some years of piloting to work out practically how land trusteeship works.

Part 1: Perspectives on Societal Threefolding

'Rudolf Steiner's Threefold Image of a Healthy Society', with 'Threefold Development at Work in Organizations', together set out the fundamental insights which underpin this book, in both macro-social and meso-social contexts. Steve Briault has worked for over 40 years in organizational, management and community development, drawing on such ideas in his work.

Andrew Scott explores 'Images of the Human Being and Their Effect on Humanity's Relationship to Power.' He argues that hidden assumptions of the nature of human beings shape the social forms in which we live and suggests that we shift our focus towards the arrangement of power within society, our own communities and organizations by taking hold of new modes of governance and emerging information and communication technologies. These have the potential to diminish the power of state authorities and corporations such that each human being can more fully develop their capacity for inner freedom.

In 'Nine Propositions in Search of a Threefold Social Order', Christopher Schaefer explores Steiner's innovative social-scientific methods with pithy, testable propositions arising from threefold thinking – such as that the more that human rights are respected and implemented, the more just and less violent a society will be. Chris, a former Massachusetts Institute of Technology academic, has worked in organizational development consultancy in business, and with many Waldorf Schools in the education sphere.

John Bloom then invites us to transform our thinking with 'Red and Blue and the Lost Primary', for thinking in three dimensions. John is a banker at the Rudolf Steiner Foundation, San Francisco.

Edward Udell then provides an in-depth historical perspective on 'Rudolf Steiner and Social Threefolding during and after the First World War'. He shows how the original threefold movement was thwarted, and how Waldorf education, now a worldwide movement, was one of the outcomes.

Part 2: The Challenges

Part 2 offers a brief analysis of some of the challenges, issues, threats and opportunities we face, to help obtain an overview of the key questions that need addressing.

Martin Large's 'Rebalancing Society for the Common Good' uses the societal threefolding map to show how respecting boundaries between the private, public and plural sectors can rebalance society, with entry-points for individuals, organizations, groups and tri-sectoral partnerships for tackling 'cathedral projects' and cities. Martin has worked 'glocally' as an academic, in business, facilitation, organizational development and community land trust development.

'The Dance of Shadows in America: Reflections on the US Presidential Elections of 2016' by Christopher Schaefer explores the challenges posed by the recent election of Donald J. Trump to the presidency.

In 'Great Again? Thoughts about the World Situation', Gerald Häfner then analyses the world situation, asking, 'We are living at a turning point. Fear and tensions are increasing everywhere in the world. How can we find a way forward?' He was a co-founder of the Green Party in Bavaria, has served in the German Bundestag as an MP, and leads Mehr Democratie, for citizen participation in legislation.

Part 3: Inspired Initiatives

Just as Quakers from the seventeenth century onwards had a profound yet quiet influence on economic and social life – for example, their work for ethical banking, prison reform and peace – so students of Rudolf Steiner have developed his educational, farming, economic and social ideas on the margins, often with others similarly engaged.

In 'SEKEM: A Model for Sustainable Holistic Development', Christine Arlt writes about Sekem, just north of Cairo in Egypt, which has made the desert green with bio-dynamic farming, social businesses and cultural development for health, education from kindergarten to university, and the arts. Sekem was awarded the 2003 Right Livelihood Prize, and has received UN awards for holistic sustainable development.

In one of this book's keynote contributions, 'A New American Revolution? Associative Economics and the Future of the Food Movement', Robert Karp draws on Rudolf Steiner's revolutionary associative economics to show practically how, starting with Community-Supported Agriculture (CSA), growers, distributors and consumers are attempting to build an associative supply chain from field to plate. Karp proposes replacing the 'invisible hand' of the free market with associative supply-chain economics. This is happening out of the dynamics of healthy buyer/supplier relationships where benefits and risks are shared.

In 'Land for People, Homes and Farms', Martin Large explores the common ground between land reformers like Henry George, Ghandi, Robert Swann and John Ruskin, and Rudolf Steiner, showing how community land trusteeship (CLT) takes land out of the market as a commodity, and can be treated as a right and then stewarded as a common asset beyond state and market. Martin has worked on several CLT National Demonstration Projects in the UK, resulting at the time of writing in 225 CLTs having been established as an alternative to the housing market and the state's failure to provide well-designed, warm, affordable homes.

In his second contribution to the book, 'Toxic Excess: Income Equalities and the Fundamental Social Law', Christopher Schaefer asks if democracy and great wealth inequality can co-exist, contrasting the nature of capitalism with Steiner's fundamental social law. He explores ways of fixing the current system more justly, and ends with the Citizen's Income or Guaranteed Basic income.

In 'Education beyond Capital and the Neoliberal State: Challenging the "Academizing" of England's Schools', Richard House argues that, whilst freeing schools from state-imposed control and from the profit-seeking free market sounds like a good idea, the reality of US charter schools and England's 'academy' schools requires searching critical analysis. Far from developing a pluralist, state-funded free educational sector as in Germany, Finland, Holland or Denmark, the academization of English schools undermines the essence of free education. Richard is an academic, and former psychotherapist and Steiner kindergarten teacher, who now helps to run the Stroud-based 'Politics Kitchen' Initiative for a new 'listening politics of the heart'.

Glen Saunders is a former CEO of Triodos Bank, which is an exemplar ethical bank. Triodos draws on Steiner's social thinking and his unusual ideas about economics and money. In 'Money and Threefold Social Order Movement', Glen explores Steiner's concepts of gift, loan and exchange money against the current financial crisis, which he considers also a crisis in our thinking about money. He asks, 'We handle money all the time instinctively. Given this, it is then surprising how strange and elusive money really is when one pauses to reflect on it. What is money actually? How is it created? How does it work socially?'

Part 4: Openings for Co-creating Our Social Future

This final part briefly indicates some ways forward, starting with relationships and encounter.

Steve Briault argues that social change works through encounter, relationships and 'Three Conversations'.

In a penetrating interview with Christoph Strawe by Martin Large, 'How Threefolding Fits – or not – with Current Political Ideologies, and Dialogue in Threefolding Developments', the authors explore what the most frequently asked questions about, and objections to, the threefold social order framework are from Left-leaning thinkers, activists and politicians; and similarly, what are the main questions and objections raised by Right-leaning thinkers, activists and politicians? In this wide-ranging and penetrating conversation, Christoph concludes that threefolding has only existed for a century – a short time historically – yet it will hopefully play an increasingly important role in the future 'struggle for a society with a human face'.

Finally, in the book's concluding chapter, 'Telling a New Free, Equal, Mutual and Earth-caring Story', Martin Large writes that the importance of stories is that we live by them: they explain who we are, our values, and how we live our human lives. John Maynard Keynes once described the dominant market fundamentalist narrative as, 'Capitalism is the extraordinary belief that the nastiest of men for the nastiest of motives will somehow work for the benefit of all'.[5] However, we can co-create an emerging 'common weal or common wealth' societal narrative from four interweaving stories by answering the following seed questions:

- How are we developing a regenerative mutual circular economy?
- How are we caring for the planet?
- How are we engaging politically for human rights, more participative democracy, social justice, inclusion, equity and peace?
- How are we enabling creative cultural life (e.g. education, health, arts, science, spirituality, media) where every person can develop and maintain their whole human potential?

These can be used as action-research questions in small ways, such as reusable water bottles instead of throwaway plastic ones, or in larger 'Olympian' ways. People can use their powers of agency, initiative, creativity and intelligence to shape relationships, and to form new social 'habits' or structures which in turn shape our structures.

The following chapters suggest that we have it in our power to remake the world. We can co-create a common-weal society where all can flourish, by rebalancing society for the common good, guided by the principles of freedom, equality and mutuality.

NOTES AND REFERENCES
1. Naomi Klein, *No is not enough: Defeating the new shock politics*, Allen Lane, London, 2017l see goo.gl/WoFKG6.
2. Ibid.; see goo.gl/ZhhSYR.
3. Cf. Paul Hawken, *Blessed unrest: How the largest social movement in history is restoring grace, justice, and beauty to the world*, Penguin, Harmondsworth, 2008.
4. Elizabeth Grice, Ellen MacArthur: 'I can't live with the sea any more', *Daily Telegraph*, 31 August 2010; available at goo.gl/fL41kP (accessed 24 November 2017).
5. Note, however, there is some considerable doubt as to whether this is indeed a direct quotation from Keynes; see goo.gl/ncLXyK.

PART ONE

Perspectives on Societal Threefolding

CHAPTER 1

Rudolf Steiner's Threefold Image of a Healthy Society
Steve Briault

Inspiration out of Desolation

A century ago, as a devastated Europe staggered to the inconclusive conclusion of the 'war to end all wars', a young man found his poetic voice – all too briefly. Wilfred Owen's poem 'Parable of the Old Man and the Young' uses the Old Testament story of Abraham and Isaac to express with deep irony and bitterness the needless cruelty of war:

> Then Abram…
> …stretchèd forth the knife to slay his son.
> When lo! an angel called him out of heaven,
> Saying, Lay not thy hand upon the lad,
> Neither do anything to him. Behold,
> A ram, caught in a thicket by its horns;
> Offer the Ram of Pride instead of him.
> But the old man would not so, but slew his son,
> And half the seed of Europe, one by one.

FIGURE 1.1: WILFRED OWEN

The 'old men', fathers of the European nations, would not slay the Ram of their national and imperial pride, but preferred to send their young men to kill and be killed on the battlefields. Four months after writing this, Owen himself became one of the slain 'seed of Europe', killed in France in November 1918, aged 25.

In this tragic historical context, Rudolf Steiner articulated a re-imagination of society based not on competing nation states and empires, but on profound insights into the nature of human beings and human relationships. He recognized that the reassertion of nationalism, 'the most unchristian impulse of all', would only lead to further violence, warfare and injustice; and he rejected Woodrow Wilson's principle of national self-determination, because '…the one and only reality befitting the present age would be to overcome nationalism, to eliminate it, and for men to be stirred by the impulse of the human universal'.[1]

This impulse of the human universal had been at work during the war in the construction of the First Goetheanum in Dornach, Switzerland, where people from 17 different nations worked together peacefully, within earshot of the cannons, while men fought and died because their leaders prioritized national competition over humanitarian unity.

FIGURE 1.2: THE FIRST GOETHEANUM

Today we see a worrying resurgence of xenophobia and nationalism in both Europe and the United States, and an urgent need for solidarity and co-operation between people from every part of the globe, if we are to stand a chance of addressing the existential challenges of climate change, sectarian conflict and financial inequality. In this situation, Steiner's social insights can be a deep source of inspiration and orientation.

This chapter offers an introductory overview of the societal vision which Steiner put forward. This is a radical alternative to the current prevailing ideology, but it can also be seen as an organic and necessary evolution of our social consciousness and practice. It gives a generalized summary of how the predominant ideologies of human society have developed and transformed over millennia, how these have led to gradually evolving social structures, and finally the ways in which Steiner's suggestions offer practical as well as intellectual ways forward in our present critical phase of human evolution.

1917: The Threefold Social Organism

CULTURAL LIFE – LIBERTY
Individual development, free enquiry, pluralism, tolerance: Overcoming antipathies

POLITICAL/RIGHTS LIFE – EQUALITY
Democracy, justice, participation, universal humanity, recognition

ECONOMIC LIFE – FRATERNITY
Mutual support, collaboration, association: New sympathies

FIGURE 1.3: RUDOLF STEINER'S THREEFOLD SOCIAL ORGANISM FRAMEWORK

The Emergence of Social Ideals

History is important. If you don't know history it's as if you were born yesterday. And if you were born yesterday, anyone up there in a position of power can tell you anything, and you have no way of checking up on it.

Howard Zinn[2]

Social threefolding, as it has become known, is not a theoretical blueprint or programme to be introduced or imposed on society. It is derived from the perception that social life inherently manifests in three distinct aspects: cultural/spiritual, rights/political and economic/commercial. These three 'members' of the social organism have evolved over the course of human civilization to the point where each of them now requires a distinct set of principles and processes, so that they can be both separated and connected in healthy ways.

Early cultures such as the ancient Egyptian and Chaldean could be described as deistic. Their leaders were assumed to derive authority directly from the gods or spirits. There was no distinction between spiritual and earthly leadership; the Pharaoh was both priest and king, a kind of intermediary between earth and heaven, and the people derived their identity and direction from that single source. This spiritually derived basis for political authority has gradually declined over the centuries, but lives on in the theocratic nature of priestly authority in certain contemporary cultures, including states and would-be states. It is perhaps also echoed in the 'heroic' status accorded to some charismatic leaders in business and political circles.

As early as the fifth century BC, the role of the autocratic leader was challenged by the first emergence of partial democracy in Greece, but up to the Middle Ages and even later, the predominant ruling principle was *monarchism*. The monarch or emperor wore the cloak of divine endorsement, from the Roman Empire to the Magna Carta and beyond. Tension between Pope and King was a recurrent theme, and the principle of the 'divine right of kings' a source of debate and conflict. Gradually, at different times and pace in different countries, monarchism has largely been abolished or reduced to symbolism, but autocratic rulers – their claims to authority now often derived from shareholders, trustees or electors rather than God – persist in many places and contexts.

Through revolution or negotiation, monarchism was typically replaced by *statism*, the emphasis on the republic or nation-state as the primary provider of social identity and due recipient of collective and individual loyalty, though in some cases still with a king or queen as symbolic head of state. Increasingly, competition between countries became competition between national *economies*, as from the industrial revolution onwards, business and trade became the main drivers of social evolution – and financial leverage gradually caught up and outstripped the influence of politics or religion. By the twentieth century, a global economy had emerged and the potential for wealth creation vastly increased; but nationalism only intensified, and the devastating wars of that century were as much about access to resources and trading rights as about political or territorial disputes.

Steiner's seminal insight was that these three competing principles – spiritual/cultural, political/legal and material/economic – each have their legitimate role in modern society, but need to be brought into a healthy relationship to each other, so that each can express itself in accordance with its fundamental nature, without trying to dominate the others. They reflect the threefold nature of human beings:

- We are dependent on each other's work to meet our material needs. As isolated individuals, most of us would hardly survive, let alone enjoy the levels of welfare and prosperity which we now take for granted. For all of our lives we are consumers, and in our working lives we are producers, in a complex and now worldwide web of interdependence.
- We are able to pursue both individual and shared cultural development. Our ideas, beliefs, tastes and personal relationships are increasingly individualized – but they develop within contexts of education and influence that we share with many others.

- We create laws and agreements to regulate our formal relationships; and today, all adults have a legitimate expectation of being able to participate in the choice and formulation of these rules. Such participation is typically seen as a precondition for our acceptance of the responsibility to follow them – as in the notion of 'no taxation without representation'.

From the French Revolution, the ideals appropriate to these three realms became a much-debated and disputed slogan: Liberty, Equality, Fraternity (or Death!). Can liberty and equality be compatible? – or must there always be an inevitable trade-off between them? People are in many respects manifestly not equal – can they be made so without coercion? And what does fraternity really mean in practice?

The elegance of Steiner's threefold vision of society is that it allows each of these ideals to find its appropriate and full expression. In cultural life, each individual can and should be free to explore and define their own beliefs, tastes, aspirations and personal path of development. **Liberty** as a social ideal means allowing others to be different; it is the principle of cultural diversity and creativity, unconstrained by political pressures or legal restrictions – but also without being distorted and manipulated by commoditization and commercialism. **Equality** belongs in the realm of human rights – and only there – where differences can and should be ignored, and people granted equal rights just because they are human.

And **Fraternity**? This is the brotherly/sisterly principle of mutual support, where human beings work for each other. Steiner's radical insight proposes that this is the true underlying nature of economic life. As I write and you read these lines, hundreds of thousands, perhaps millions, of people all over the world are working, at this moment, for our benefit. They are producing and transporting the fuel we will use, the clothes we will wear, the food we will eat, the vehicles we will travel in and all the products we will consume in the next days, months and years. They are working for us, right now. Of course, their motives for doing so may be largely egotistic – they are earning money for themselves and their families – but the de facto reality is an altruistic, other-oriented activity.

In order to be productive economically, I have to direct my actions to the needs of others. Mundanely, this is called 'customer orientation' and is central to all successful business: in the economic process itself, I have to turn my own egoism inside out; to imagine – and then act to fulfil – the needs of other people. This discipline – made necessary by our own dependency on others' work – can be a moral educator: this is the developmental benefit of productive work. A truly fraternal economic life would make this altruistic principle more and more explicit, gradually replacing the abstract workings of markets manipulated by self-interest with direct dialogue and agreements between producers and consumers.

Evolution of Social Forms: The Emerging Individual

Underlying the long-term societal developments described above – from deism to monarchism to statism to corporatism – is what Rudolf Steiner termed the Basic Sociological Law. It could also be called the law of social development. He describes it in this way:

> *In the early stages of cultural development, human beings strive to create social groupings; initially, the interests of the individual are sacrificed to the interests of these groups. Further development, however, leads to the emancipation of the individual from the interests of the group, and to the free unfolding of the needs and strengths of single human beings.*[3]

This universal 'law' can be observed on many levels and in many contexts, from the evolution of whole civilizations to that of organizations and communities, down to the development of marriages and personal partnerships. Its essence is *individualization*, and its implication is that to be sustainable, any social structure needs to include the requirement to allow and support the growing demand for personal self-expression, choice and fulfilment. The choices we are offered as *consumers* can only very partially meet this requirement: we want to express our individuality also in what and how we learn; where, how and with whom we work; and, crucially, in our personal relationships.

In the ongoing, long-term transition from a power-based to a bargaining-based society, relationships have gradually been liberated from the control of social laws and norms, and entrusted increasingly to individual self-determination. Historically, interpersonal relationships were highly regulated and prescribed: first by the race, tribe or sect into which one was born, and later by social class. There is a rich cultural narrative in countless dramas, novels and stories – from Chaucer's *Troilus and Criseyde* to Shakespeare's *Romeo and Juliet*, Jane Austen's *Pride and Prejudice* to E.M. Forster's *Maurice* – rehearsing the struggles of individuals and couples to release themselves from the constraints of tradition, law or family and seek fulfilment in self-chosen relationships.

In parallel with this, individualism and personal choice have become increasingly the norm in work life. With some exceptions, we are no longer expected to follow the family trade – our parents may be a little disappointed, but cannot insist that we follow the same profession that they inherited. Work relationships are increasingly changeable and negotiated – long-term loyalty to a single employer is now a rarity, and most young people today will change not only jobs but profession several times in their working lives. Within organizations, moreover, role flexibility and portfolio workloads are increasingly common.

These healthy and inevitable developments in personal and work relationships are not without problems and threats, however. Individualism brings uncertainty and insecurity, and for many it is tempting to seek reassurance in old forms of community – racial, national or sectarian – which then all too often leads to rejection of, or even violence against, other groups and individuals – from rival football supporters, to immigrants, to members of other religions.

In work life, a parallel but opposite tendency is the fragmentation of organizational identity: when each person is their own tiny business, individually marketing their skills to a succession of employers and customers, a sense of being part of a working community is increasingly elusive. This can create a social-Darwinistic context of exploitation, commoditization of people and, on a macro-social scale, what has become known as elite globalization.

The Inner Experience of Human Encounter

How can we as individuals learn to navigate these accelerating trends and tensions? Again, Rudolf Steiner's surprising insights can offer support. Also in 1918, he described the 'archetypal phenomenon of social science' – that in the encounter between human beings,

> …*a certain force works from one person to the other.… We cannot confront another person in life with indifference, not even in mere thoughts and feelings, even though we may be separated from them by distance. If we have any kind of relation to other people, or any communication with them, then a force flows between us creating a bond. It is this fact which lies at the basis of social life and which, when broadened, is really the foundation for the social structure of humanity.*
>
> *One sees this phenomenon most clearly when one thinks of the direct interchange between two people. The impression which one person makes on the other has the effect of lulling the other to sleep. Thus we frequently find in social life that one person gets lulled to sleepiness by the other with whom he has interchange. As a physicist might say: a 'latent tendency' is always there for one person to lull another to sleep in social relationships.*[4]

This rather startling statement becomes more accessible as he explains further (hence the longish quotation):

> *Why is this so? Well, we must see that this rests on a very important arrangement of man's total being. It rests on the fact that what we call social impulses, fundamentally speaking, are only present in people of our present day consciousness during sleep.… Thus there exists a permanent disposition to fall asleep precisely for the building up of the social structure of humanity.*

> *On the other hand, something else is also working. A perpetual struggle and opposition to falling asleep in social relationships is also present… . In this situation a tendency to keep awake has an anti-social character, the assertion of one's individuality, of one's personality, in opposition to the social structure of society. Simply because we are human beings, our soul-life swings to and fro between the social and the antisocial.*

As described further in *The mystery of meeting – relationships as a path of discovery*,[5] this 'pendulum' process is a threshold phenomenon. It takes us beyond our separate, self-enclosed consciousness into a different world – the world of another person's soul; of their thoughts, feelings and intentions, which may be quite alien to our own. The further the evolutionary process of individualization advances, and consequently the more inwardly distant from each other we become, the more essential it will be that human beings develop the capacity consciously to navigate this sleeping–waking, threshold process.

This ability has become known as *empathy*. It is distinct from the 'social' force of sympathy, by which we are 'put to sleep' in an encounter, and also from the 'anti-social' force of antipathy, by which we continually reawaken ourselves. It is an integration, a dynamic balancing of the two. Only this can allow us genuinely to meet another person without losing our own integrity and self-responsibility.

The capacity of empathy expresses itself most fully in the process of deep listening, the skill of paying selfless attention to another person's reality, without agreement or disagreement, collusion or judgement. Whether with our colleagues, clients, family members, friends or opponents, this ability is central to the creation and maintenance of healthy relationships.

It is this experience of meeting others that awakens in us the feeling for human rights. Why should we treat others as equal, when they are obviously not? Why should we reject slavery, exploitation, exclusion, injustice, if these do not affect us personally? Because if we meet enough people deeply enough, we may start to perceive – directly, not theoretically – the essential humanity which each different individual shares with us and each other; which calls on our own humanity to acknowledge and respect, and which can create a sense of unity amidst the vast diversity of human identity, personality and experience.

The Renewal of Economic Thinking and Practice

The historical, ongoing process of individualization and personal freedom must be the basis for a modern cultural life. The inner phenomena of human encounter, and their manifestation in the social quality of empathy, underpin the principles of equal human rights. In the economic dimension of society, its 'youngest' but now most powerful member, the conventional image of 'economic man' – described by Kate Raworth as 'standing alone, money in hand, calculator in head, nature at his feet, and an insatiable appetite in his heart'[6] – needs to be replaced by 'a hologram of humanity' willing to give as well as receive, to collaborate more than to compete, to act out of responsibility as well as out of need. In questions of human rights, and the health and well-being of humanity and the Earth, individual freedom must be balanced by shared responsibility.

In 1922 Rudolf Steiner gave a series of lectures which, building on the threefold image of society as a whole, laid the basis for a transformation of economic thought and activity. He saw that the 'invisible hand' of the market needed to be complemented by the conscious, 'associative' collaboration of producers, traders and consumers. This collaboration should neither be left to market forces nor controlled by the state, but should be placed in the hands of stakeholder groups who, between them, can carry responsibility for ensuring that economic processes genuinely serve the needs of human beings. This would require the removal of 'non-economic' factors – specifically land, labour and capital – from the market, and making them available to business on a different basis.

In relation to work, for example, Steiner regarded the wage system as a kind of hangover from the time of slavery. 'Wagery' is not only an injustice, but also an economic untruth:

> [People] actually speak as though a kind of sale and purchase took place between the wage-earner who sells his labour and the man who buys it from him. But this sale and purchase is fictitious. It does not in reality take place.... [In reality] it is values which are exchanged. The worker produces something directly; he delivers a product, and it is this product which the entrepreneur really buys from him. In actual fact, down to the last penny, the enterpriser pays for the products which the workers deliver to him. It is time we began to see these things in their right light.[7]

Trading land as if it were an economic commodity is another untruth, because it has not been produced by human beings: what is actually being 'sold' is the *right* to occupy and use the land. Elsewhere in this book [see, for example, Chapters 10 and 12], practical examples are described of systems which ensure that land is no longer treated as a commodity to be bought and sold as if it were an economic product, but must be cared for in ways which are environmentally sustainable as well as humanly beneficial; and of organizations in the field of ethical investment, social banking and co-operative ownership that administer capital not via the 'money market' (the third untruth, treating money as if it could be traded in the same way as actual goods or services), but in line with real human needs (see Chapters 12 and 15).

Weaving Together the Three Dimensions

Steiner's rationale sees this liberation of capital as the key to the healthy reciprocal relationship between the cultural and the economic aspects of society. Personal development and creativity, supported by education and the wider cultural context, make available mature, skilled individuals who are able to contribute to economic productivity. They bring their gifts to the service of others through work. Fruitful economic activity – in which not only labour works on nature, but also human intelligence continually makes labour more productive – leads to an objective surplus of value (usually referred to as 'profit') which, after meeting the legitimate needs of the producers and the requirements of re-investment, can be made available as 'gift money' (Steiner's term for this surplus – not the same as 'donations') to support education and culture. This balancing, mutually fructifying exchange of resources between cultural and economic life can be objectively mediated by rights processes, without the state trying to control or manage either of the other two realms.

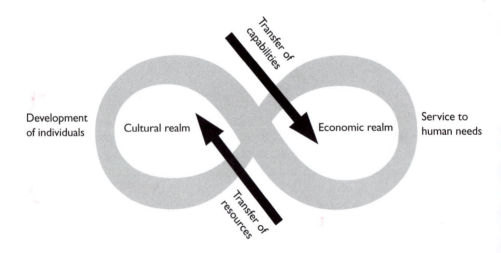

FIGURE 1.4: TRANSFERS OF SURPLUSES BETWEEN CULTURAL AND ECONOMIC ACTIVITY

In this brief outline, a first indication has been attempted of what a healthy society, based on the threefold reality of human relationships, could look like: a free cultural life, liberated from state control or commercial manipulation; an economic life based on mutual responsibility and collaboration; and a political system which genuinely ensures equality of rights for all. It is a simple image which can help us make sense of the complexity of social phenomena, and is capable of inspiring and informing concrete actions and creative participation in every aspect of human society.

Respecting Boundaries – the Key to Societal Health

A central tenet of social threefolding is that each realm of society should apply its own appropriate principles within its own realm, and not try to 'invade' either of the other two. Such invasion leads to social pathologies – for example:

- When the power of money manipulates cultural processes (newspaper and media proprietors, advertising);
- When the state restricts freedom of expression (for example in Turkey, China and many other countries), or imposes political control of education (e.g. the UK's National Curriculum and testing regime; cf. Chapter 14);
- When economic interests unduly influence electoral processes or national policy (through professional lobbying or party political sponsorship, prevalent in the USA);
- When governments try to manage national economies as if they were businesses (as in the nonsense expression 'UK plc', which dresses up the political structure of a nation-state in the clothes of a corporation);
- When individual freedom becomes the freedom to exploit and marketize natural resources (purchase of land rights, destruction of habitats for profit);
- When religion tries to make itself the basis of national regimes (Islamic republic, Jewish state, Christian Democratic party…).

Within their rightful spheres, Liberty, Equality and Fraternity can be unequivocally and fully pursued, without corrupting or inhibiting each other. This is the ideal of the threefold society.

NOTES AND REFERENCES
1. Rudolf Steiner, 'The blood-relationship and the Christ-relationship', in his *The festivals and their meaning*, GA 198, Dornach, 3 April 1920, Rudolf Steiner Press, London, 1996, pp. 140–51.
2. 'You can't be neutral on a moving train', 2004 documentary; available at goo.gl/TRze4c (accessed 15 November 2017).
3. Steiner, *Collected essays on culture and history*, 1887–1901, GA 31, 1966, 247ff (see goo.gl/cKURZL).
4. Steiner, 'Social and anti-social forces in the human being', Bern, 12 December 1918; GA 186 (available at goo.gl/QfPk6b; accessed 15 November 2017).
5. Steve Briault, *The mystery of meeting: Relationships as a path of discovery*, Sophia Books, Forest Row, East Sussex, 2010.
6. Kate Raworth, *Doughnut economics: Seven ways to think like a 21st century economist*, RH Business Books, London, 2017, p. 96.
7. Steiner, *World economy*, Lecture VII, Dornach, 30 July 1922; available at goo.gl/wPcLUY (accessed 15 November 2017).

CHAPTER 2

Images of the Human Being and Their Effect on Humanity's Relationship to Power
Andrew Scott

Introduction

The mostly hidden assumptions of the nature of human beings shape the social forms in which we live. Five so-called 'noisy images' inform how society is organized today. Three 'quiet images' stand behind societal threefolding. This chapter advocates that we shift our focus towards the arrangement of power within society, our own communities and organizations by taking hold of new modes of governance and emerging information and communication technologies. These have the potential to diminish the power of state authorities and corporations such that each human being can more fully develop their capacity for inner freedom.

The purpose of this chapter, then, is to help the reader make the connections between their individual self and societal threefolding, with the aim of providing new insights and new drive to make a difference – that is, to co-evolve with other beings the development of themselves and the Earth.

The essential premise of this chapter is drawn from a study published by the Center for the Study of Social Policy at Stanford University in 1982,[1] as follows:

> All public and private policy decisions necessarily embody some view (or compromise of views) about the nature of man, society and the universe. The kinds of educational systems and goals a society sets up, the way in which it approaches the problems of material distribution (poverty and wealth), how it treats the welfare of its citizens, the priorities it gives to various human needs - all these

aspects and many more are affected by the image of humankind that dominates the society.

For most people, assumptions about the nature of human beings are held beneath the conscious level of awareness. However, only when these hidden assumptions are recognised and brought into awareness can the images be examined and with perspective, retained, discarded or changed.

The 'Noisy' Images

My assertion is that the seemingly intractable problems humanity and the Earth face are the product of the following five 'noisy' images of human being, drawn from the aforementioned Stanford paper, that are expressed in the current social constructs surrounding us.

1. **Human as Separate from God and Nature** – the Abrahamic view that within oneself is not divinity but only 'soul', which may or may not find a proper relationship with God. A proper relationship can be achieved only by obedience to God's commandments and membership in God's chosen tribe.
2. **Humankind over Things** – the Renaissance and Reformation view of reality, articulated most convincingly by Descartes and Newton, being made up of the human being and nature, with nature regarded as an objective reality, observable in every aspect, unaffected by either observation or observer – the emergence of duality – subject/object and the predominance of measurement.
3. **Economic Man** – leading from the Renaissance and Reformation view of reality, the human being is viewed as individualistic, materialistic, rationalistic and utilitarian.
4. **Humankind as Beast** – a combination of Darwinian and Freudian views that instinctual drives predominate, where the human being is a creature of evolution whose survival depends on competitive adaptation and/or the suppression of base instincts.
5. **Human as Mechanism** – the behaviourist view of the newborn human as a clean slate on which is written the results of conditioning, whereby the actions of an organism are brought under control by giving it a reward, if it behaves as specified.

Manifestations of the 'Noisy' Images Today

The litany of seemingly intractable problems is well-known and well-rehearsed. However, for the sake of context, see the digest in Table 2.1, below.

TABLE 2.1: MANIFESTATIONS OF THE NOISY IMAGES

Problem	Description
Environmental Degradation	The consequences of human activity are externalized because exchange value trumps experiential value, and a debt-based money system makes economic growth the essential imperative.
Hot and Cold Military Conflicts	The geo-political self-interest of ruling regimes, grounded on the 'noisy images', creates false differences and assumptions. Military conflict, or the threat of it, is a way of achieving or holding on to power over the members of their societies as an end in itself.
Concentration of Assets	Asset classes such as capital and land are in the hands of a few people and corporations mediated by centralized captured institutions.
Dysfunctional Class System	Developed economies have stratified into a dysfunctional class structure as reciprocity and solidarity have weakened. This assertion and what follows are drawn from *A Precariat Charter* by Guy Standing (2014), his basic thesis being that as humanism and capitalism have separated, no longer can a broad swathe of the population rely on political franchisement, civil, cultural, economic and social rights. A plutocracy of global super citizens (individuals and corporations) has arisen, enabled by senior salaried staff who manage the so-called 'precariat' – workers in insecure low-paid jobs in receipt of heavily conditional, inadequate benefits and social care. These non-work sources of income are constrained by the plutocracy not contributing sufficient taxes to support the common good and locking capital and other asset classes within tax-havens outside of national jurisdictions. While a class of mobile self-entrepreneurs, employees of Non-Governmental Organizations, health and social care professionals and civil servants sit outside of these class structures, they constitute a minority.

Problem	Description
Suckered by Consumerism	The 'Bread and circuses' approach, coined as it was by Cicero, is not new by any means, but the rise of individuation of the movements of the 1920s and 1960s, which showed so much promise at these times, stuck at the level of meeting material needs only, and did not pursue the flourishing of the human soul. We see an intolerance for anything other than comfort, convenience and choice on the one hand, and on the other, corporate-funded celebrity culture provided as a proxy for our unfilled desires. *Plus ça change, plus c'est la même chose.*
Organization Management Technology	Social technologies such as the management hierarchy promote egotism, where sociopathic behaviour is a competitive advantage.
Surveillance and News Manipulation	Access to worldwide instantaneous information and communication is virtually free at the point of use, but only in exchange for personal identification data enabling psychological targeting of political messaging and a boon for the surveillance state.
Nihilistic Terrorism	Initially a reaction to the hegemony of the West, and the unholy alliance between the United States and Saudi Arabia following the Bitter Lake Conference of 1946 (see Adam Curtis's documentary 'Bitter Lake'),[2] the terrorism we are seeing is an expression of the striving youthful social will not being met in ways that allow for the free human being to unfold. This has led, and is leading, to extreme alienation and nihilism.
The Built Environment	The built environment is far uglier than it could be. Land use is a mess, and infrastructure is either inadequate or too expensive to access. Great architecture and civic-planning examples almost always start with the conception of a commonwealth.
Education	This last issue is the most important. Many young people are subjected to a largely utilitarian education system and therefore either cannot conceive of, or are not motivated to accept, anything other than the status quo.

Characterization of Societal Threefolding

There is a multitude of ways in which societal threefolding can be characterized; for the purposes of this chapter the following definition is offered:

> Arranging power relationships such that we move beyond the sterile battle between state actors, owners of capital and owners of labour so that each human being can develop their capacity for inner freedom.

To be clear, this is a process of evolution, and not an end state, as the more capability every human being has for inner freedom so the more optimized can be the arrangement of power.

The 'Quiet' Images

It is my lived experience that to make sense of social threefolding, it is the 'quiet' images that have significance: whilst looked at it through the lenses of the 'noisy' ones, it makes little sense.

My hypothesis is that only through individuals collectively holding and living out of the worldviews expressed in the 'quiet' images that follow will the current social constructs that surround us melt away – to be replaced by social forms and processes requisite for humanity and the Earth to meet the potential coming from the future.

1. **The Knower** – the Zoroastrian view that human beings have the capacity for extraordinary and experientially intimate knowledge of the mysteries of existence
2. **The Individual** – the Greek view that one acts from a sense of duty to oneself striving after excellence, based on the perfection of divine intelligence from within, rather than looking to any supernatural authority
3. **Human Being as Evolving Holon** – arising from systems theory, this view is that all natural systems are open and therefore complex (rather than closed and therefore complicated), and have a holarchic structure, meaning that the whole is in the part and the part is in the whole

Changing the Wallpaper of Our Lives

Were the prevailing images of the human being and the nature of the universe to shift fundamentally from 'noisy' to 'quiet', it is my contention that the social constructs set out in Table 2.2 would no longer be considered laws of nature, as is mostly the case today in mainstream discourse.

TABLE 2.2: FROM SELF-EVIDENT CURRENT TO SELF-EVIDENT NEW PARADIGMS

Self-evident Current Paradigm	Self-evident New Paradigm
Labour treated as a commodity	Labour is not treated as a commodity. Labour 'price' is not set by markets. Income is a rights issue.
Land is an asset class and treated as a commodity	Land use and allocation are a rights issue. Capital sunk into land is recognized as inherently unproductive.
Money treated as a commodity where money makes money	By societal agreement, the roles of money are limited to medium of exchange, as a store of value, and as a unit of account.
Debt treated as a commodity that can be wrapped into derivatives for speculation	By societal agreement, trading debt is not allowed; and furthermore, periodic debt write-off is a societal feature.

In these regards, this recent quotation[3] from Yanis Varoufakis, the academic and past Greek Syriza Finance Minister, is illuminating:

> *As soon as land and labour were commodified [at the time of the enclosures], instead of the distribution of surplus coming after production, distribution began before production had even started, which turned debt into the essential lubricant of the industrial revolution. This is how profit became an end in itself. The essential transition was from a society with markets to a market society.*

Suggested Areas of Focus

We are starting to see that this chapter is not a counsel of despair. For the reader who is already an activist or wishes to become one, what follows are two recent beneficial societal developments that are already underway. The opportunity exists to join with others in worldwide communities of practice to bring these seeds, and others like them, to maturity.

New Modes of Organization-Level Governance

Two organizations and their methods, known to and practised by myself, are Holacracy[4] and Encode.[5] Holacracy, a way of getting work done, is proven to work in organizations large and small; and Encode – with ways of assigning property rights, including earnings based on equity allocation for all co-workers, and caring for the people associated with an organization – is work in progress.

The key features of these approaches are as follows:

- The radical redistribution of power where authority is vested in a constitution, operating agreements and association agreements – 'the rules of the road' – and not a person or persons.
- Eliminating the monarch principle of organization that we've lived with for centuries in many cultures, and from the industrial revolution the adoption of command-and-control organization in business borrowed from the military, whilst still being able to organize at scale.
- Role autonomy replacing the need to build consensus – the organizational sickness of the modern age where any decision of significance needs to be socialized with the formal and informal power holders to receive their blessing.
- Operational and governance tensions felt by a role-holder are processed one at a time, thus using the whole human being: every human being who has connected their purpose to the purpose of the organization is a sense-maker for the whole.
- In this way also, conflicts of interest and loyalty that are so prevalent in conventional organizations are overcome.
- The ultimate potential in the context of societal threefolding, which is being realised today in a few organizations around the world, of the elimination of the employer/employee construct.

Distributed-Ledger Technologies

Very much in the early stage of their development, perhaps five to eight years away from maturity, technologies like Blockchain and Holochain have the potential significantly to disrupt the power relationship between state actors, corporations and individuals. The foundation of distributed-ledger technologies is certainty – an immutable record of transactions between parties is established between individuals without the need to build trust, where consensual rules are established using decentralized security based on computation and cryptography.

When a central authority mediates access to any right or asset, it sets the rules for the interactions between it and participants, be they in the role, for example, of consumer, producer, citizen, researcher or artist. These technologies have the potential to shift the balance of power away from state/institutional/corporate actors and towards networked individuals in these and more roles.

Blockchain has received a lot of media attention in recent times as the underpinning of crypto-currencies like Bitcoin. However, commentators in this space are of the view that multiple sectors of human activity will be disrupted by distributed-ledger technologies and the design principles and practices that underpin them.

TABLE 2.3: INDICATIVE DISRUPTIONS BY SECTOR

Sector/Activity	Indicative Disruption
Banking and Payments	May do to banking what the internet is doing to the media. Enables access for the unbanked.
Charity and International Aid	The potential to reduce inefficiency and corruption by providing transparency for the donor that the funds they provide reach the intended recipients.
Crowd Funding	Elimination of the need for expensive intermediaries serving start-ups and projects that need capital investment.
Energy Management	Enables producers and users to buy and sell electricity directly from each other.
Governmental Operational Systems	Could increase the security, efficiency and transparency of services. A good contender for the practical implementation of universal basic income.
Healthcare	Offers a secure platform to store and share sensitive data.
Insurance	For insurance that relies on real-world data, the potential exists to significantly reduce fraud and therefore premiums.
Peer-to-peer Car-and-ride Sharing	The likes of Uber and Zipcar collapse.

Sector/Activity	Indicative Disruption
Supply Chain Management	Better management of environmental impact, verifying the authenticity of fair-trade products.
Retail	Elimination of the need for intermediaries like Amazon and eBay.
Voting	Voter registration, verification and vote counting much more robust.

Whether any of these projections come to pass is not just a function of the technology maturing but a shift of perception within and across societies globally. However, the technologies are a catalyst for seeing and arranging social relationships differently.

They may be co-opted or regulated to the point of neutering by central authorities, and/or they may be subverted and diluted by corporations; however, the promise remains of the following essential features of distributed-ledger technologies becoming manifest:

- Commercial and rights relationships becoming peer-to-peer without the need for intermediaries.
- Not requiring the permission of state or corporate actors to participate or innovate.
- No requirement to share personal data.

What is described in this section is largely informed by the articulate explanations of Anton Antonopoulos,[6] a leading Bitcoin commentator.

Call to Action

My invitation is to:

- Reflect on your images of the human being and of humanity, and the areas of focus offered.
- Look to where and how you will change the status quo around you more fully.
- Take new or revised initiatives that move society to somewhere new and better.

Notes

1. See http://www.global-vision.org/papers/changing-images-of-man.pdf (goo.gl/JDJq74).
2. Adam Curtis's documentary titled 'Bitter Lake' – see https://www.youtube.com/watch?v=VRbq63r7rys (goo.gl/9bwq8S).
3. *Talking to my daughter about the economy*, Penguin Books, Harmondsworth, 2017.
4. For more information, see https://www.holacracy.org/.
5. For more information, see https://encode.org/.
6. Two YouTube videos of Anton Antonopoulos' worth viewing are at: goo.gl/kzVTNu and at goo.gl/QgRGHA.

Reference

Standing, G. (2014) *A precariat charter: From denizens to citizens*, Bloomsbury, London.

CHAPTER 3

Nine Propositions in Search of a Threefold Social Order
Christopher Schaefer

What kind of institutions must exist for people to be able to have the right thoughts on social matters, and what kind of thoughts must exist that these right social institutions can arise?
                                                                Rudolf Steiner

Introduction

We live in the time of 'The Long Emergency' when the threats of climate change, mass migrations caused by starvation and war, widespread terrorism and a re-emergence of nuclear brinksmanship fuse with economic insecurity to breed feelings of uncertainty and despair. Since 9/11 there is a growing recognition that the post-World War II period has ended, and that the political and economic institutions on which we have relied for so long in the Western world are not functioning well in bringing peace and prosperity to millions of people. The rise of a global media intent on manipulating our fears and distracting us from looking more seriously at the basic issues confronting us enhances the sense of crisis, and provokes authoritarian and nationalistic responses to the need for reform. What adds poignancy to this widely felt need is that the dominant models of societal structuring – socialism and capitalism – are both over a century old, and have demonstrated marked deficiencies.

In this chapter I articulate a set of principles or propositions about social life based on the recognition that we continuously create and re-create society in a dialogue of social creation. In this dialogue with others and the world, we externalize who we are, our own nature as human beings, as well as that of our ideas and values. At the same time as we imprint who we are and our consciousness and values on the social world, it shapes our consciousness. The difficulty is that we are largely unconscious of this reciprocal relationship between ourselves as social creators and the social world which we have created. I argue that by bringing central aspects of the social-creation process to awareness, a new threefold imagination of society emerges which offers quite new possibilities of social reform, as well as meeting the deeper longings of the human soul and spirit. In making this argument I rely on the traditions of social phenomenology, on critical theory and on the social and philosophical insights of Rudolf Steiner.[1]

Proposition 1: The social world is a humanly created world.

The natural world of mountains, sunsets or a grazing deer is given to us by a divinely created world. We are part of that creation. We, however, create the world of road signs, living-room conversations, families, post offices, amusement parks and multi-national corporations. In the twentieth and twenty-first centuries, we increasingly inhabit this humanly created world, often losing our living connection to nature.

Proposition 2: The social world carries the imprint of our characteristics as human beings, for we are continuously externalizing who we are in the process of social creation. — Competition

As we are the creators, the artists, of the social world and of society, it reflects our nature and mirrors our consciousness. First, all social events and happenings take place in *space and time*; I meet my friend on a Tuesday afternoon in September at James Baird State park near Pougkeepsie, NY, or on 8 November 2016, a Presidential election took place in the United States with millions of people voting in their individual communities.

Just as we each have a *unique identity, an I*, so does every family, group, city and nation. No two families, towns, companies or countries are the same. They each have a moment of birth: the United States was born in 1776 with the signing of the Declaration of Independence, and Germany as a nation was formed in 1871 under the leadership of Count Bismark. Or if we married on 2 December in 1990, our immediate family was born on that date.

Each social entity also has a *distinct history, or biography*, just as we do as individuals. The history of Ford Motor Company is different from that of General Motors or of Volkswagen, and your biography as well as that of your family is different from mine.

What we also share as individuals and with all institutions and societies is that we go through *stages of development*; birth, childhood, young adulthood, maturity, decline, old age and death. The time-periods for each stage vary between that of individuals and institutions, and indeed between institutions and societies; but the characteristics of different phases are discernable and can be described, as Arnold Toynbee has done for civilizations, Bernard Lievegoed for organizations, and Erik Erikson for individuals.[2] For example, we know about the improvisational pioneer period of young organizations and their often crisis-filled transition to a more rational administrative or managerial phase of development, whether in schools, social-service agencies or companies. Even groups have a natural life cycle, neatly captured in the phrase 'forming, storming, norming and performing'.[3]

PROPOSITION 3: As we have a body, soul and spirit, so do communities, organizations, cities and countries.

Because human beings are the creators of the social world and because we externalize our nature in the process of social creation, all social entities also have a *body, soul and spirit*. The body of the social world is our home and neighborhood, the beauty of the Sussex countryside, the street canyons of lower Manhattan, or the sleek corporate headquarters of IBM or BMW. For nations it is the landscape of a country, and the built architecture of its cities, towns and villages. It also comes to expression in agriculture, manufacturing and the economic life of a country. We can't help but be aware of the Dow Jones Industrial Average or of the economic consequences of Brexit. Indeed, a concern about the production, distribution and sale of goods and services is the main fixation of our consumer society and of many societies in the West, a 'body' consciousness expressed in the financial and fitness culture of our times.

The soul is expressed in the quality of relationships, in festivals and celebrations, and in the mood of discourse in families, groups, institutions and society. It is manifest in Bastille Day or Washington's birthday, and finds articulation in the governing norms and laws of societies and groups. Will religious restrictions on immigration or a watering down of affirmative action laws occur under a more conservative Supreme Court in the United States? Will political discourse harden and the mood of extremism grow in our increasingly divided societies? All questions to do with the 'soul' of our society.

It seems to me that spirit is found in the mission and purpose of groups and institutions, in the uniqueness of our individuality, and in the genius of the language and culture of a people. It comes to expression in the history of a country: the legacy of manifest destiny from the nineteenth century, for example, is still with us in our present dealings in the Middle East. The genius of the English language as expressed in Shakespeare or Dickens is part of Great Britain's identity which we share as English-speaking people, whereas we as Americans are not bound by Britain's long and complex relationship to France and French culture.

Because language plays such a central role in the dialogue between people, and in the social-creation process, its effect on how we perceive the world and how we relate to others needs to be especially noted. I experience the world and myself differently when I speak German rather than English, and when in China I cannot help but wonder how writing vertically in pictographs affects how the Chinese think and perceive the world, and how this in turn affects the culture and society they have created over thousands of years.

By externalizing our body, soul and spirit we create an economic life, a social and political-legal life and a cultural life, no matter how imperfect. In some societies, cultural life is dominant as in Iran or in ISIL-controlled territories in which religious principles are most important. This is also true in many fundamentalist Christian communities and in Orthodox Jewish settlements. In other countries the state is dominant and controlling, as it was in communist societies before 1989 and still is in some socialist nations. In the United States and to a lesser degree in Britain and Germany or Japan, it is economic life which controls the state and, to a significant degree, culture. So the relationship between cultural, political and economic life matters greatly in terms of what kind of society we are part of. Is it the mullahs or clerics, the politicians or the businessmen, who ultimately call the shots and determine the national agenda, or is there a reasonable balance between these different parts of society?

PROPOSITION 4: There is an outer and an inner side to the social world, or an objective visible dimension and an internal, more subjective dimension, just as there is for us in our experience of the world. When the outer and inner dimension of a social order deviate too much, the pressure for social change builds.

We grow and become human through acquiring language and learning to understand the meanings and taken-for-granted nature of the social world through a process of socialization.[4] Post offices are not restaurants, and you do not wear ripped shorts to a wedding reception – examples that offer a succinct rendition of this reality. Everything in our social environment has significance and meaning which, because we have internalized it, allows us to function with a minimum of fuss. This taken-for-granted knowledge of everyday life is internal to us and yet guides our behavior and action. In a sense this more internal (subjective) understanding of society gives legitimacy and support to the outer world of offices, work, elections, policemen, shopping, and communication.

Social change happens when there is a growing disconnect between the outer (objective) dimension of how society functions and our internal thoughts and expectations of how it should function. We say we support and promote democracy and yet in America we allow uncontrolled amounts of money to affect election outcomes, and as a country have financed and supported the overthrow of democratically elected governments in Chile, Iran, Egypt, the Ukraine and elsewhere. At some point this glaring contradiction becomes intolerable. This is occurring in regard to a number of quite central questions facing the USA and some other Western societies, issues such as income inequalities, economic opportunity, immigration and international trade.

The first step in bringing about social change is to create public awareness of a discrepancy between actual behavior and the values affecting the issue. The Occupy movement was able to do this very successfully with the slogan of the 1 percent and the 99 percent, promoting a public awareness that for most people the American Dream had died. The progress on LGBT rights is another example of dramatic shifts in our understanding of gender questions and of legal protections against discrimination.

PROPOSITION 5: Humanity's ability to transform and indeed to destroy the natural world and its central role in creating a social world call for a new level of responsibility and consciousness in developing a healthy and environmentally sensitive social order.

In the last century we have moved from a predominately rural, village life style, lived in connection with the patterns of nature, into an urban, industrial or post-industrial society. In the past, instinct, tradition and religion guided the greater portion of humanity in creating families, villages and towns, thus creating the fabric of social life. The rapid growth of technology and our new capacity to control and exploit as well as to destroy the earth proclaim a new era of human responsibility in co-creating the natural and social worlds. We have become gods in our ability to either husband or to destroy the planet and ourselves. It is time to replace tradition and social instinct with a new ecologically aware social consciousness and capacity, to become conscious social artists in the dialogue of social creation.

PROPOSITION 6: The central activity in the dialogue of social creation is the meeting and conversation between two or more people. It is the archetypal social phenomenon through which the social world is created and its most important inner dynamic revealed.[5]

All activities in the social world take place through the medium of dialogue, either directly or indirectly; the buying of groceries or of stamps, the making of appointments and agreements, and the evening conversation with children and friends. In conversation all aspects of the social world are exercised or revealed. Our body, soul and spirit are re-engaged by the other. We exercise our thinking, feeling and willing in words and gestures. And through the process of speaking and listening, a level of mutual understanding is achieved.

Indeed, a true miracle occurs in dialogue, which we take largely for granted – namely, that you and I are able to take an invisible idea, experience or intention, and turn it into audible speech which is heard by the other, internalized and understood before being responded to. It is through language that we understand the world and each other, and it is through dialogue that relationships, families, schools and organizations are built. It is language and conversation that both build and sustain the social world.

Dialogue, conversation and the meeting between people also reveal three other essential aspects of social life. *The first of these is that there is always an interplay between social and anti-social forces in every conversation, and indeed in social life as a whole.* When I speak I am aware of my ideas and intentions, of what I wish to communicate, and less aware of the other person and their thoughts and intentions. So I am awake to myself and less aware of the other. This is a more anti-social gesture. The other, in listening consciously, is directing their awareness towards me, seeking to understand my thoughts, feelings and intentions. They are more awake to the other and in some sense more asleep to self. This is a more social gesture as they seek to let me into their soul. Listening is harder and more demanding than speaking, hence our tendency to listen for a moment or two and then begin formulating our responses.

When we reflect with consciousness on our anti-social nature in dialogue with others we can notice the functioning of critical intelligence in our thought life – 'Yes, but have you thought of… that can't be right' – and we have stopped listening and are off stating our own views.

Turning to our feeling life, we can notice strong likes and dislikes, both toward ideas and people – 'consensus doesn't work, does it?', or 'Helen isn't a responsible person'. Likes and dislikes tell us how we feel, but generally they do not accurately reflect the quality of events or of other people, being strongly coloured by moods and projections. In our will life, our behavior, we can observe our desire to get our way, a certain egotism and also, at times, a fear and uncertainty. We can notice these three anti-social qualities at work in others and in social situations, but also in ourselves if we reflect on conversations which did not go well, or on conflicts and disagreements. We can also be conscious that while these qualities close us off from others and the world, they do give us self-consciousness and deepen our sense of individuality.

Social qualities come to our awareness when we reflect on our experience of deep listening. I have a few friends who are such good listeners that I feel wiser and more authentic than in normal conversations, and I am sure that you have similar experiences. As Brenda Ueland, a gifted writer and journalist, remarked many years ago, 'And so try listening… It will work a small miracle. And perhaps a great one.'[6]

Social life offers us this opportunity, this invitation, to develop interest, empathy and ultimately love and compassion through conscious listening. Conversation therefore makes visible both our egotistical and selfish sides and provides an opportunity for developing empathy, for practising a culture of selflessness. This dynamic is summarized below.

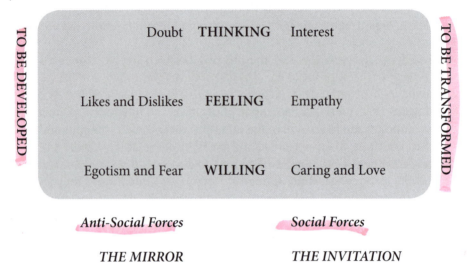

FIGURE 3.1: SOCIAL AND ANTI-SOCIAL FORCES IN THE HUMAN BEING

While the interplay between social and anti-social forces is visible in every conversation and encounter, it is also a basic dynamic in society, especially in an age devoted to self-interest, consumption and the forces of the market. A central question facing all efforts at social reform is whether the reform and the resulting policies and structures will strengthen the forces of egotism and selfishness, or encourage individuals and groups to develop interest and empathy towards others. Conflict, exploitation and poverty are the result of the anti-social forces of egotism and greed. They are like forces of nature in us and in society. Social qualities, such as empathy and compassion, need to be practised and consciously developed by us as they are no longer a natural heritage of being human. The opportunity for doing so is given in every conversation and relationship. Developing a caring culture, a culture of selflessness is the great task of the present and the future, and all social reform efforts must be judged on the basis of whether they promote a deeper, more caring connection between individuals and groups.

A second central aspect of social life revealed in human dialogue and encounter is the reality of karma and reincarnation. We meet a lifelong friend at summer camp when we are 12 and have a feeling I have known you for ever, or we meet a future colleague on Thursday morning in 1994, coming down the stairs of an office building, and have an immediate sense this person will play an important role in my life. Or perhaps we have a special relationship to a sixth-grade class teacher who seems to see and understand us from the time of our first handshake. We all have such experiences, and perhaps acknowledge that there is a kind of synchronicity to events or meetings, but shy away from recognizing the deep bond of mutual karmic intention that is present but not conscious in our lives.

I have also had other experiences in which a sense of spiritual energy and connection was so palpable that I could not help but be aware of something important happening. In 1970 I was sitting in an apple orchard with two Waldorf teachers from Toronto and a group of us from the Boston area discussing whether to start a Waldorf school in Cambridge. In this conversation we made a decision to start the school a year into the future, and to devote ourselves fully to this endeavour. All who were present could sense a karmic intention coming to conscious awareness. The Waldorf School in Lexington was started as a kindergarten a year later.

A similar experience occurred for me over a decade ago when a group of 10–12 young Chinese students, some in teacher training at Sunbridge College, met in our living room every other month to plan to bring Waldorf education back to China. My wife and I watched and attempted to hold a positive space and mood, sensing that we were witnessing an important spiritual and human event because the psychic and spiritual energy felt so powerful. Two years later the Waldorf school in Chengdu was started and now, 12 years later, there are over 50 Waldorf schools, 500 kindergartens and many training centers in mainland China.

Rudolf Steiner, in describing human meetings as the archetypal social phenomena, also points to the experience that just below the surface of consciousness when we listen deeply to the other, images of our future karmic connection are present, and that as we speak something of our past connections comes alive. While this is not yet a common experience, I have had several such experiences in my life when I felt that out of such images I was for a moment able to sense something of the true being of the other, and to speak to the other in such a way that I was addressing an essential question in their life. Put differently I had the feeling that their higher self was speaking through me.

How can we know whether reincarnation and karma are real, that the social world is the tableau on which the reality of our mutual karma is exercised? We can reflect on our life experiences, on our biography, to see if we can find clear patterns of destiny, from life themes and challenges to unexpected and deep friendships formed instantaneously. We can see whether the perspectives and meaning offered by the teachings of reincarnation and destiny as a path of learning and development make sense to us, not so much in providing specific answers but as a goad to deeper questions. Why was I born a mixed-race person or why did I become an immigrant at seven? How did the accident I had with my father play into my life and career choices? By asking such questions we take greater responsibility for our life, recognizing that our life has intentionality and purpose.

While there is no conclusive proof of the reality of reincarnation and karma, there is a growing body of personal and empirical evidence to support it. I was quite moved by a book titled *Old souls: The scientific evidence for past lives* by Tom Schroder, who examines the very detailed research of Dr Ian Stevenson who looked at over 3,000 cases of young children's recollections of previous incarnations.[7] I was also touched by *Expecting Adam* by Martha Beck, in which she describes her inner conversations with her joyous, light-filled and handicapped son both before and after his birth.[8]

If we do in fact elaborate a kind of life plan of mutual intentions with our community of familiar souls prior to incarnation, then the dynamics of our network of mutual destiny is the single most important factor in the forming of social life. I am quite certain that in the future this will be seen as a staggering omission in judging current forms of social enquiry, as for the most part people do not yet possess the organs for perceiving this reality.

The third significant dimension of social life that is revealed through a deeper reflection on conversation and human encounter is that it can bring to our consciousness the deep longing for human freedom, equality and sisterhood and brotherhood that live within the human soul. If we listen deeply to another we can come to experience the value of another's thoughts and opinions, and when we are listened to with care we recognize the importance of being allowed to express our thoughts freely. In this manner we know from experience that freedom of speech and religion is an important human birthright. As we deepen our awareness of what occurs in conversation, in genuine dialogue, a deep sense of gratitude can arise for the freedom which allows our individuality to unfold and wish to see others have the same opportunity.

As our relationship to another deepens and we feel empathy for their journey and their struggles, we experience their essential equality as a brother or sister on the road of life, and wish to honour it and safeguard it. We can do so by listening, by giving equal time, by not interrupting, and by judging our own behaviour and that of others through the lens of whether the experience of equality is enhanced or limited. The undemocratic nature of the American political system, or the excessive discrepancy of salaries and wealth inequalities in many societies, then become a source of pain for us.

Through developing empathy towards another in our feeling life, we bring alive a sense of compassion and service in our will toward the less fortunate. They are our brothers and sisters, and as Martin Luther King said many years ago, 'we are all caught in an inescapable network of mutuality, tied in a single garment of destiny. Whatever affects one directly affects all indirectly…'.[9]

By experiencing this deeper dimension of conversation we bring to consciousness the longing for inner and outer freedom, the desire for the mutual recognition *of equality between human beings and the wish to serve others in thought and deed.* These three ideals of freedom, equality and sisterhood/brotherhood can then become the guiding star for our own behaviour, and indeed for all efforts at social reform.

PROPOSITION 7: There are three formative principles to do with human motives and consciousness that were formulated by Rudolf Steiner as the Sociological Law, the Fundamental Social Law and the Motto of the Social Ethic, all relevant to the challenge of forming a healing society.

1. In 1898, Steiner formulated what he called the Basic Sociological Law:

> *At the beginning of culture, humanity strives to create social arrangements in which the interests of the individual are sacrificed for the interest of the whole. Later developments lead to a gradual freeing of the individual from the interest of the community and to an unfolding of individual needs and capacities.*[10]

This law, or principle, exists in time, covering the whole of known history. Certainly, when one ponders the sweep of history and the gradual emergence of individual rights from Greco-Roman times to the present, it appears justified, and points to one of the central aspects of historical evolution: the emergence of individual consciousness. Based on my observation of institutional development, I would also say that it applies to the life cycle of institutions, which require the energy and sacrifice of individual interests in order to be established, and are then in later years more able to respond to the needs of individual members. Put simply, no pension and overtime in the start-up period of many organizations.

The implication of this principle is that organizations and society will have to reckon with ever-greater demands from individuals for the meeting of their rights and needs. The growing expectation that freedom of speech and religion, free elections and free health care and education as well as unemployment insurance and old-age pensions are human rights is evidence of this development in our time.

2. In 1905, Steiner described a second principle, calling it the Fundamental Social Law:

> *The well-being of a community of cooperatively working human beings is the greater, the less individuals demand of the proceeds of their work for themselves or, in other words, the more they make over these proceeds to their co-workers and the more their needs are met not by their own work but from that of others.*[11]

This complex and awkwardly phrased law is concerned with motives, suggesting that when labour is a commodity and self-interest becomes the motive force of economic activity, suffering, poverty and want are the result. One might ask about the degree to which the poverty in the Third World, or in our inner cities, is the result of this social law not being understood and worked with. Certainly, my own research into income inequalities in the United States suggests the truth of Steiner's insight as poorer health, decreased longevity, greater levels of psychological distress and higher prison populations result from high levels of wealth and income inequalities.[12]

The interest in a Basic Guaranteed Income, now being experimented with in a number of countries, and the existence of a Living Wage Movement point in the direction of turning remuneration into a rights question rather than an economic one. Such a development is critical in overcoming the egotism and fear built into much of Western economic thought and practice since neoliberal economic orthodoxy sees economic life as a competitive struggle for survival in the market place.[13]

3. In 1918 Rudolf Steiner formulated the Motto of the Social Ethic, proposing that:

> *The healing social life is found when in the mirror of each human soul the whole community find its reflection and when in the community the virtue of each one is living.*[14]

Out of our experience in family life we know that families thrive when parents devote their consciousness, energy and their financial resources to the well-being of their children and the family as a whole. I know from experience that the Marxist dictum 'From each according to their abilities, to each according to their needs' is a healing approach to family resource allocation. We also know that social illness, conflict and heartbreak result when families and organizations are built around the principle of a competitive struggle for survival. However, if families, communities, organizations and societies are organized in such a way that each individual is allowed to develop their mind and spirit in freedom, to experience their equality in the sphere of rights, and is called upon to give the results of their labour to others through meaningful work, then the virtue of each one is indeed truly living.

The call to develop an individual social consciousness towards others and a community awareness that society exists to serve the development of the free individual, then, is made explicit in this social maxim. We can picture our colleagues, children and clients, and the members of our community, and let them appear in the mirror of our soul; and we can ask how our community and organization foster and honour the development of the individual.

PROPOSITION 8: The nature of modern consciousness as well as the threefold nature of the human being requires an explicit threefolding of society at this time; an independent life of culture based on freedom, a legal political life committed to true equality, and an economic life devoted to serving human needs based on principles of mutuality. Steiner summarized this demand by calling for 'socialism in economic life, democracy for the life of rights and individualism for spiritual life'.[15]

The principles of a threefold social order were elaborated by Rudolf Steiner in many lectures between 1918 and 1922, and in his book translated as *Toward social renewal*.[16] While he did not directly formulate the threefold social order as a law, except by inference, it could be expressed in the following way:

> *The health of a group, institution, or a society is the greater, the more it works with principles of freedom in cultural life, equality in the sphere of rights and politics, and brotherhood and sisterhood in the area of work and economic life.*

If this is true, groups, institutions and societies working with these principles will be characterized by higher levels of creativity and greater health, and will produce higher levels of commitment and satisfaction amongst their members and their clients. Health is not synonymous with efficiency or profitability, although such factors need to be considered.

Christof Lindenau, a German sociologist, has formulated these principles in more detail as follows: 'The meeting of human needs within a group, institution, or society of cooperatively working human beings is the greater the more it is based on the practice of brotherhood or sisterhood.'[17] This principle refers to the conscious division of tasks within an institution or society based on competence, in which each person contributes her or his talents to serving the needs of the whole, and to remuneration based on need, as opposed to status, hierarchy or power.

Next (Lindenau again), 'Agreements on rights and responsibilities within a group of co-operatively working human beings are most binding and effective, the more they are based on the practice of equality'. (Referring to the life of rights.) This principle suggests that a conscious rights life – for example, spelling out the rights and responsibilities of parents and teachers within a school, or management, labour and capital in companies – is most effective when based on dialogue and consensus.

It also applies to societies for when true democracy exists and extends to the making of laws and the articulation of rights and responsibilities; there is less conflict and violence, in families, groups, institutions and nations. A strong rights life in any social setting is the road to peace and co-operation. Its absence leads to dysfunction and the struggle for power.

Finally, 'The creative working together of people in a group or an institution is most fruitful when it can proceed from the exercise of freedom'. (Referring to cultural life.) When individuals are granted substantial autonomy or freedom of initiative within a generally accepted mission or set of goals, they will be more creative on behalf of the whole.

It is important to note that there is an inherent tension within each sphere: in economic life between service and efficiency; in the rights life between rights and responsibilities; and in cultural life between individual freedom and a set of cultural norms or institutional goals. A balance between these polarities is essential for health.

In working with a wide variety of institutions over the years, I have also experienced an essential interdependency between the three spheres. If the goal or mission of an organization is not clear or shared (cultural life), the rights life suffers in the sense that power-plays and personality conflict become more pronounced (social life), which in turn makes the trust or delegation required for an effective work life based on brotherhood and sisterhood more difficult (economic life.) Equally, if the resources in economic life are ongoingly too limited, it will over time erode both the relational and the spiritual life of the organization or of society at large.

PROPOSITION 9: By becoming more conscious social artists, and social scientists, and by recognizing that we create and sustain the social world by externalizing our nature as well as our values, we have the possibility of creating healthier families, communities, organizations and societies.

While it is likely that the large formal institutions of society will not relinquish their power easily, and will certainly not be in the vanguard of social change, the millions of groups and institutions around the world that make up civil society offer a 'blessed unrest', a fertile ground for social reform. Through a deeper understanding of the dialogue of social creation, and through the principles I have described here, a new image of what it means to be human, and a new imagination of what a healthy threefold society looks like, can emerge. The beginnings are visible everywhere, from a recognition that neither socialism nor capitalism serve human needs effectively, to experiments in direct democracy, to co-operative and worker-owned enterprises, and to growing demands for cultural freedom.

The regressive power of economic and political elites and the authoritarian tendencies of religious fundamentalism are rising to counter this new awareness, and are seeking to develop the tools to repress and control the longing for freedom, democracy and economic justice. Yet I sense a ferment for change, and I see around me active and widespread social experimentation occurring that is seldom reported on. I agree with Rebecca Solnit that 'what we dream of is already present in the world'.[18] Yet we must learn to see and be aware it – and here, the propositions which I have outlined in this chapter can be an aid.

As we go about our life we can ask ourselves questions like the following: What furthers community and a sense of human connection? What are the values we seek to practise in family and community life? How can I listen more deeply and bring to awareness my destiny connections? What are the biographical themes of the institution of which I am a part?

Social practitioners are usually ahead of social theorists and academics, and so if we look we will find many beginnings of a new and healthier society. This can give us courage, and help awaken us to the truth that it is only individuals in alliance with others who bring about social change. So let us engage in action learning, in being both more courageous in taking initiatives and in reflecting on what brings health and healing to the social world, in a new, more conscious social art, and a new, more human social science.

By engaging in such a process and meeting others deeply and listening carefully, we will also awaken the dynamic of mutual destiny that will allow us to bring social healing. And we will bring to awareness that it is ultimately more loving, moral human beings who create a better world.

NOTES

1. My political and social thinking has been strongly influenced by Hannah Arendt, by critical theory and the work of Herbert Marcuse and Jürgen Habermas, by social phenomenology (in particular Alfred Schutz), by Peter Berger, and by the many insights of Rudolf Steiner.
2. Arnold Toynbee, *A study of history*, 12 volumes, Oxford University Press, London, 1947–57; Bernard Lievegoed, *The developing organization*, Tavistock, London, 1976, Erik Erikson, *Childhood and society*, 2nd edn, Norton, New York, 1994, in particular Chapter 7; and Signe Schaefer, *Why on earth?: Biography and the practice of human becoming*, Chapter 4, Steiner Books, Great Barrington, Mass., 2013.
3. See Christopher Schaefer, *Vision in action: Working with soul and spirit in small organizations*, Steiner Books, Great Barrington, Mass., 1996, Chapters 2 and 6.
4. Peter Berger and Thomas Luckman, *The social construction of reality: A treatise in the sociology of knowledge*, Random House, New York, 1966, pp. 129–63.
5. Quoted in Dieter Bruell, *The mysteries of social encounters*, AWSNA, Fair Oaks, Calif., 2002, p. 164.
6. Brenda Ueland, 'Tell me more: on the fine art of listening', *Utne Reader*, Nov–Dec. 1992.
7. Tom Schroder, *Old souls: The scientific evidence for past lives*, Simon & Schuster, New York, 1999.
8. Martha Beck, *Expecting Adam: A true story of birth, rebirth and everyday magic*, Random House, New York, 2000.
9. Martin Luther King, 'Letter from a Birmingham Jail', reprinted in *The Atlantic*, April 2016.
10. Contained in GA31, Dornach, Switzerland, p. 147 (translation by the author).
11. Contained in GA34, Dornach, Switzerland, p. 160 (translation by the author).
12. See 'Toxic excess, Income inequalities and the Fundamental Social Law', my Chapter 13 in this volume.

13. George Monbiot, 'Neoliberalism – the ideology at the root of all our problems', *The Guardian*, 15 April 2016; see goo.gl/rRCSav.
14. The Motto of the Social Ethic is contained in Rudolf Steiner, *Verses and meditations*, Rudolf Steiner Press, London, 1985, pp. 116–17.
15. Rudolf Steiner, *Education as a force for social change*, Steiner Press, Great Barrington, Mass., 1997, p. 10.
16. Rudolf Steiner, *Toward social renewal*, Rudolf Steiner Press, London, 1987.
17. See Christof Lindenau, *Soziale Dreigliederung*, Verlag Freies Geistesleben, Stuttgart, 1983 (author's translation).
18. Rebecca Solnit, *Hope in the dark: Untold histories, wild possibilities*, Haymarket Books, Chicago, 2016, p. xvi.

CHAPTER 4

Threefold Development at Work in Organizations
Steve Briault

Three Dimensions of Organizations and Communities

The threefold nature of social life is a discovery of Rudolf Steiner's, rather than an invention. Although for a few years he tried to promote it as a programme of political reform, its significance today is not primarily historical, but flows from its profound insight into the underlying realities of human society and the developmental forces and processes working in it. These find their expression on every level – macro, meso and micro – of social phenomena.

However, as Steiner himself pointed out, one cannot simply transpose what he described for society as a whole on to the organizational or small community level. We cannot expect to create a distinct, self-regulated cultural, rights or economic realm in each institution. Organizational cultures are embedded within wider cultural contexts; rights issues are governed by national laws as well as organizational policies; and every business is integrated within many wider economic systems. Moreover, most organizations have their basic identity within *one* of the three realms of society – i.e. they are commercial, political or cultural in their primary purpose (although some Non-Governmental Organizations, for example, may straddle more than one of these).

So where can we observe and validate social threefolding on the meso-social level? What follows are my own perceptions, conclusions and approaches based on many years' practice of organization and community development, as member, manager and consultant.

The Rights Life of Organizations

Every human grouping, if it is to be more than an informal crowd, needs *structure*. This is expressed through the legal, financial, constitutional and internal forms, policies and agreements that regulate how people work together. There are physical, administrative and leadership structures in most organizations. These represent the 'rights' dimension – who can decide what; how activities are to be carried out to ensure quality and safety; the guidelines on behaviour that apply to everyone, and so on. Included in this is remuneration, which from a social threefolding perspective is a rights rather than an economic issue (because work is seen to be a contractual responsibility rather than a commodity to be sold at a price).

The Economic Life of Organizations

Any organization which does not exist purely for the benefit of its own members contains and manages work processes which benefit others. These others may be customers, beneficiaries, patients or students, and the organization itself may be commercial, cultural or political in nature. However, the work processes represent its *economic* dimension, because they are carried out to create value for other people. In a factory this is obvious, but in a school perhaps less so. The *teaching*, together with all the administrative and physical support processes, is the economic aspect of the school. This may seem surprising in a cultural organization, but the core *cultural* process is learning, not teaching. Teaching and studying (including the teachers' professional development) serve the primary purpose of promoting learning and development in the students. In a police force, the work involved in safeguarding and law enforcement is the expression of its economic dimension (which does not make the public – or criminals – into customers!), although its primary purpose lies in the rights sphere.

It is important to emphasize that what we are here calling the 'economic' dimension of an organization is not the financial aspect. Money flows – in different ways – through all three dimensions of a social organism. This theme is treated in more detail in Glen Saunders' chapter (see Chapter 15). In Steiner's threefold image, the essence of the economic realm is *work processes which serve other people's needs*.

The Cultural Life of Organizations

Thirdly, every enduring organization or community develops its own particular *culture*. Where structure is the objective aspect of relationships – the rules that govern behaviour – culture is the *subjective* aspect. People live and work within structures; culture evolves and expresses itself within and between people. It can be observed externally in how people dress (if uniforms are not prescribed!), how they speak to each other and to outsiders; and it manifests internally in people's feelings and attitudes towards their work and the organization of which they are part. Where structures can be *designed*, culture can only be *cultivated and influenced*; this is why so many 'culture change projects' in organizations fail to achieve their aims.

FIGURE 4.1: THE THREE SOCIAL DIMENSIONS OF AN ORGANIZATION

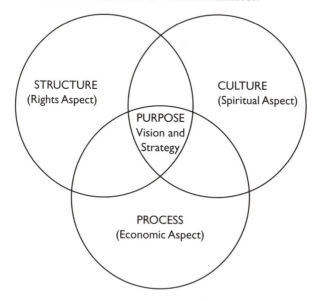

Caring for the Structural Dimension

If one has identified this inherent threefoldness in an organization, it is important to explore how each of the three aspects needs to be managed and developed; and also how they can find their right relationship to each other. Structures, for example, need to be designed and when necessary redesigned, to support the processes which take place within them – following the principle that 'form follows function'. This is usually obvious in the case of physical structures – a gymnasium is designed differently from a theatre – but not always so clear in the case of social structures, such as work-group composition, management remits and reporting lines, decision rights, meetings, group and individual responsibilities. The principle of equality here does not mean that everyone has equal authority – the organization does not need to be a democracy – but that everyone is treated with equal respect, everyone has a right to be heard, to pursue equal opportunities, to be paid through an equitable system.

Organization design is both an art and a science. Done imaginatively and effectively, it can create the social conditions in which collaboration, initiative and individual development can thrive. Done mechanistically or unreflectingly, it can stultify personal responsibility and sub-optimize the value stream. If jobs, for example, are defined in a rigid, over-prescriptive manner so that the post holder has very limited discretion in what tasks they can undertake, and how their work is to be carried out, then motivation is undermined, and opportunities for professional and personal development limited. If work-groups are composed by function rather than complementarity of role, genuine teamwork is impossible – a 'team' of sales people, for example, all carrying out the same tasks with different customer groups or geographical patches, are more likely to compete than co-operate with each other. They are like a 'team' of goalkeepers.

Healthy social and organizational structures support empowerment by allowing every individual to take on a role – or better, a range of roles – matched to their aptitudes, potential and preferences (this is the cultural aspect) as well as contributing appropriately to the organizational purpose and needs of customers/beneficiaries (the economic aspect). Equality expresses itself in the principle that every colleague, from the grass roots to the boardroom, carries 100 percent responsibility for their work. If the Chief Executive is negligent or dishonest, he or she is less valuable to the organization than a single shop-floor worker who carries out their tasks conscientiously.

Caring for the Process Dimension

In work processes, the principle of fraternity/sorority means that workers should be as clear as possible about the identity and needs of those who receive the outputs of their work. In a manufacturing context, this includes the next stage in the production process – the individual or work-group who receives the semi-finished product – as well as the ultimate customer at the end of the value stream. In service organizations where there is direct contact between staff and external customers – for example, retail, insurance, personal or professional services – employees are often trained in 'customer focus' or similar disciplines. They are taught how to be courteous, friendly, show interest, apologize appropriately, and so on. It is interesting, however, that as a customer it is nearly always possible to tell the difference between a service provider who is genuinely interested in one's situation and needs, and one who has just been trained to appear so. Formulaic behaviour is no substitute for real human good will.

Fabio Brescacin, founder of EcorNaturaSi (a supermarket chain specializing in organic products) states that: 'in economic life, efficiency is morality'. He explains this surprising statement on the basis that the more efficient a business is – i.e. the more effective its work processes – the more value can be created for customers, and the use of resources minimized. This principle holds good for all businesses, not just 'ethical' ones. This is a purely economic principle – i.e. to serve the demands of customers as efficiently as possible. Ethical questions, such as the treatment of workers and the protection of the environment, need to be addressed by legal/rights provisions; and the education of consumers so that their choices and preferences are informed by social morality is a matter for the cultural life. This is why Steiner jokes that one should not 'pour moralic acid' into the economy. Of course, in our present society the cultural life is constantly distorted and manipulated by economic interests – most obviously by advertising, much of which is hugely wasteful for the economy (because it adds cost without adding value) and toxic for our culture (because it misuses attractive imagery to manipulate behaviour).

In a healthy organization, work processes will be under continual review, involving everyone in an ongoing quest to reduce waste and improve quality. There will also be a regular dialogue between customers and suppliers along the whole chain of demand and supply – what Jones and Womack in *Lean thinking*[1] call the 'continual conferencing along the value stream'. Such dialogue and the resulting improvement efforts exemplify the essential collaborative nature of economic life. Economic value streams – from Mother Nature to consumer (and back again) – are like river systems, where multiple tributaries converge in a growing confluence towards the ocean of the market. Waste and egotism are the primary pollutants in this global flow of value. Through the financial system, the inherent altruism and mutuality of productive work are obscured: the pseudo-purpose of generating profit usurps the centre of attention, reducing the true purpose of meeting human needs to merely a means of maximizing the return on investment. In a capitalist economy, the 'freedom' principle is extended from the legitimate self-interest of the consumer into the freedom of investors and corporations to exploit the earth and other human beings. Movements such as fair trade, ethical investment and sustainable consumerism struggle to counter the overwhelming power of money seeking to multiply itself.

Caring for the Cultural Dimension

Processes and structures can be made visible, be studied, analysed and consciously transformed. Culture is different: it is an outcome of, not an input to, an organizational system. It can be influenced but not determined by management design. Its sources as well as its ultimate expression lie within human souls. Organizational culture emerges and evolves organically as a result of many inner and outer factors – demographics and personal backgrounds, management communication and behaviour, training and staff development, reward systems, job design and team structures, physical conditions, professional standards and norms, as well as the professed values and strategic vision articulated by the leadership. This complex picture means that it is neither possible nor appropriate to 'manage' the culture directly: only totalitarian systems try to do this, and their attempts are always ultimately unsuccessful.

However, culture can be, and always is, influenced by management actions. Such influence may be more or less conscious and more or less appropriate. An effective approach to nurturing an organization's culture will involve diagnosing the existing culture, describing the desired direction of development (for example, 'people feeling more empowered to take initiative' or 'sense of real team working') and then identifying the mix of factors which can promote the intended direction of change. These influencing factors need also to be 'matched' congruently; otherwise contradictions will cause the culture to become infected with cynicism – for example, when an ideology of teamwork is espoused, but the remuneration system is based on individual pay for performance.

In organizational culture, the social ideal of Liberty means that each person must be able to express their individuality within the common ethos which unites them with their colleagues. Any attempt to create 'corporate clones' or uniformity of behaviour runs counter to this. The ideal means that every individual should be able to act intelligently and autonomously in the service of the whole community and its beneficiaries, and participate in a culture of continuous improvement. This completes the 'benign cycle' between the three dimensions.

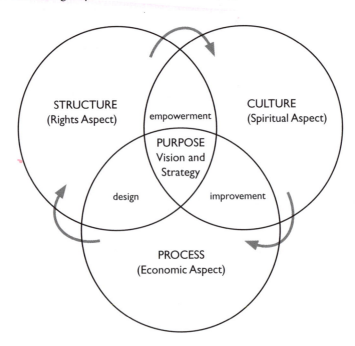

FIGURE 4.2: ORGANIZATIONAL DEVELOPMENT CYCLE THROUGH THE THREE DIMENSIONS

Britain's National Health Service (NHS) – a Study in Institutional Threefoldness

The three words which make up the name of the UK's most beloved and beleaguered institution are a wonderful illustration of its threefold aims, which are simultaneously political, cultural and economic:

- NATIONAL: through the NHS, the British Government has since 1948 guaranteed the equal right of every citizen to healthcare, 'free at the point of use'. This remarkable social experiment has been admired, criticized and stress-tested, subjected to massive demographic and financial challenges, but survives and attracts passionate defence whenever it appears to be under attack. To the British population, the principle just *feels right*, and is a source of enduring national pride. One trade union leader even described as 'barbaric' the idea of healthcare being a commodity, with the best treatment only available to those who could afford it.
- HEALTH: healthcare, health education, medical research and therapeutic practice are cultural activities.[2] Medicine is arguably both an art and a science, and its practitioners are rightly protective of their freedom to do what they believe is right for their patients. The Hippocratic oath is entered into by free individuals, and the quality of person-to-person relationship between patients and carers is an important expression of individual responsibility, compassion and commitment – as is the self-responsibility of citizens in informing themselves about risks and factors affecting their own health, and making life-style and treatment choices accordingly.
- SERVICE: the NHS and its staff deliver a wide range of services to the population, both the sick and the healthy. These services are its economic dimension: although they are not directly purchased by the recipients, they are valuable and highly valued, and contribute directly to the physical and mental well-being of many millions. In this aspect (only) of the NHS, the economic principle of efficiency applies: the service uses vast amounts of national, human and material resources, and its managers have a responsibility to deliver the maximum value with the minimum of waste, for the benefit of patients and the whole national population.

With its 1.4 million employees and more than 60 million beneficiaries, the National Health Service is somewhere between an institution (actually it is composed of several hundred discrete institutions) and a whole society; and it is therefore important to differentiate between its three dimensions, and allow each of them to develop and operate according to their distinct principles. Politicians, for example, notoriously create confusion, dysfunction and resentment when they try to impose ideologically driven restructurings; clinicians justifiably resist the marketization of their profession, but often fail to appreciate the economic (not the same as commercial!) nature of service delivery.

When in the 1990s academics and consultants (including myself) started to introduce 'lean' process disciplines into hospitals – perhaps unwisely mentioning Toyota as the exemplar of value creation and waste elimination – a typical reaction from clinicians was: 'We're not Japanese and we don't make cars…'. Both points are true, despite the unfortunate national stereotyping; but what this reaction overlooked was the reality that clinical and care services are delivered through human and technological work processes; that these processes were riddled with wasted effort, error and unnecessary delay; that process improvement could significantly enhance clinical benefit and the value derived from inevitably limited resources; and that much could be learned from industrial best practice in such improvement efforts. On the other side, many lean enthusiasts failed to appreciate the fundamental differences between a production and a clinical environment, and to respect the special culture and ethos of the caring and therapeutic professions.

So here also, the importance of respecting boundaries is paramount: service provision should be truly, altruistically economic and efficient; access to advice and treatment should be genuinely equitable and universal; and professional expertise and development should be in the hands of practitioners, not politicians or managers. Then, patients and citizens would experience prompt, cost-effective service; clinicians would be free to develop and deploy professional best practice within agreed resources; and the role of the state would be limited to guaranteeing universal access and appropriate levels of public funding. What a national treasure such a service would be!

Notes and References
1. D. T. Womack and J. P. Jones, *Lean thinking: Banish waste and create wealth in your corporation*, Simon & Schuster, London, 2003.
2. Why cultural, and not an economic service? Because the medical practitioner has to retain the freedom to work according to their knowledge, skill and conscience. This is a necessary limitation to "patient choice": choosing a course of treatment is more like commissioning a work of art than engaging a decorator.

CHAPTER 5

A Primary Approach to Threefold Thinking, or Red and Blue, and the Lost Primary
John Bloom

Introduction

The purpose of this chapter is to stimulate a transformation of our thinking in order to be in a social world that recognizes the inherent value of every human being and supports working together more harmoniously in the ecosystem of human relationships. Given our conventional Western training in dualism we will need tools, examples and imagination in order to cultivate this important transformation.

One such imaginative exercise comes from what might appear as a diversion – an exploration into Goethe's colour theory. Through Goethe's work and the subsequent development of his colour theory, we can find that experience complements appearance. Taken together, the simultaneous experience can awaken in us how we are actively part of the colour system. What Goethe did was expand the definition of how we know things to include not only what we are looking at but also what we are experiencing as we are looking. That is, Goethe included the inner experience as an essential part of our understanding and knowing.

The purpose of this chapter, then, is to use colour experience as a replicable experiment in new ways of knowing, with the understanding that we need to open new pathways of understanding if we are to transform how we grasp and engage in our daily world. The hope is that this exploration will support the transfer of this changed awareness to the fullness of social life. One simple but difficult outcome will be that we can discover our agency in bringing a threefold perspective as a reorganizing principle in our relationships and organizations.

Experiential Background

Figure 5.1: Typical Pharmacy Show Globes from the 1950s
Note: *For colour images online see goo.gl/4MYv8q*

I remember as a child in the 1950s the red and blue show globes at the pharmacist's counter or in the drug-store window. Glowing red and blue liquids were a sure sign of profession and health, and an intriguing vestige of the seventeenth-century apothecary. I never knew what was actually in the containers, though I made up stories. However, I came to think that the red and blue were emblematic of the arterial and venous states of blood flow – again a conjecture, but generally agreed-upon explanation.

This red–blue view about human blood circulation is what we learned in school. I remember the illustrations in our general science textbook. As an imagination, I guess it was easy to teach, but in its simplicity, it is nonetheless dualistic. Blood sustained life: renewed and red on its way out from the heart–lung complex, exhausted and blue on the way back. This approach characterizes, rather than accurately describes, and is tailored for didactic purposes in the name of science. The dualistic imagination emanates from and serves to reinforce the dominant Western paradigm: polarities as a primary framework for explaining not only the circulation of the blood but also electricity, magnetism, and a host of other scientific concepts that are part of our vernacular understanding of how the universe works. But it is time to move past the simplicity and power of dualistic mind–body dichotomous thinking. It is not serving us any more, and there is no better example of this than our current political systems.

The red–blue modality has come to frame the contrast between the two most visible political parties in the USA and UK (though they are reversed from each other in how they are used), and is told as a story of opposition in a manner eerily similar to, and equally as simplistic as, the story of blood circulation. That red and blue are construed as opposites is a complete distortion of what they represent of human vitality. In the blood, the descriptive colours are not in opposition but merely stages in a continual transformative process that never physically or chemically divides. We are stuck with a misleading meme that is a blunder, both metaphysically, metaphorically, scientifically and probably emotionally.

A Theory of Colour

Bear with me through a brief foray into pigment-based colour theory, as articulated by Johann Wolfgang von Goethe in the eighteenth century and still relevant today. First and foremost, there are three primary colours: red, yellow and blue. Right away you can surmise that yellow is the primary lost in the proverbial political shuffle. But Goethe wanted to seat colour theory in perceptual and conceptual experience – the full dimensions of human reality. This means that we see colour optically, and simultaneously experience a certain soul resonance. In other words, colour bypasses the typical path of intellectual knowing, and instead speaks directly to our feeling. We do not need to think blue to experience blue. That is the inbound pathway. The outbound pathway is that colour serves as a manifest expression of soul life. In short, Goethe indicated that colour is the language of the soul. If you doubt this, I encourage you to try working with colour in a way that is both fluid and open. Be advised that while the materials are easily attainable, the actual aesthetic discipline is both challenging and profound.

To understand this Goethean approach, one has to be open to the direct experience of colour and be willing to live with and scientifically observe that experience as it informs daily life. A big ask. But without a big ask, how do we imagine change will happen? Goethe recognized that yellow has a quality of light (day) and blue the quality of darkness (night). One could say that this is a kind of base polarity. However, he does not stop there. He goes on to posit that red has a similar effect on both yellow and blue. It serves both, equally, as an intensifier. That is, if I have a field of yellow and into that flow a bit of red, the red will mix with the yellow to bring it to orange. But orange is not a discrete colour here as you might find it in the crayon box. Rather it is an intensification of the yellow, and the eye will move through the field of yellow to land on the red-orange. A similar process happens when you add a bit of red to a blue; in which case, violet is an energetic concentration of the blue. This is a lot to digest – but easily reproduced with even the simplest water-colour kit.

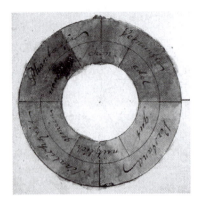

FIGURE 5.2: GOETHE'S COLOUR WHEEL, CIRCA 1809
NOTE: Goethe's Colour Wheel can be seen online at goo.gl/dL8ZX9.

This fluid and unified view of colour is very different from the way colours are commonly named, as discrete entities. As a teaching tool, artists are asked to work with the three primary colours in such a way as to produce what is called a colour wheel or circle, such that the pigments keep their identity and blend into the next. In its completeness, the wheel constitutes a colour system.

However, the wheel bears about the same relationship to aesthetic experience as the periodic table does to chemistry. The whole of the system is there, but one has to see past the charts to the living experience behind it. Furthermore, as the basic elements come to life in combination, their meaning emerges from our participation in and perception of those life forces.

Colour Experience

Let me take another step in this exercise with the three primary colours – red, blue and yellow – from the viewpoint of one's experience of them. We know the primary colours are primary because they are the irreducible elements from which all others emerge. The mix of any two primaries gives us what are known as 'secondary colours'. Red and blue produce violet; yellow and blue, green; yellow and red, orange.

Next is the concept of complementary colours. People commonly define complementary colours as opposite one another on the colour wheel. This understanding is true in one sense, although it fails to grasp what 'complement' means, which is to complete or make whole. If we take the 'opposites' view, the complementary pairs are red-green, orange-blue and yellow-violet. But are they really opposites, an idea that resides soundly in the dualistic mindset? In reality, no.

Let's take one pair, red-green, as an example. Red is the primary colour, and in green the other two primaries – yellow and blue – are co-present. In other words, in the complementary 'pairs', all three primaries are present, albeit in different proportions. So the three are found in the two.

Now it gets a little more complicated, but no less wondrous. There is a principle called 'simultaneous contrast'. An example of this phenomenon occurs when you put a neutral grey card next to a red one: the grey appears greenish. Place a yellow card next to the same grey one, and the grey will take on a violet hue. This experiment illustrates how, in looking at a primary colour, we also 'see' the complement as projected on to the neutral grey. The Impressionists used this optical reality to enhance the experience of colour. To make an orange paint-mark more intense, they placed it next to a mark of blue. The marks then mutually reinforce each other through the principle of simultaneous contrast. The orange became more orange, the blue bluer.

Here is the last and most important piece of this exercise, the concept of the so-called 'afterimage'. The afterimage is what we experience when we close our eyes after looking at one colour for an extended time. If we have looked at red, for example, we will see green when shutting our eyes. The green, in this instance, is what is called the afterimage. Given the reality of simultaneous contrast, what is actually happening is that we are experiencing the green even as we are looking at the red, though we are conditioned to tune the complementary 'afterimage' out. So the word afterimage is actually a misnomer.

We are always experiencing wholeness. Here is why this is the case. While we are looking at the red, having a simultaneous image of the green, we are *experiencing* all three primary colours that are co-present. The nature of colour is such that in our perceiving of it, it generates simultaneously within us an experience of its complement. What this then means is that all three primaries are present even if we think we are looking at one colour. The three are present in the one. To awaken this unified experiential reality requires a major shift in awareness.

From Colour to Threefold

To move beyond dualism, we have to look at our experience of both inner and outer as equally valid. Science is slowly getting to the place where the observer is also a participant, and therefore never really outside of the system. What this means is that we affect what we perceive even as what we perceive affects us. It takes a particular consciousness to hold an objective–subjective awareness of this *both–and* relationship. Recognizing this shift of consciousness is a step towards shifting the paradigm of knowing. Colour, since it is the language of the soul – and the soul embodies the inner life – is a great medium and exemplar for such a consciousness shift.

How do we take this learning back to reconsider the false polarity of red and blue? And, how might the inclusion of yellow foster a truer reflection of human experience beyond the dualistic paradigm? And what does colour theory have to teach us about life, anyway?

To address these questions, I will refer to a threefold imagination of social life as first posited by Rudolf Steiner, the Austrian philosopher, scientist and archivist of Goethe's work, early in the twentieth century. As discussed elsewhere in this book, Steiner's approach in 1917, which he called 'the Threefold Commonwealth', was an attempt to rectify the chaotic cultural, political and economic state, which had already led to the disasters of the First World War (1914–18). Without addressing and transforming those three primary domains of social life, Steiner imagined that Europe would plunge again into another disastrous war. He died in 1925 and thus did not live to see how prophetic his words had been.

What Steiner suggested was a way of being in the world that is unified in its threefoldness, yet respectful that not all experiences are the same. Rather, we are constantly in a dance between ourselves and the world, our inner voice and the messages and sense impressions we receive from the external. Further, since we are all social beings, our relationships vary in depth and purpose. Steiner's purpose was to set a framework with which to understand this and to provide us with tools with which we can create a new level of creative clarity for managing social and organizational life beyond dualistic or oppositional conflict.

First, Steiner looked at the three basic domains of social life: cultural/spiritual, rights and agreements (political), and economic. This framing in itself is not particularly unique. What was radical – in the sense of connecting to the roots of human wisdom – was his applying the three principles of the French Revolution – i.e. freedom, equality and brotherhood – not solely to the political realm as the French had done. Rather, he associated each principle with its appropriate realm in the following way: freedom in culture and spirit, equality in rights and agreements, and brotherhood in the economy.

In the cultural sphere, we have to remain free to develop our individualities, create our rites and rituals together, our modes of expression, and all the educational processes that support our evolution of consciousness. Such freedom would produce chaos in the realm of rights and agreements. Instead, the principle of equality should govern how we govern. Each human being brings his or her perspective to the creation of agreements or laws. But in the actual decision-making process, it is 'one person, one vote', a mark of democracy.

In economic life, the reality is that we are completely interdependent. Someone makes my clothes and builds my car so that I can do my work in finance (for example) on behalf of others. The imagination here is that economic life is driven by being aware of others' material needs and bringing our own capacity in service to meeting those needs. This is not the normal way that economics is taught. Self-interest is usually at the centre; but, from an economic perspective, self-interest is a myth – one of the stories at the heart of materialism and dualistic thinking. Threefolding has much to say from micro to macro, in how we guide our lives to how we work in a community and, furthermore, how we arrange the functions of government, economics and culture.

Integration of Colour and Social Threefolding

While the practice of threefolding could occupy much more attention, let me return to the unity of the three primary colours. If we could imagine assigning one of the primary colours to each of the threefold domains, we might gain some insight into how we could work with each of them, remain true to the character of each, and yet operate with an awareness of the full complementarity or afterimage that includes the other two. I would like to reiterate an important principle here: viz. *the nature of colour is such that in our perceiving of it, it generates within us simultaneously an experience of its complement.* Assignment for the purpose of this imagination:

blue to rights and agreements;
red to economics;
yellow to cultural-spiritual.

These connections are not prescribed. Rather, they are based on my experience as a painter: yellow has a quality of light and consciousness, blue of water and equanimity, and red of fire and enterprise.

If we hold the principle of equality in rights, how can it be that some people are treated as less equal, especially when predicated on their choice of religion or present life circumstances, both of which are in the domain of culture and spirit and therefore guided by the principle of freedom? No one should be told who they are by someone other than themselves. If that were the case, it would be an exercise of power over another's individuality. Yet this happens all the time. For example, when politicians (blue) and the business leaders (red) determine educational curricula (yellow) that serve their ideologies, it constitutes a pollution of the educational process. The truer purpose of education is to support individuals in their own becoming, so to speak, and to develop a citizenry capable of participating in democratic processes with respect for the value of each other's freely formed views. Following the logic here, if education is misdirected, how could we imagine the realms of politics and economics as not debased, since the three sectors directly affect each other through the principle of complementarity. Those who have painted know that if you start with a muddy yellow, the rest will be muddy too.

If we look at how the economic world currently operates based upon the myth of self-interest and unlimited natural resources, we can see why we get such disparity of wealth. Part of the self-interest story is that, as an individual, I can exercise my power over others to accumulate wealth for myself. That seems to be at the heart of the free-market concept. But in the economic world, we are not absolutely free, as we are in the cultural domain, because we really would not get very far without others working to make the material aspects of our lives possible. The truer (primary red) picture of economics is one of compassionate interdependence – a web of transactions and interactions in which each of us freely chooses to participate. Once we have made that choice as an individual, we are no longer free in the same way. There are many examples of how, when the colours are mixed up, the domains are confused. An experience can be politicized (think education), or the formulation of our identity can be besieged by commerce (think advertising). And so much can be driven by fear that the only way we feel safe is when we believe that we have power over others.

Shifting Consciousness

The whole point of the colour exercise and this threefold analysis is that it is a framework that, if carefully taken up, can set us on a path to having power *with* each other, rather than over one another. How might the false red-blue political duality change? Imagine two politicians discussing education. Instead of talking about how and with what content children should be educated – a discussion driven by ideology and standardized testing – they would consider how to assure every child's right to an education; one that respects a free cultural life and the need for each child to be seen as a human being striving to contribute her or his gifts to the world. Or imagine a world in which corporations come together, not to control the market-place and maximize profits (self-interest), but to look at their own needs in relation to what is needed in the world. The ideal would be to find an equitable relationship between self and community interest that recognizes the reality of mutuality and regeneration.

Conclusion

We need to imagine a world that can be different. But first, we need to change our own thinking and practice. If we can hold the reality that the circulation of blood is a complexity of processes that goes well beyond the input–output, red-blue reductionist view, and instead operates as a whole system capable of self-renewal and supporting consciousness through clearly defined interdependent functions and interactions with both internal and external environments, then perhaps we can move beyond a dualistic win–lose paradigm.

I have never met a human being who did not want to be seen as a whole person – red, yellow and blue. Can we be whole and support each other by recognizing when we are building culture out of our inner freedom, when we are creating agreements as equals, and when we are economically active with an awareness of interdependence? It's a big ask. But without the big ask, we won't change. And without the change… – well, I prefer the challenge of change to the loss of any primaries.

CHAPTER 6

Rudolf Steiner and Social Threefolding during and after the First World War
Edward Udell

On 15 May 1922, Rudolf Steiner gave a lecture in the concert hall of the Four Seasons Hotel in Munich. According to the *New York Times*, 'organized reactionaries, Nationalists, and anti-Semitics attended the lecture in force'.[1]

The 33-year-old Adolf Hitler was in Munich that day[2] and had been leader of the Nazi Party for about ten months. Whether or not he had any link to what took place in the hall that evening, he was certainly aware of Steiner. In an article signed by Hitler and published 14 months earlier, on 15 March 1921, the Nazi Party's newspaper *Völkische Beobachter* referred to 'Anthroposophist Rudolf Steiner himself the adherent of the Threefold Social Order which is one of the many completely Jewish methods of destroying the peoples' normal state of mind'.

Steiner was neither anti-Semitic nor Jewish. In any case, the radical right in Germany considered him a traitor to the nation in part because in early 1921, he had led a movement for the autonomy of Upper Silesia, a region both Germany and Poland wanted to absorb and were acrimoniously contending for. Thus, during a lecture tour by Steiner through Germany in 1922, radicals had been trying to disrupt his lectures on various subjects.[3] He had been informed in advance of the risks that would attend the Four Seasons lecture 15 May, but he had refused to cancel it. Walter Beck in his memoirs described the scene that evening:

> *The hall was all filled up. The lectern was toward the front of the stage.... Rudolf Steiner spoke as he always took care to do with such lectures, leading in slowly,*

and explaining the spiritual science he had founded. After a half hour the lights went out – most listeners were in suspense as to what would now happen.... Rudolf Steiner stood above at the podium and, to the astonishment of all, spoke on as if nothing were going to happen. Absolute quiet ruled and it was dark in the hall, but Steiner spoke further without the slightest interruption in his tone of voice or sentence structure. This behavior by Steiner seems to have so astonished his foes that they initially attempted nothing. It was helpful that in the dark hall, beneath the lectern, on the table of the stenographer, a small lamp burned, so that this area was not fully in darkness. Steiner spoke on unhindered. After say ten minutes, friends who kept watch out on the floor had managed to get the lights back on. Rudolf Steiner spoke until the end and was discharged with great applause. He went out over the stage toward the left exit door at the back of a sidewall – and in that moment three or four young people rushed via some small steps up onto the right side of the stage and in the direction of the left exit door, which Steiner had just reached. We of the youth group, prepared for adverse events, jumped onto the stage as well and cut off the attackers' path to the exit door; I myself, coming in the middle of the second rank, could reach the stage center with some other friends as quickly as the attackers coming from the right side. A small scuffle broke out; meanwhile the stage filled up; our friend Hans Wohlbold and others were particularly involved; nothing happened, and silently the opponents disappeared out of the crowd, which had gathered on the stage.[4]

The *New York Times* story reported that just before the stage was stormed, firecrackers and stink bombs had been thrown at Steiner, and that the ensuing fracas continued until police cleared the hall. The *Times* writer found the events amusing, and colourfully described the attack on 'the long-haired Theosophist', who was speaking to an audience 'more than half composed of women'. The next morning, the would-be attackers seem to have shown up for the departure of the train on which Steiner had been scheduled to leave Munich – but he had intentionally left on an earlier train.[5]

In January 1920, Steiner – architect, creator of Waldorf Education, and humanitarian polymath who by the time of his death had brilliantly transformed a half-dozen core fields of human endeavour – explained that his threefold idea of social reform was

not a program or system for society as a whole, requiring the old system to cease suddenly and everything to be set up anew. The threefold idea can make a start with individual enterprises... – the threefold idea is not utopian.[6]

In April 1919 his main book about the threefoldness of the social order had been published, and had demonstrated a similar spirit:

> *Perhaps imperfections are contained in what is presented here. Then let them be found. It is not the function of a way of thinking which corresponds to reality to formulate perfect 'programs' for all time, but to point out the direction for practical work.*[7]

With regard to social ideas, that book is perhaps what Steiner is most known for. It has been translated into English under various titles, the most recent of which is *Towards social renewal*.[8] His struggle for social reform went well beyond writing the original German version of that short, great work; but it is worth recalling that when one of the early English translations appeared, it became the subject of a 14 January 1923 *New York Times* Book Review that said the book had 'novelty and bigness as a contribution to sociological literature – the most original contribution in a generation.'[9]

W.F. Lofthouse, writing in the January 1923 *London Quarterly Review*, said the work was 'perhaps the most widely read of all books on politics appearing since the war'.[10] *Towards social renewal* and a number of brilliant lectures Steiner gave on social and economic reform remain cutting-edge.[11] At least equally remarkable, however, is what Steiner *did* with his sociological discoveries: on several occasions he came within shouting distance of altering the course of twentieth-century history massively for the better.

In May 1917 the Russian Revolution was unfolding, the United States had recently entered the Great War on the French and English side, and Count Otto von Lerchenfeld was concerned about a certain frantic helplessness he observed amongst German officials inside Bavaria's consulate in Berlin. In a diary entry he recorded his impression of

> *how tiredly, hectically, restlessly – as if the tongue were hanging out of the mouth – everyone seeks in his little department or sub-department for the all. For thoughts – no time! Of ideas – no trace! They count on the war and on victory as with numbers. To gain courage, they look to the military. They dream only: Victory – Victory – Victory!*[12]

Otto was a minister to the court of Bavaria (the southeast region of Germany), and his uncle, Hugo Phillip von Lerchenfeld, was Bavaria's representative in Berlin and one of Bavaria's delegates to Germany's national parliament.[13] Partly because of his observations at the consulate, Otto, who had been a student of Rudolf Steiner's anthroposophy for a decade, met with Steiner in Berlin in June 1917 to ask what could be done about the social and political situation.[14] Thus, as was the case with most of Steiner's practical initiatives, this one developed in response to a request.

Further meetings ensued, during which Steiner for the first time spoke in detail of society's fundamentally threefold character and the need for policies that were in harmony with that fundamental reality.[15] Another of Steiner's associates, the Austrian Ludwig Polzer-Hoditz, whose brother Arthur was one of the chief advisors to the Austrian emperor, also participated in some of these discussions.[16] Otto von Lerchenfeld soon asked Steiner to write a memorandum that could be circulated among leading political figures.[17] Steiner wrote two – one for Austrian and the other for German statesmen.

Contents of the Two Memoranda of 1917

The memoranda rejected the notion that the Central European powers alone were to blame for the world war that was in progress. The issue had grave ramifications, because if Germany and Austria-Hungary should lose the war and be assigned exclusive blame for the conflict, as many signs indicated could happen, then it might be impossible to stop the war's victors from breaking up the two Central Powers into a collection of small states with boundaries based on ethnic and linguistic criteria. To divide Austria-Hungary into the various national ethnic groups within the empire meant to Steiner a backward step that would 'bring the European peoples to ruin'.[18] It would amount to a barbaric reduction of individuals to ethnic categories,[19] and would actually exacerbate the very problems that had led to the First World War in the first place.

Steiner instead supported 'federalizing' governance in Austria-Hungary. emphasizing that the way to bring about freedom for the many ethnic and linguistic groups in the Austro-Hungarian empire was not by separating them into independent states, but by establishing complete cultural freedom for the individual.[20] Steiner held that cultural life, including languages and ethnic cultures, needed to be separated from state power.[21]

In both memoranda, Steiner supported the introduction of political democracy limited to 'political matters', law enforcement, and control of the military.[22] At this early stage, he did not elaborate on what he meant by 'political matters', but in 1919 in *Towards social renewal* he would characterize politics as concerned with human rights and law, including labour law and other legal boundaries within which economic life would need to operate.[23]

The memoranda did not fully express Steiner's social thinking, but his outlook as it came to light over time included three orientations that he perceived as part of the half-conscious will of modern humanity: 1) government requires democracy and equal rights for all persons who are of age; 2) cultural and educational life need to be removed from state control and management and given over to individual freedom, but all families, not just the well-off, should have freedom of choice among non-state schools for their children; and 3) economic life, to be healthy, needs to be separate from the state, but based on freely contractual co-operation rather than on competition, and must operate within the legal and regulatory boundaries the democratic state develops.

Steiner held in the two memoranda that behind the high-toned moral propaganda employed by the alliance of nations at war with the Central Powers – thus behind President Woodrow Wilson's words in support of democracy and the freedom of nations – was an Anglo-American impulse to economically and culturally dominate the extraordinarily diverse community of peoples in Central Europe. Steiner believed this to be the purpose behind seeking to divide the Central Powers into small states with provincialized, weak cultures and economies.[24] He repeatedly warned that taking this ethnically fissiparous path would lead to further wars in Europe.[25]

Steiner's view was simultaneously conservative and progressive, because he hoped the two great Central European states would continue and remain whole but be profoundly transformed by a decentralizing federalism to be achieved via threefolding.[26] Steiner held that Central Europe, by which he meant not just the Germans but the great many peoples and linguistic groups of the region,[27] had a contribution to make to civilization that was distinct from the Anglo-American social pattern of often letting economic life have the upper hand over political life (laws and rights) and cultural life (science, art, religion, education and the media). Steiner believed that through social threefolding, Central Europe had the potential to achieve better balance amongst the three domains of culture, economy and state.

Would Steiner have supported the current European Union? Perhaps. But the question is beyond the scope of this account.

German and Austrian Leaders and the Two Memoranda

In July 1917, Ludwig Polzer-Hoditz, who had participated with Otto von Lerchenfeld in some of the Berlin discussions in which Rudolf Steiner first explained the threefold social order, gave Steiner's second memorandum to Arthur Polzer-Hoditz (Ludwig's younger brother), who was cabinet chief for the 29-year-old Austrian Kaiser, Karl I.

In a 1929 book, Arthur wrote that when he finally brought Steiner's memorandum and the threefolding idea forward at a November 1917 meeting with the Kaiser, the latter listened closely and asked Arthur himself to write a memorandum explaining 'the whole system of threefolding'.[28] At another meeting on 14 February 1918, the Kaiser asked Arthur for another copy of one of the memoranda expressing Steiner's social ideas. According to the former cabinet chief, the Kaiser wanted to show the memorandum to Ernst Seidler, the Austrian prime minister.[29] Arthur soon gave the requested copy to the Kaiser and then went to Prime Minister Seidler to prepare him:

> I had studied the idea of the threefolding of the social organism during my vacation and thought about how it could be executed, so I was in a position this time to make very concrete proposals to the prime minister. Seidler listened attentively and spoke with me very interestedly about the matter.[30]

Little seems to have come of all this, yet the Kaiser's interest apparently persisted. Hans Kühn writes that the Kaiser asked yet again – nine months later, on 10 November 1918, the day before he was compelled to relinquish power – about Steiner's social proposals. According to Kühn, the Kaiser called for Steiner's memorandum to be brought for study from a state archive.[31]

It should be noted that the English-language translation of the original German edition of Arthur Polzer-Holditz's 1929 book about the Austrian Kaiser omits all of the German passages having to do with threefolding, and the fact that the Kaiser, his cabinet chief, and the prime minister all had some interest in the idea.

Two distinct but not necessarily contradictory accounts explain how Steiner came to have conversations about social threefolding with Prince Max von Baden, who soon became chancellor of the German Empire. Von Baden would hold the office for five weeks, and then announce the abdication of the German Kaiser, Wilhelm II – to Wilhelm's surprise. According to Albert Schmelzer, Steiner probably met von Baden through the military officer Lieutenant Corporal Hans von Haeften.[32] Hans Kühn, however, in *Dreigliederungs-Zeit (Time of threefolding)* (Kühn, 1978) describes how he, Kühn, arranged the meeting, which then took place at the end of January 1918. Kühn also writes that speaking with Steiner 'must have left an impression' on von Baden, because

> the prince before the start of his chancellorship met again with Rudolf Steiner, at 17 Motz Street in Berlin. When the prince left the dwelling, he gave his hand to the accompanying housekeeper, Anna Samweber, and congratulated her that she 'could be of service to such a significant man'.[33]

Von Baden was appointed Chancellor of the German Empire on 3 October 1918. Did he want to propose threefolding instead of Woodrow Wilson's Fourteen Points as the basis for peace in Europe? In his later memoir, von Baden did not mention Steiner, and said only that after the war, Germany had needed its own programme for reorganization, not what Wilson in the West or Trotsky in the East were offering.[34]

To judge by Hans Kühn's account, Steiner had high hopes that von Baden would propose threefolding in his inaugural address as chancellor. Thus Kühn writes:

> According to the statements of Rudolf Steiner, what mattered was that the new chancellor before the beginning of the impending revolution [which started in early November 1918, a month after von Baden became chancellor] would find

> the right words, that is, would have the courage to immediately proclaim the idea of threefolding as a demonstration of the German people's readiness for peace and for a profound new orientation.
>
> Rudolf Steiner was intensely interested in the content of the inaugural address when he got hold of the newspaper. But nothing was to be found therein that might even have pointed in such a direction! I never again saw Rudolf Steiner so deeply shaken as he was by this disappointment, which to him prefigured suffering and downfall for the German people.[35]

In a lecture on 29 November 1918, not quite three weeks after the war's end, Steiner himself more than hints that von Baden had indeed intended to adopt threefolding as the future path for Germany. In the lecture Steiner indicates that von Baden had been prevented from doing so by General Erich Ludendorff, who for about two years had been the most powerful man in the German Empire. At the moment in early October when von Baden was about to assume his position as chancellor, Ludendorff warned him that the German front lines could collapse at any moment, and told him that he must seek an immediate armistice. However, US President Woodrow Wilson would only agree to an armistice quickly if his Fourteen Point programme, not a Central European alternative, were adopted by the Germans.[36] During the lecture of 29 November 1918, Steiner said:

> *Prince Max von Baden wanted to go to Berlin and* do something completely different. *But Ludendorff declared that an armistice must be proposed within twenty-four hours, or else the greatest misfortune [collapse of the German army] would come. Prince Max von Baden went against his own earlier decision. After five days, Ludendorff declared: he had been completely mistaken, it [the armistice] had not been necessary at all!*[37] [emphasis not in the original]

In the above passage, Steiner is clearly if discreetly saying that von Baden had originally decided to publicly support threefolding as a new basis for Germany and Central Europe. No doubt in giving the lecture, Steiner had to be somewhat indirect in revealing what von Baden had told him privately; the conversations with von Baden would have taken place under the assumption that they were confidential. In addition to the lecture passage just quoted, Steiner's great disappointment in finding von Baden's inaugural address devoid of any mention of threefolding makes clear that Steiner believed that von Baden had originally decided in favour of threefolding. Von Baden's above-mentioned remark to Anna Samweber, Steiner's housekeeper, congratulating her that she 'could be of service to such a significant man' suggests moreover that Steiner was perhaps correct, and that von Baden had indeed adopted Steiner's threefolding proposal as the path to be championed for Central Europe.

Be that as it may, by the time Ludendorff reversed himself on the danger of military collapse, von Baden was determined to go ahead with the armistice and seems to have surrendered to the inevitability of some version of Wilson's plan.

Steiner and his associates communicated with a number of statesmen in addition to those discussed above. In 1917 and 1918 an outline of Steiner's social-reform ideas gained a remarkable amount of attention amongst people at the pinnacles of power in Germany and Austria, but in the end the relevant leaders did not move on Steiner's suggestions.

To the Grassroots amid Revolution

Nevertheless, interest in Steiner's social views grew, and at the end of 1918 and the beginning of 1919 Swiss lawyer Roman Boos and German industrialist Emil Molt, among others, approached Steiner with the intention of helping to actualize his proposals. Again in response to requests, Steiner became a social activist, and the threefolding movement took off in Germany amid social chaos. The German Kaiser had been forced to abdicate on 9 November 1918; the Austrian Kaiser lost his throne on 11 November. A naval mutiny early in the same month had led to the takeover of many German cities by soldiers', sailors' and workers' councils. A weak social-democratic government had emerged and was backed by the army, which put down more than one rebellion of communists. The latter were seeking to bring about a dictatorship in line with Soviet Russia.

In the first months of 1919, armed revolts broke out in various parts of Germany. In March, as many as two thousand were killed in Berlin in clashes between the new government, communists, right-wing paramilitary forces and workers. Also in March, what must have amounted to hundreds of thousands of copies of Steiner's *Appeal to the German People and the Civilized World*, a petition supporting threefolding, were distributed as newspaper inserts and flyers. The *Appeal* had been signed by several hundred notable Germans of the time (including novelist Herman Hesse, who had gone to school with the above-mentioned Emil Molt).[38] In April, Steiner's *Towards social renewal* (German title: *Die Kernpunkte der sozialen Frage*) was published in Switzerland, Germany, and soon in Austria, and sold some 40,000 copies or more in the first year.[39]

In the same month that the book came out, Steiner was invited to speak to thousands of workers, particularly in Stuttgart and the surrounding territory of Württemberg, where several industrialists were allies of Steiner. During one stage of these talks, some 10,000–12,000 workers adopted a resolution calling on the Württemberg government to appoint Steiner to get to work immediately on social threefolding in the region.[40] A few days later the Württemberg government's Socialization Commission invited Steiner to come to the Interior Ministry to participate in a meeting with their 'Subcommittee 4' studying the question of workers sharing in company profits.[41] Nothing – at least on the government side – seems to have directly resulted from this meeting.

Transcripts of Steiner's talks to workers during these months indicate that one reason why he was popular among them was that he was leading them at times in the direction of choosing their own managers, and was speaking of managers and entrepreneurs as just another kind of worker.[42] The details of Steiner's economic proposals in his writings and in later series of lectures show that he was always moving in a direction distinct both from state socialism and competitive capitalism. He was striving for a co-operative capitalism, or what might also be described as a voluntary 'socialism' outside of the state.

Unfortunately, his talks with workers in 1919 were gradually shut down because the threefolding movement was increasingly demonized by both the right and the left. Extreme forces on the political right wanted to find a way back to something like the old imperial order. On the left, social democratic party leaders and union functionaries feared loss of influence over workers.[43]

General von Moltke's Memoir and Steiner's Efforts to Prevent the Next War

Towards the end of May 1919, while he was engaged in so many other activities, Rudolf Steiner arranged for the publication in early June of memoirs written by General Helmuth von Moltke (a.k.a. von Moltke the Younger). Von Moltke had died in 1916, and had been the top German military officer at the start of the First World War. Steiner considered it essential to publish the memoirs because they contained evidence that the Germans had not been solely to blame for the start of the war, had not been warmongers, and thus had the right and the opportunity, now that the war had ended, to take a path to social reform different from Woodrow Wilson's and the Entente's plan to ethnically segment Central Europe.

Von Moltke's widow, Eliza, had been a student of Steiner's anthroposophy since 1903, and von Moltke himself seems to have been at least to some degree an anthroposophist. He first met Steiner in 1904, and after reading two or three of Steiner's works, including *Theosophy*, the general wrote to Eliza that 'no other philosophizing author has so far been more comprehensible to me than he'.[44] Thereafter Steiner sometimes visited the von Moltkes at Eliza's invitation.

Von Moltke had a number of private meetings with Steiner. One of these took place in Niederlahnstein, a few miles from the German military headquarters in Koblenz, on 27 August 1914.[45] That was about one month after the start of the war. Less than two weeks after that meeting, it would become clear that Germany had lost the decisive First Battle of the Marne. This was almost tantamount to losing the war itself, since the whole German strategy depended on a lightning victory against France. The failure at the Marne made that quick victory impossible. Some in the German press would later accuse Steiner of interfering on 27 August with von Moltke's military judgement and bringing about the loss at the Marne. However, Steiner, in a 1921 interview with Jules Sauerwein of the French newspaper *Le Matin*, said that the meeting with von Moltke had been about purely human concerns.[46]

On 14 September 1914, soon after the loss of the Battle of the Marne, the Kaiser informally relieved von Moltke of his position as Chief of the General Staff. Von Moltke again met with Steiner on 27 or 28 September, and on later occasions,[47] and described to Steiner a scene that had taken place on 1 August 1914 between the German Kaiser, the chancellor, some advisors, and von Moltke himself at the critical moments right at the start of the war, when Germany had just begun mobilizing its military to invade Belgium and France.[48] In addition to telling Steiner about the scene, Von Moltke recorded it in his memoir. It was this scene that Steiner wanted the public to know about. In Steiner's view it demonstrated, among other things, that Germany had sought to avoid war against France, England, and Belgium.

To understand fully, it is necessary to know that the Kaiser had received a message that seemed to show the British to be offering a guarantee that they and the French would not attack Germany, if Germany did not invade France or Belgium. The message seemed to mean that Germany could go to war with Russia, which was at that moment mobilizing against Germany, and the British and French would stay out of it.[49]

The Kaiser, who learned this from his diplomat in Britain, was happy that war with France and England could apparently be avoided, and so decided to interrupt the ongoing German mobilization toward Belgium and France. The sight of the Kaiser and the chancellor happy and excited about this interruption greatly disturbed von Moltke, for several reasons. First, he thought it foolish to suppose that Britain – even if the British had sent the message to the Kaiser in good will – had any power to guarantee the neutrality of France, not least because France had already begun the almost irreversible process of mobilization against Germany.[50] Secondly, Von Moltke also thought that moving the bulk of the German army to meet Russia in the East, as the Kaiser then suggested doing, would leave Germany absurdly vulnerable to French attack from the rear. Finally, the general believed that interrupting German mobilization to the West would be disastrous for logistical reasons.

Having long feared being forced to fight a war with France and Russia simultaneously, the German leadership had for decades prepared for the possibility of that two-front war. Military mobilization had been planned with tightly timed co-ordination of huge numbers of trains, vehicles, supplies and people in order get to the Western front in the quickest and most organized fashion possible. To interrupt mobilization to the West and embark upon a completely unplanned rerouting of an army of millions, von Moltke thought, would transform Germany's battle-ready troops into a disordered mass of hungry, armed men.[51] The German strategy envisioned a rapid defeat of France that would free up much of the German military to turn in orderly fashion, by pre-arranged schedule, to meet the slower Russian mobilization in the East without having to fight France simultaneously.

To Steiner, it was of great significance that the Kaiser, in the hope of peace with France and Britain, had taken the risk of interrupting German mobilization. It proved that Germany was not the evil belligerent demonized by the Allies' propaganda. In one sense, though, Germany's attempted peace did not matter: within a few hours of pausing mobilization, the Kaiser heard from the king of England that Britain in fact could *not* guarantee French neutrality towards the impending war between Germany and Russia.[52] The Kaiser now surrendered to what seemed unavoidable, and allowed von Moltke to proceed with mobilization towards Belgium and France.

On the same day, 1 August 1914, a telegram written by the British Foreign Secretary to the British ambassador in Germany appears to show that the British were partly culpable for the start of the war, and that it had not all been the fault of Germany. The last two paragraphs of the telegram form the most significant part of this communication between two British officials:

> *The [German] Ambassador pressed me as to whether I could not formulate conditions on which we would remain neutral. He even suggested that the integrity of France and her colonies might be guaranteed.*
>
> *I said that I felt obliged to refuse definitely any promise to remain neutral on similar terms, and I could only say that we must keep our hands free.*[53]

Thus, on 1 August the Kaiser and his chancellor wanted to avoid war with France and Britain, while British officials remained aloof from German feelers for peace.

Steiner, who had tried in various ways since 1916 or before to present evidence that Germany was not solely to blame for the start of the war, now sought at the beginning of June 1919, about a month before the conclusion of the Versailles negotiations, to publish von Moltke's memoirs.[54] Steiner believed that for threefolding to have any possibility of adoption in place of Wilson's plans, the non-German world would need convincing reasons to stop demonizing Germany and start granting that nation some modest measure of understanding.[55]

By early June 1919, Steiner had printed 10,000 copies of a 34-page booklet that contained a preface he had written and von Moltke's brief memoirs.[56] Hans Kühn later recalled that the Württemberg delegate to Versailles, a Dr Schall, who later became finance minister, was to be part of the effort to make the von Moltke document known. Schall was ready, wrote Kühn, 'to lay the document there on the [Versailles] negotiation table. Rudolf Steiner said Germany's signature under the war-guilt lie could not be demanded if this document were on display.'[57]

One day before copies of the memoirs were to be sent to Versailles, however, the surviving elder of the von Moltke family forbade publication.[58] In addition, the German Foreign Office and top military officials got wind of it. A General von Dommes, who had worked with General von Moltke at the beginning of the war, was sent to Steiner and had an extended conversation with him. Von Dommes alleged to Steiner that von Moltke's memoirs contained errors.[59] Steiner did not find that convincing, but felt he had no choice but to pulp the 10,000 copies of the document, because of the elder von Moltke's prohibition on publication, and because if the German General Staff was going to impugn von Moltke's accuracy, the document's chance of changing things at Versailles would be substantially reduced. The General Staff seems not to have wanted the Kaiser's abortive actions and misjudgements, as observed by von Moltke, to become public, although the Kaiser had gone into exile in Holland months before.

Many historians today believe that the final Versailles Treaty, by attributing sole responsibility for the war to Germany, played a major role in the rise of Adolf Hitler. Perhaps in 1919 no single human being could have come anywhere near to preventing the Second World War. Yet Steiner may have come as close as anyone, not only because he nearly managed to publish General von Moltke's memoir of the Kaiser's attempts to avoid war, but also because Steiner's prescient effort to bring about a threefold order and avoid the dismemberment of Central Europe into a collection of ethnically defined states nearly came to fruition through German Chancellor Max von Baden, and was looked upon with interest by the Austrian prime minister, as well as repeatedly considered by the Austrian Kaiser and his cabinet chief.

1917 to 1919: An Evolution of Proposals

There is not space here to consider every development of Steiner's social thinking and action, but from mid-1917 to mid-1919, when he was in certain respects most active on behalf of social reform, three phases may be distinguished in his approach to the *economic* side of social threefolding.

First Phase

In his 1917 memoranda to the ruling statesmen of Central Europe, Steiner did not refer to transforming the relationship between entrepreneurs, workers and consumers into a co-operative one. As far as economic life was concerned, he argued that ending the intermingling of Austro-Hungarian political forces with the economy would help resolve ethnic conflict within the multi-national empire.

Second Phase

Then in spring 1919 in the context of the ongoing German revolution, Steiner addressed himself to all levels of society through his main work on social reform, *Towards social renewal*. He proposed the abolition of wage labour, and argued that workers should in effect become partners in enterprises and share in profits. Moreover, the idea that workers should have a say in who would manage industry is at least latently present in *Towards social renewal*, in so far as the book called for a truly free contractual relationship between workers and entrepreneurs.[60] The implication was arguably that workers in Germany's emerging new order could be in a position to hire entrepreneurs and management perhaps as much as management and entrepreneurs would hire workers. On the other hand, in contrast to any such implication, *Towards social renewal* stated that when a successful enterprise manager was to retire, that manager, or another successful manager, would be the person best equipped to judge who was qualified to step into the vacant managerial spot. Within certain limits successful managers were therefore to choose their successors and colleagues.[61]

The book's proposals for the empowerment of both workers *and* managers were not self-contradictory, however, but a reflection of the two sides of a genuine polarity: on the one hand, talented managers need freedom to lead if they are to be effective for the benefit of all; while on the other hand, employees need to be considered as more than mere means to others' ends: workers need the equality of a partnership relation rather than an instrumental relation to those providing managerial and entrepreneurial leadership.

To an extent, a synthesis between managerial freedom and worker equality is contained in *Towards social renewal*'s call for a democratically based state that is independent of economic life, and which develops and enforces labour laws. But the book also makes clear, for example in emphasizing a truly free contractual relationship, that in Steiner's view, worker dignity was not to be only an external imposition by the state. Participatory relationships were inherent in the very nature of economic life itself, and thus needed to be an integral, though not too rigidly fixed, aspect of enterprise organization.

The book, and the second phase it embodies, also described a new kind of capital ownership for companies above a certain size. In such companies, a significant part of capital accumulation would be no one's personal property, nor would the state own or control it. Instead, capital of this kind would be designated to serve two broader social purposes: enterprise managers could use it to develop or expand the enterprise for the benefit of workers, consumers and society, and to support cultural and educational institutions and scholarships. This kind of capital – which groups unconnected to Steiner's work have also independently conceived and developed[62] – circulates productively, for the benefit of all, through the economy, and gives new meaning to the ideal of a 'commonwealth' society.

For Steiner, there was nothing arbitrary about conceiving the matter in this way, because capital results not only from the genius of entrepreneurs, but in significant part through their collaboration with workers, consumers and many parts of society.[63] The concept of ownership thus did not apply to such accumulations of capital. There was only access to the right to manage and develop it. The state's role would not be to select which people were qualified to exercise that right, however.[64] The democratic state's part, Steiner said, was to ensure that a manager did not choose his or her own blood relations as colleagues and successors, and did not remain as manager if unsuccessful or in breach of the fiduciary entrepreneurial role.

For a share of the profits, the manager or entrepreneur would freely negotiate with others in economic life who required managerial talent, but in any case the manager's share of gains – at least in a society recognized as threefold – could not properly amount to more than an interest-like percentage of company profits.[65] Such profits also needed to be distributed to company reserves, to new investment, to workers, to research initiatives, and to scholarships in support of society's independent cultural domain.

Third Phase

Thus, the ideas in *Towards social renewal* that were concerned with economic life – the book also had seminal things to say about cultural and political life – were focused to a significant extent on relations *within* enterprises. By contrast, the idea that comes into its own in the next, and third, phase of Steiner's economic proposals is barely mentioned in *Towards social renewal*. Steiner was soon to develop the new emphasis in some detail while addressing large assemblies of workers in Stuttgart and the Württemberg region of Germany during the revolutionary summer of 1919.

Steiner knew how to engage his audiences, and was capable of an entertaining retort to those who attempted to bad-mouth threefolding. Thus, at a discussion evening on 5 June 1919 to which Steiner had been invited by the 'worker committees of the great companies of Stuttgart', a Mr Armbruster was reported as saying that he found, 'like the *Social Democrat*' – apparently a party newspaper – that Steiner's statements were 'plum-soft'. In response to this claim, which seems to have meant that his utterances were vague, Steiner told the audience of workers,

> Yes, that stood in the *Social Democrat*, that my statements were 'plum-soft'. I could make nothing of that. I said to myself: With respect to all possible socialistic and social programs there have already been so many statements that tasted like sour plums, that it seems to me actually not at all so inadmissible to bring the plums for once to ripeness; and then, as is well-known, they are soft.[66]

In this third stage the focus would be less on co-operation within enterprises and more on co-operation amongst producers, consumers and traders across a whole geographic area. And Steiner did more than express that idea. He strove to have workers immediately start organizing themselves in specific ways for action in that direction. He was conscious that time was short. The void of firmly established law and authority in Germany would fairly soon be filled, and when that happened the nation's relative openness to implementing new social ideas would evaporate. Steiner believed the government would soon lay down laws that would in effect hobble new potentials for worker participation, and prevent economic life from becoming fully self-managing, co-operative and independent of the state. Progress towards such an economy was essential to a threefold social order. Steiner therefore wanted workers and sincerely co-operating managers to take quick steps to lay the foundations of a self-organizing economic life that would no longer be controlled by old-style capitalists pursuing their own narrow interests. If enough progress were to be made quickly, the government would be presented in Württemberg with a worker-backed *fait accompli* that would make it difficult for the dominant political parties to impose, as they were inclined to do, a mixture of the old capitalism and state socialism, which Steiner recognized as two sides of the same pfennig.

The way Steiner spoke to assemblies of worker committees of the large companies of Stuttgart during seven discussion evenings[67] between May and July 1919 may sometimes surprise people who are acquainted with his social ideas only through *Towards social renewal*. There was much discussion in revolutionary Germany of 'socialization' of the economy, and Steiner also started speaking of it, although the socialization he sought to instigate amongst workers was to take place voluntarily, and outside the coercive purview of the state. But he now sometimes sounds rather radical in the claims he stakes for workers, and in the challenge his talks present to managers' and entrepreneurs' prerogatives. Thus, at the 5 June discussion evening, Steiner at one point speaks of the German word for 'employer', *Arbeitgeber*, which literally translated means 'workgiver':

> *Now, the concept of the workgiver – you can gather this from my earlier lectures and also from my book about social questions – the concept of the workgiver must actually disappear through socialization. For someone can only be a workgiver if he is a work owner, and a work owner there simply may not be. There can only be a* work leader, *which means people who are active in the organization of the work, so that the physical worker knows how to apply his work power in the best way and so forth. Of course the work in an enterprise cannot run on in such a way that everyone simply does what he pleases. Leadership must be there, the whole company must be penetrated with spirit and intellect [durchgeistigt], but these are no workgivers, they are work leaders, that means* workers of another kind. *The greatest value is to be placed now on grasping at last the actual concept of work. For in reality a workgiver who does not himself collaborate does not belong at all to the enterprise, but is a parasite on the work.*[68] [emphasis in the original]

We find Steiner in Württemberg seeking to actualize associative economic life on a fairly grand scale, as he speaks to large (and sometimes very large) numbers of workers who, in the still-revolutionary setting, have gained new powers in the companies in which they work. Thus, during a discussion evening with workers on 23 July 1919, Steiner discusses the need for all the workers, both physical and intellectual, of each enterprise in the Württemberg region to elect from within their enterprises councils that possess, or are able to gather full knowledge of, the business's operations, inventories, and financial and economic situation.[69]

In a threefolding perspective, all workers are eligible to be elected to these councils, Steiner declares, and the entrepreneur too, provided he is not obstructive of the change-over to an associative economic order.[70] Depending on size, each enterprise would thus elect and send forth one or more councils, and these were then to meet together in a great gathering representing all the enterprises of the Württemberg region. Such plenary gatherings were to include consumer- and trader councils[71] at the earliest opportunity. Steiner explained that in such a plenary assembly, the councils, along with consumers, would together create an overall picture of the whole economic situation in the region.[72] By mutual consultation, they would then co-operatively negotiate and plan the next months' and year's prices and production. The councils would also choose a central council,[73] which would be an economic body only, without the coercive enforcement powers that a state political body could bring to bear. In this purely economic gathering of councils, therefore, co-ordination of all the interests would for the most part not be possible through the central council's bureaucratic fiat, nor by majority vote, but would depend on more horizontal processes of co-ordination and negotiation among all the freely associating participants.[74]

In tune with the foregoing, Steiner said that using elections to determine who would serve on each company's works councils – a selection method that was necessary to begin with – would in future gradually change into a process of delegation more suitable for federative and associative organization. Elections tended towards greater centralization, which would be undesirable or impossible for economic processes in a region of any size.[75] In any case, it would be for the plenary assembly itself to decide whether a change from election to delegation should later take place.[76]

National Majority Needed for Threefolding

During the course of the same talks with workers, Steiner told them that if an entrepreneur in an enterprise – meaning a medium- or large-sized enterprise – failed to recognize the region's plenary collaborative body of works councils as the real leader of the enterprise, the entrepreneur would have to retire.[77] In making that and similar statements during the third phase, Steiner was in no way supporting lawless compulsion, much less revolutionary violence. The changes in property relationships he envisioned could in his view only succeed in the long run if accepted democratically by a majority of the nation.[78] Drumming up support and engagement among as many workers as possible was a stage on the way to achieving that democratic approval. Steiner also supported compensation for entrepreneurs called upon to give up some of their rights in an enterprise.

As Steiner describes the associative economy, it would obviously entail significantly increased economic transparency among enterprises and individuals, since otherwise a plenary assembly of works councils would be unable to carry out one of its main tasks: continual development of an economic overview of the region. Without increased economic transparency, it is difficult to conceive moving from competition towards voluntary co-operation and collaborative price formation.

Real Differences?

The so-called third phase of Steiner's economic proposals, as distinct as it may appear to be from what preceded it, arguably only fleshed out what was already implicit in the second phase represented by *Towards social renewal*. Like that book, Steiner's talks to workers of the Württemberg/Stuttgart region strove for balance between managerial freedom, on the one hand, and worker equality and power on the other, but now on a more macroeconomic, society-wide scale. In the book, the polarity in question had been resolved up to a certain point. In the talks with workers, elaboration of the idea with respect to a concrete situation permitted the manager–worker polarity to be further resolved, in part through Steiner's distinction between elections and centralization, on the one hand, and delegation and federative association on the other.

Elections for the councils would tend over time to be transformed by workers themselves into a simpler, less centralized, and more informal delegation process, Steiner said, because workers would generally come to know and agree, without need of elections, who in their own branch were the people qualified and unqualified for management roles. In their own economic interest workers would then delegate management to the most qualified persons.[79] Such delegation would in turn dovetail with federative and associative forms of management rather than with more strongly centralized forms.

In these talks Steiner also warned against any separation between 'intellectual workers' [geistigen Arbeiter] and 'physical workers', lest an 'aristocratic stratum formation' result.[80] Such a division would be 'monstrous', he said.[81] He affirmed that

> there must be a sense of belonging together among all workers in the individual enterprise branches. We will not progress if the intellectual workers of the different enterprise branches separate to fry special sausages, for the category of 'intellectual worker' has no justification.[82] [emphasis in the original]

For economic life to prosper, managers would need to possess ability, as well as technical and other forms of expertise acquired through education in an independent cultural domain.[83] Those with such skills would not, however, be able to impose themselves. Expertise could not lead to an economic aristocracy dominating workers, since the plenary assembly of works councils had no state powers, nor was it ever meant to have such powers in the future. In the scenario Steiner seeks to establish, therefore, there would be nothing to prevent workers from combining to withdraw support from their current managers, should those managers fail to serve the whole economic life in a reasonably unselfish way. The independent democratic state that Steiner characterized as a key aspect of threefolding would safeguard workers' rights as well.

Steiner's talks to workers thus display graphically, as it were, a good deal of what he had in mind about how managers and other workers would interact within associative economic life. In this third phase we see just how committed Steiner was to carrying through a voluntary, federative socialism that was to be independent of the state. As noted earlier, groups to Steiner's political left and right made sure that the experiment would not gain support broadly enough and quickly enough.

Did the Threefolding Movement End?

By mid-June 1919, the crystallization of opposition to the threefolding movement – opposition from industrialists, the government, the unions, and the various political parties – had made clear to Steiner and some of his collaborators that a breakthrough transformation of Württemberg would be all but impossible. And by September 1919 at the latest, the revolutionary opening in Germany had closed.[84] The Weimar constitution had come into effect, and new power structures had been established. Steiner and his colleagues had tried by tremendous exertions to sprint through the revolutionary gap and activate threefolding in a whole region of Germany, but it was not to be.

So the intense campaign they had been waging wound down. Only in that limited sense did the threefolding movement come to an end. Though on a somewhat smaller scale than before, Steiner continued with his collaborators to develop various threefolding initiatives, such as the Waldorf school, the effort to gain autonomy for Upper Silesia, and the organization of The Coming Day joint stock corporation. He also gave a series of valuable and original economics lectures. Social reform in tune with threefolding continues to this day through many people and organizations, and not only amongst students of Steiner. Many social reformers who have never heard of him, or of threefolding, are nevertheless currently moving society forwards in one or more of the directions to which Steiner pointed: freedom in culture and education; co-operative economic life independent of the state; and impartial democracy in political life.

The Coming Day Stock Corporation for the Support of Economic and Spiritual Values

Founded in March 1920 by Rudolf Steiner and a number of his economically active associates, The Coming Day was a union of economic enterprises with research and cultural enterprises. The industrialists who joined their companies to the Coming Day renounced ownership, received shares in the Coming Day in compensation, and continued to manage the enterprises they had brought in. In return for continuing as managers, they received a fixed income.[85] Shares, like loans, received not more than a 5 percent return.[86] To assure retention of The Coming Day under the leadership of people supportive of the spiritual intentions of the founders, from the beginning a category of preferred shares was created with 25 times the voting power of other share categories, but no advantage financially.[87]

The wage system for workers remained provisionally intact.[88] In his account of the events, Hans Kühn seems to attribute this to a reluctance on Steiner's part to interfere in the management of the subsidiary companies.[89] Steiner initially did not stipulate a voice for workers in management, but by 1922 two representatives of the workers and employees were part of The Coming Day's supervisory board.[90] Part of the profits of The Coming Day went to the support of the Waldorf School recently founded in Stuttgart. The school had initially been created for the children of people working in one of the factories of The Coming Day, but under Steiner's pedagogical guidance the school grew rapidly to include many other students as well. Profits from The Coming Day went also to support its research laboratories, which worked along lines proposed by Steiner and others.[91] It was hoped that these laboratories would create new products that could in turn support the economic enterprises.

Leadership problems, combined with German hyperinflation and the government's measures to stop it, led by 1925 to the dissolution of The Coming Day and the unbundling of the various enterprises within it, some of which continue to this day. The multinational company Weleda, which won Germany's 2016 Sustainability Award as 'Germany's Most Sustainable Brand',[92] produces beauty products and naturopathic medicines, and traces its origin back to The Coming Day.

Threefolding, Past and Future

Steiner maintained that human society fundamentally *is* threefold, but that many institutions, as leftovers from the past, have been structured unconsciously and hence mask society's underlying threefold character. Thus, threefolding in a sense introduces nothing, but merely seeks to bring institutions into harmony with fundamental social realities.

Steiner noted that threefolding had been proceeding by small unconscious steps for thousands of years. For example, in ancient Egypt the pharaoh had simultaneously been king, high priest, and owner of all Egypt, but later, in ancient Rome, through the development of secular law, the political system became to some degree independent of the cultural domain. In medieval Europe, as feudalism waned, economic life grew more distinct from the political order represented by the nobility.

In the nineteenth century, the end of slavery in the United States and the British Empire meant human rights (the political system) became more independent of economic life. In the late twentieth century, the re-birth of democracy in Eastern Europe ended the fusion of a cultural impulse (communist ideology) with political and economic life. The co-operative and socially responsible forms of capitalism that have been emerging in recent decades may in time become widespread enough to increase the threefold articulation of society by reducing the need for state intervention in economic life, as well as by reducing the concentration of wealth in the hands of economic elites, who have often used their economic power to manipulate the state.

Future possibilities and historical examples of progress towards threefolding could be multiplied almost indefinitely (see elsewhere in this book). Recognizing these patterns can make us more aware of how social reform can be accelerated in many salutary ways, and alert us that the future of threefolding still beckons to social reformers today.[93]

Notes

1. 'Riot at Munich lecture: Reactionaries storm platform when Steiner discusses Theosophy', *New York Times*, 17 May 1922.
2. Harald Sandner, *Hitler, Das Itinerar*, Berlin Story Verlag, Berlin, 2016.
3. Rudolf Steiner, *Die Anthroposophie und ihre Gegner* 1919–1921, Collected Works Vol. 255b, Rudolf Steiner Velag, Dornach,1981, p. 575. See goo.gl/eGVGY3 (accessed 10 January 2017).
4. Walter Beck, *Rudolf Steiner – The last three years*, Dornach, 1985, as quoted in Rudolf Steiner, Die Anthroposophie und ihre Gegner, pp. 575–76, my translation.
5. Ibid., p. 576.
6. Rudolf Steiner, *Renewal of the social organism*, Anthroposophic Press, Spring Valley, NY, 1985, pp. 47–8. (A collection of essays from 1915 to 1924.) For the passage in the original German, see the Collected Works, Volume 24, p. 262. See also the German Rudolf Steiner Online Archive, here: goo.gl/uFGm2W.
7. See goo.gl/Jrozac.
8. Rudolf Steiner, *Towards social renewal*, 4th edn, trans. Matthew Barton, Rudolf Steiner Press, London, 1999. Other translations or editions have been titled *The threefold commonwealth; The threefold state; The tri-organic social order; The threefold social order*. The last-named is an abbreviated edition.
9. Raymond G. Fuller (a pseudonym of Genevieve May Fox), 'New scheme of social organization', *New York Times*, book review, 14 January 1923.

10. Stephen Usher refers to the Lofthouse review in *Rudolf Steiner: Social and political science*, ed. Stephen E. Usher, Rudolf Steiner Press, London, 2003, p. 1.
11. Besides *Towards social renewal* (note 8, above), see the following three works: *The social future: Culture, equality, economy*, Steinerbooks, Great Barrington, MA, 2013); *Rethinking economics: Lectures and seminars on world economics*, Anthroposophic Press, Great Barrington, MA, 2013; and *Renewal of the social organism* (note 6, above).
12. My translation of the quotation in Albert Schmelzer, *Die Dreigliederungsbewegung 1919: Rudolf Steiners Einsatz für den Selbstverwaltungsimpuls*, Verlag Freies Geistesleben, Stuttgart, 1991, p. 60.
13. See goo.gl/iF4pNe (accessed 17 May 2016); Christoph Lindenberg, *Rudolf Steiner: A biography*, Steinerbooks, Great Barrington, MA, 2012, p. 466.
14. Albert Schmelzer, *Die Dreigliederungsbewegung* 1919 (note 12), p. 60; Hans Kühn, *Dreigliederungs-Zeit: Rudolf Steiners Kampf für die Gesellschaftsordnung der Zukunft*, Philosophisch-Anthroposophischer Verlag, Dornach, Switzerland,1978, pp. 14–16.
15. Kühn, *Dreigliederungs-Zeit* (note 14), p. 14; Usher, *Rudolf Steiner: Social and political science* (note 10), p. 5.
16. Schmelzer, *Dreigliederungsbewegung* 1919 (note 14), p. 60.
17. Stewart Easton, *Rudolf Steiner: Herald of a new epoch*, Anthroposophic Press, Hudson, NY, 1980, p. 231.
18. Rudolf Steiner, 'Memoranda 1917', in *Rudolf Steiner: Social and political science* (note 10), p. 86.
19. Peter Selg, *Rudolf Steiner: Life and work, Vol. 4 (1914–1918): The years of World War I*, SteinerBooks, Great Barrington, MA, 2016, p. 223.
20. Steiner, in Usher, "Memoranda 1917' (note 18), pp. 68, 82, 97–9, 104, 106, 112, 114.
21. Ibid., pp. 81–2.
22. Ibid., pp. 79, 99–100, 113.
23. Rudolf Steiner, *Towards social renewal* (note 8), pp. 47–8.
24. Steiner, in Usher, 'Memoranda 1917' (note 18), pp. 78, 90–3.
25. Ibid., p. 68.
26. Ibid., pp. 68, 81, 97–8, 113.
27. Rudolf Steiner, *Der Dornacher Bau: als Wahrzeichen geschichtlichen Werdens und künstlerischer Umwandlungsimpulse*, Rudolf Steiner Verlag, Dornach, Switzerland, 1985, p. 38 (Volume 287 in the Collected Works); Selg, *Rudolf Steiner*, Vol. 4 (note 19), p. 53.
28. Schmelzer, *Dreigliederungsbewegung 1919* (note 14), p. 62, quoting Arthur Polzer-Hoditz, *Kaiser Karl*, Amalthea, Vienna, 1929, p. 537.
29. T. H. Meyer, *Ludwig Polzer-Hoditz, a European: A biography*, Temple Lodge, Forest Row, Sussex, 2014, p. 161. See also: goo.gl/JF1C4p.
30. Ibid.
31. Kühn, *Dreigliederungs-Zeit* (note 14), p. 16.
32. Schmelzer, *Die Dreigliederungsbewegung 1919* (note 14), p. 63; see also Lindenberg, *Rudolf Steiner: A biography* (note 13), p. 475.
33. Kühn, *Dreigliederungs-Zeit* (note 14), pp. 16–18, my translation.
34. Lindenberg, *Rudolf Steiner: A biography* (note 13), p. 476.
35. Kühn, *Dreigliederungs-Zeit* (note 14), p. 20, my translation.
36. Ibid.
37. My translation of a passage from Rudolf Steiner, *Die soziale Grundforderung unserer Zeit in geänderter Zeitlage, Zwölf Vorträge, gehalten in Dornach und Bern vom 29. November bis 21. Dezember 1918*, Rudolf Steiner Verlag, Dornach, Switzerland, 1990, p. 35; Volume 186 in the Collected Works; see goo.gl/8f3AVM (accessed 23 May 23 2016).

38. Kühn, *Dreigliederungs-Zeit* (note 14), pp. 162–6.
39. See goo.gl/Qg9QGS (accessed 31 December 2016).
40. Rudolf Steiner, *Betriebsräte und Sozialisierung: Diskussionsabende mit den Arbeiterausschüssen der großen Betriebe Stuttgarts*, Rudolf Steiner Verlag, Dornach, Switzerland, 1989, p. 20; Volume 331 in the Collected Works.
41. Ibid.
42. Ibid., p. 114.
43. Christoph Strawe, 'Die Dreigliederungsbewegung 1917–1922', p. 7; see goo.gl/2kRqux (accessed 13 November 2017).
44. T. H. Meyer (ed.), *Light for the new millennium: Rudolf Steiner's association with Helmuth and Eliza von Moltke*, Rudolf Steiner Press, London, 1997, p. xvi.
45. Selg, *Rudolf Steiner* (note 19), Vol. 4, p. 26; Schmelzer, *Die Dreigliederungsbewegung* 1919 (note 14), p. 186.
46. Rudolf Steiner, *Aufsätze über die Dreigliederung des sozialen Organismus und zur Zeitlage 1915–1921*, Rudolf Steiner Verlag, Dornach, Switzerland, 1982, p. 404; Volume 24 in the Collected Works.
47. Schmelzer, *Die Dreigliederungsbewegung* 1919 (note 14), p. 186.
48. Ibid.
49. Ibid., p. 191.
50. Ibid., pp. 191–2.
51. Ibid.
52. Ibid., p. 192.
53. Stephen Usher points this out in *Rudolf Steiner: Social and political science* (note 10), pp. 10–11. The telegram was from British Foreign Secretary Edward Grey to E. Goschen, the British ambassador in Germany, 1 August 1914 (Catalogue ref: FO 438/2), UK National Archives, goo.gl/GkkG2n (accessed 30 May 2016).
54. Schmelzer, *Die Dreigliederungsbewegung* 1919 (note 14), p. 185.
55. Ibid., p. 187.
56. Ibid., pp. 187–8.
57. Kühn in *Beiträge zur Rudolf Steiner Gesamtausgabe*, '1919 – das Jahr der Dreigliederungsbewegung und der Gründung der Waldorfschule', 34, Heft 27–8, 1969, goo.gl/CYxQzo (accessed 29 May 2016).
58. Ibid.; Schmelzer, *Die Dreigliederungsbewegung* 1919 (note 14), p. 188.
59. Ibid.
60. Steiner, *Towards social renewal* (note 8), p. 69.
61. Ibid., p. 81.
62. See, for example, discussions of the 'indivisible reserve' here: goo.gl/zL9jLv (accessed 30 December 2016). See also: goo.gl/x9ZKn6 (accessed 30 December 2016).
63. Steiner, *Towards social renewal* (note 8), pp. 78, 82.
64. Ibid., p. 81.
65. Ibid., p. 80.
66. Steiner, *Betriebsräte und Sozialisierung* (note 40), p. 120.
67. As yet these discussion evenings appear to be unavailable in English. In German: *Betriebsräte und Sozialisierung*, Vol. 331 of the Collected Works. See goo.gl/oJVDo1 (accessed 30 December 2016).
68. Ibid., pp. 113–14.
69. Ibid., pp. 277–8.
70. Ibid., p. 272.

71. Ibid., p. 278.
72. Ibid., pp. 274–5.
73. Ibid., p. 279. See also the other discussion evenings in the same volume, 92, 105–7, p. 123.
74. Ibid., pp. 279–80.
75. Ibid., pp. 279–82. See also the other discussions, pp. 170, 252.
76. Ibid., p. 274.
77. Ibid., p. 281.
78. Steiner, *Betriebsräte und Sozialisierung*, 69 (note 40); Schmelzer, *Die Dreigliederungsbewegung 1919* (note 16), p. 176.
79. Steiner, *Betriebsräte und Sozialisierung* (note 40), p. 282.
80. Ibid., pp. 45–6.
81. Ibid., p. 103.
82. Ibid., p. 45.
83. Ibid., pp. 277, 279.
84. Christoph Strawe, 'Die Dreigliederungsbewegung 1917–1922 und ihre aktuelle Bedeutung', p. 7; see goo.gl/b2xHVE (accessed 13 November 2017). For an English translation, see p. 9 of goo.gl/aQDGAQ (accessed 13 November 1917).
85. Kühn, *Dreigliederungs-Zeit* (note 14), p. 101.
86. Ibid., p. 103.
87. Ibid.
88. Ibid., p. 103.
89. Ibid., p. 253.
90. Ibid., p. 124.
91. Ibid., pp. 101, 103.
92. See goo.gl/NPGuky (accessed 30 December 2016).
93. A few of the author's preferred current examples: in economic life, the certified B Corp movement; in political life, movements for greater transparency with respect to the influence of money on politics; in cultural life, movements to increase the educational freedom of parents and teachers, and in particular to make it possible for all families to send their children to independent schools.

PART TWO

The Challenges

CHAPTER 7

Rebalancing Society for the Common Good
Martin Large

Society is out of balance. We live in a corporatocracy (i.e. rule by corporations) where the market has captured much of the state and the plural sector. Privatization means that the boundaries existing between public (state) and private (business) on the one hand, and between the civil society or plural and private sectors on the other, are being torn down as the market gets everywhere. Schools, hospitals and universities are being turned into businesses, as are government departments. We have the best democracy money can buy – and, increasingly, a National Health Service Plc. The barriers have been removed that kept advertising out of schools and kept the commercialization of childhood in check, kept profit-making businesses out of healthcare or prevented the news media from becoming purely propaganda vehicles for a handful of wealthy owners.

Despite societal imbalance, we hold on to our constitutional balances, and understand the need for this threefold design. The threefold separation of the constitutional powers of the state – into the judiciary, legislature and government – is designed to create dynamic checks and balances. The outcome is political health, transparency and respect for human rights. When some politicians call judges the 'enemies of the people' and thus cross boundaries illegitimately, this arouses resistance.

However, the design of social threefolding between the economy, politics and culture, or the private, public and plural sectors, was traditionally implicit rather than explicit, taken for granted. Such *de facto* social threefolding was widespread in Britain before the advent of Margaret Thatcher in 1979. The state guaranteed its citizens free healthcare, through resourcing an autonomous public-service NHS that was rooted in the plural sector. State-maintained schools and universities respected educational and academic freedom (cf. Chapter 14, this volume). However, since 1979 this form of a balanced, social democratic society with a welfare state and mixed public/private economy has been progressively eroded by the implementation of the neoliberal market state.

The purpose of this chapter is to suggest ways of rebalancing society for the common good, avoiding either revolution or breakdown. First, it analyses our destabilized society; and secondly, it explores the importance of respecting boundaries between the three sectors. Thirdly, it gives examples of unhealthy boundary-crossing or capture, and it lastly shows how respecting boundaries can enable the private, public and plural sectors to contribute their strengths for the common good of both people and planet.

Destabilized Society

Our destabilized society is dominated by the 0.1 percent, led by the eight billionaires who own as much wealth as the poorest 3.6 billion people.[1] This is called elite globalization. In the West, a kleptocratic plutocracy (defined as rule by the super rich, driven by the urge to own ever more things) controls society through a corporatocracy and a bankocracy (or rule by the banks), which captures the state for tax breaks and sweetheart regulations, and the corporate media for influence. We are corporate serfs paying through the nose for once-affordable things such as privatized water or housing, because these were formerly publicly protected and owned. Such inequality matters, because society is then fundamentally unstable.

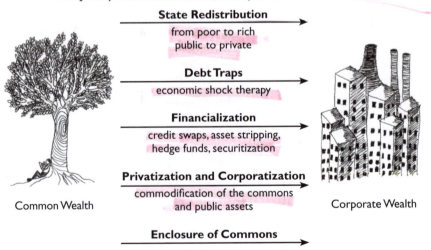

FIGURE 7.1: PRIVATIZATION OF OUR COMMONS AND PUBLIC WEALTH

Thomas Piketty observes that there are few checks to reverse these processes.[2] He argues that capitalism automatically generates arbitrary and unsustainable inequalities that radically undermine the meritocratic values on which democratic societies are based. He famously asked not only who earns what, but also who *owns* what. Piketty describes two kinds of households – those that only own their labour, generating wages, and those which own the capital of land, housing and financial assets which generate rents, dividends and interest with minimal effort

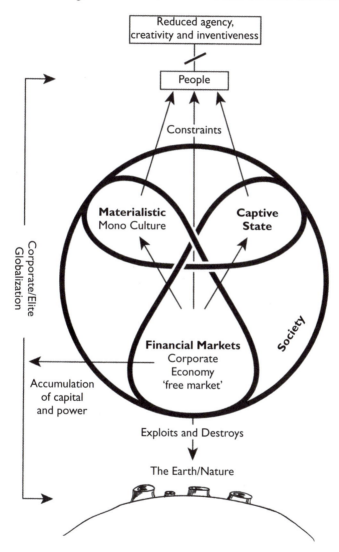

FIGURE 7.2: ELITE GLOBALIZATION: CAPTURE OF CULTURE AND RIGHTS BY THE CORPORATIONS AND THE BANKS

REBALANCING SOCIETY FOR THE COMMON GOOD 101

by owners. He researched historic trends, concluding that Western economies are inevitably leading to high levels of inequality, because the returns for capital grow more quickly than the economy, and so wealth then becomes concentrated. Political influence, corporate lobbying and funding political parties secure benefits for the wealthy; it's socialism for the rich.

A society that is out of balance cannot survive, let alone reverse climate change and the planetary destruction unleashed by rampant capitalism in the search for more profits. Corporate and government leaders hang on to crisis capitalism, believing that 'more of the market' is the answer. It's like the Titanic captain, having hit an iceberg, saying, 'Well, we'll just put up the prices of life jackets and lifeboat seats'.

Corporatocracy is where the market economy dominates the state and culture, and corporations rule the world. We see this with the US Trump presidency dominated by rentier capitalists, by Goldman Sachs bankers and by corporate CEOs such as Rex Tillerson, the former CEO of Exxon. Theocracy or deism is where ideology dominates, as with the mullahs' Iran, or ISIS, or where Communist Party ideology dominates the state, economy and culture, as in North Korea and China. 'Statism' is where bureaucracy and red tape dominate business and culture in a paternalistic way. A balanced society, however, needs a thriving business sector, effective government and a vibrant cultural life.

Respecting Boundaries between the Three Sectors

Just as there are healthy checks and balances in the constitution between the three powers of the judiciary, legislature and the executive government, so there is also need for a healthy balance between the three pillars of society – between the state or public sector, the private or business sector, and the plural or cultural sector. A healthy society has clear boundaries between state, business and the plural sector, sometimes called the third, cultural, community or civil society sector because it is so diverse.

To regain balance, we first need to change the way in which we see society, from the lens of a two-legged stool of business and state, to seeing a three-legged stool with the plural sector as the third leg. The plural sector is normally invisible to people who see society through statist or corporatist lenses. When, for example, at least 1.5 million citizens demonstrated in London against the Iraq War on 23 February 2003 and around 25 million worldwide, this was an expression of the global plural sector, speaking truth to power.

We see the one-sided corporate, market state at work here in Gloucestershire, England, with a secretive Gloucestershire County Council contract with UBB Plc to build and run a white-elephant incinerator that's taller than Gloucester Cathedral. GCC guarantee UBB profits for 25 years. These are odious profits extracted by GCC from tax-paying members of the community. The all-party GCC Planning

Committee voted 16:0 against the incinerator, but this was overturned nationally by the Conservative-run central government.

A group of activists and groups have been campaigning against the incinerator, as there is no 'social licence' for this development from the community, and there are cheaper, healthier, greener, proven alternatives. This is an example of the toxic anti-democratic, two-legged corporate market state at work, as is the British government's pushing through a costly, unproven, risky nuclear power station at Hinckley Point in Somerset. These kinds of toxic two-legged contracts are known the world over, with such debt-enslaving projects as big dams and nuclear power plants, as documented by John Perkins in his *New confessions of an economic hit man*.[3]

FIGURE 7.3: THE AUTHOR AND JOJO MEHTA PROTESTING AGAINST THE JAVELIN PARK INCINERATOR OUTSIDE GLOUCESTERSHIRE COUNTY COUNCIL'S SHIRE HALL

Another way of framing of the two-legged state/market stool is the Left/Right straight line, which has limited our societal thinking for so long.

FIGURE 7.4: STATE/BUSINESS DUOPOLY

REBALANCING SOCIETY FOR THE COMMON GOOD 103

This oppositional, polarized framing stems from the time when commoners sat to the left of the speaker in the French parliament, and the wealthy *ancient regime* sat to the right. The endless debates between polarized state or market, left vs right, nationalization or privatization, communism or capitalism, and the swings in politics between state and market solutions, are not helpful.

However, changing the way we see society and politics can help, by thinking in three dimensions. There are three sectors, not two, and the assertion of the third, plural sector is crucially important for restoring dynamic societal balance and renewal. This has long been a design principle of building three-way partnerships for tackling complex challenges, as an effective way of getting business, government and the plural sector together.

Rudolf Steiner is not alone in seeing society in a threefold way, when he observes that the public state, private/business and the plural/cultural spheres have quite different dynamics. Henry Mintzberg, a globally respected management professor, uses the tri-sectoral model to illustrate how a rebalanced society can work.[4]

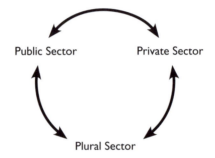

FIGURE 7.5: TRI-SECTORAL SOCIETY: PUBLIC, PRIVATE AND PLURAL SECTORS

Minzberg uses the concept of the plural sector to include the vast number of associations that are owned and run neither by the state nor by private business, such as NGO's, trades unions, religious bodies, schools, health organizations, social movements, social initiatives, the free media and more. This is the sector of *the commons*, of common property, held jointly and together – an associational space that is beyond both state and market. One remarkable feature of the plural sector, perhaps because of its cultural and communal essence, is that despite its cultural power, it remains largely invisible to people of a statist or corporate mindset. Like fish, such people just don't recognize the culture they are swimming in.

Unhealthy Boundary-crossing and Capture

Boundaries are important, and good fences make good neighbours. If you confide in a friend, you want personal secrets and boundaries to be respected. You declare a conflict of interest as a director if you might benefit, say, from a company board decision to avoid potential corruption. The toxic speculation in financial derivatives was caused by the 1999 repeal of the US Glass-Steagall Act, which put a wall between retail banks and merchant banks. This prevented the use of ordinary customer's deposits for speculation, until repeal unleashed speculation by bankers using other people's money.

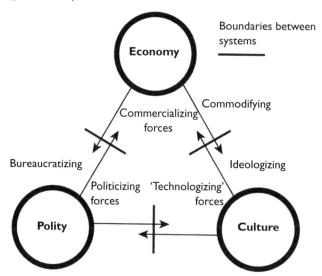

FIGURE 7.6: OVERSTEPPING HEALTHY BOUNDARIES: COMMERCIALIZING, BUREAUCRATIZING AND IDEOLOGIZING FORCES

Setting boundaries between personal life and paid work is a big issue for many people. The rise of laptop computers, email and mobile phones has resulted in people having to work without clear boundaries between their work and personal lives, 24/7. Fuzzy boundaries can mean that you don't have a life – you are all over the place.

Just as clear personal boundaries are important, so maintaining appropriate boundaries between the private, public and plural sectors is vital for societal balance. We have a gut-level sense for healthy boundaries, and also a sense for when negative boundary-crossing happens. Here are some examples of, first, the marketization of cultural (plural) life as unhealthy boundary-crossing, as business overstepping fences:

- **Commercialization of personal life:** you have been invited to a friend's party, only to discover that it's in fact a book-sale party in their home. Friends, who get rewarded by marketing firms, send you messages about products, or people 'spread the word' via social media.
- **Commercialization of childhood:** As a parent, you have to constantly counter pester-power from your children and their peers, as advertisers invade the

free cultural space of your family using all media means possible to get at you through manipulating your children. Some countries like Sweden have media rules that protect children from marketeers, and a child-centred culture backed by children's rights.

Privatization and marketization of health: according to University of York research, the introduction of the market into the English NHS has increased costs by 14 per cent. The market doesn't belong in healthcare, let alone as a way of improving health services – quite the opposite; the more the market is introduced into the health service, the more costs will go up. Caroline Molloy of Open Democracy writes about the extra costs of,

Administering the hugely expensive artificial 'marketplace' created by successive governments to allow both NHS and private 'providers' to compete with each other to offer services to NHS and other 'purchasers'.... No-one knows the exact cost of this bureaucratic 'marketplace'. A recent estimate by rebel Lib Dems put the figure as high as £30 billion a year. Dr Jacky Davis and other doctors and campaigners including the National Health Action Party have put it at £10 billion a year. The Centre of Health & the Public Interest put it at a 'conservative' £4.5billion a year. In 2010 the Health Select Committee found that running the NHS as a 'market' cost the NHS 14% of its budget a year.

The Select Committee noted that the NHS would have some administration expenses even if it didn't run itself as a 'market'. But they noted evidence from the NHS Chief Historian, Professor Charles Webster, that in the pre-market late-1980s, the NHS spent only 5 percent of its budget on administration. The difference in administration costs pre- and post-market – 9% of the NHS budget – is over £10 billion a year of the current £120 bn budget. That's more than the entire cost of every General Practitioner in the land.

The government tried to suppress the 14% figure, which was in a York University report it commissioned then refused to publish for 5 years. The York study found that 'market' mechanisms like 'the purchaser–provider split, private finance, national tariffs...mean...transactions costs of providing care have increased, and may continue to increase'.[5]

Another reason why the privatization and marketization of the NHS will cost much more to run is that they shift the NHS from being a free, semi-autonomous public service with primarily a health and 'cultural' focus, led by doctors and health professionals that we all 'give' to via national insurance and taxes, to a profit-making business. This was researched by Richard Titmuss, who found that donating blood was the cheapest, most timely, effective and high-quality way of sourcing blood, rather than people being paid for selling their blood through commercial systems.⁶ What goes against the market theory of 'rational economic man' is the health workers who give themselves over 100 per cent to their work – often unpaid for the extra time; or the volunteer blood, breast milk and plasma bikers who transport such priceless gifts all over the country to save lives.⁷

- **Commodifying education:** there was once a time in England when higher education was a public investment in young people, so that it was free of fees, with grant support being given. Charging fees with expensive student loans has helped marketize higher education and turn universities into businesses, which are now the most expensive in the world. Students are 'consumers', and staff 'deliver' and are rated on output, rather than on quality. The academies programme is privatizing schools and public property into private, often indirectly profit-making, academy chains (cf. Chapter 14, this volume).

- Michael Sandel, in *What money can't buy*, says that market triumphalism can have a toxic moral effect on culture. According to him, we drifted away from having a market economy to becoming a market-run society.⁸ So a love of learning for its own sake may be undermined by paying children to read. He asks about the moral limits to markets, which is one way of pushing back the market from areas of life where it does not belong.

However, the market can also capture the state. Here are some examples:

- **We have the best democracy money can buy? State capture:** business uses the revolving door of seconding staff, lobbying, the implied promises to 'helpful' politicians and civil servants of future jobs after a parliamentary career, contributing to political parties for favourable legislation, regulation, grants, tax breaks, tax avoidance loopholes and guaranteed profits.
- **Cognitive capture:** market-oriented thinking can dominate politicians and civil servants. When we of Stroud Common Wealth proposed a 78-home cooperative affordable housing scheme in 2007 in Stroud, Gloucestershire on government-owned land that was earmarked for housing, the UK Treasury insisted that they wanted a market price for the land. This meant that we couldn't build many social rental homes which local-government housing policy was saying were a top priority.
- **Nature is commodified and marketized** when an ancient, beautiful wood that people love is priced as an 'ecosystem service'.
- **Citizens are regarded as consumers** and voting is likened to consumer buying-behaviour.
- **The military-industrial complex** gets contracts by making sure politicians

are influenced by arms jobs for votes. War is privatized by the state outsourcing to mercenaries and corporations.
- **Company-dominated cities** can extract subsidies and planning gain benefits from the statutory sector

The above examples are of negative boundary-crossing. Fences between the sectors are torn down. However, a clear understanding of the boundaries between the economic, political and cultural systems or spaces prevents confusion. This in turn enables the private, plural and public sectors to focus on what they do best. The triangulation between the three sectors creates a healthy dynamic of checks and balances, of countervailing forces.

Fortunately, most people have an intuitive grasp of social boundaries. We have a 'feel' for the conditions for the healthy development of the economy, political system and culture. However, the sense for where boundaries are drawn changes over time. For example, as formal religion declines, many people feel there is no longer a place in Britain for a state church, for a Church of England, as religion is now a cultural, individual concern. So they feel it is high time to dis-establish the Church of England with its 26 bishops sitting in the House of Lords as a theocratic relic, to separate it from the state and political system. The Church can then stand on its own feet in the plural, cultural sector, as a self-supporting church with a religious purpose. The separation of church and state has been part of the US Constitution since the first amendment of 1791 – the founding fathers clearly saw the potential mayhem that could be caused if Congress were to be dominated by religious factions, as had happened in some of the short-lived Puritan theocracies of New England. Thomas Jefferson considered that 'building a wall of separation between church and state' was the 'expression of the supreme will of the nation on behalf of the rights of conscience'.[9] And as Alastair Campbell, former Prime Minister Tony Blair's Press Secretary, once observed, 'We don't do God'.

Rebalancing Society

The clarifying of boundaries can help people with an intuitive grasp of boundaries spot unhealthy boundary-crossing such as the captive state. So people campaign for 'getting the money out of politics' as a way of redrawing the boundaries between public and private sectors, or proactively protecting creative-commons licences from corporate intellectual property grabs, so that we can freely access the Linux operating system or Firefox as opposed to paying high fees through to Microsoft. Here are some more ways of social rebalancing to consider, which go from the individual, through organization, city and sectoral levels

First, as consumers or producers we can assert our own agency in the economy to choose the likes of fair trade, banking with mutuals, social businesses, low-carbon options, directed investment and companies engaging responsibly with their context, and we can try to avoid predatory, extractive corporations. You can choose the Phone Co-op and the ethically and environmentally designed and sourced Fairphone. As citizens, we can play an active political role, engaging with decisions and policies that affect us, participating in political parties and movements in local and national political life, working for a rights-based politics that could have exposed the rights grab behind the Brexit campaign. As individuals, we can engage with plural community and cultural life with our creative interests. We can join social initiatives and movements, what Paul Hawken in *Blessed unrest* calls a worldwide movement of movements and people for making a difference.[10]

Just consider Dr Bronwyn King, the Australian oncologist who has successfully campaigned for medical pension funds divesting from tobacco companies. The spark for this initiative was asking where her pension money was invested, and connecting the six million people dying from tobacco-related cancers per annum with her own cancer patients and her pension money. Everyday life offers many opportunities for such forms of subtle activism. Just relating to people convivially with respect, as opposed to transactionally (what's in this for me?), is a way of pushing back the market from everyday relationships.[11]

Secondly, society recovers balance not just by developing its economy, or by government intervention, but by plural-sector initiative and agency. Groups of activists develop social initiatives and movements to improve the environment, and enrich cultural and social life. Just think what society would be like without the huge variety of voluntary associations. The dramatic rebalancing of the Eastern European communist countries in 1989 was the outcome of many years of patient work by unofficial trade unions, churches, artists, musicians, journalists, writers, environmental and human-rights groups. They collectively eroded the legitimacy of the despotic state communist regimes over many years.

The one-sided, market fundamentalist capitalism that was then unleashed after 1989 is endangering the planet, as we have entered the Anthropocene or 'Capitalocene' Age. Despite a series of intergovernmental climate agreements, the real power to change lies with the plural sector, as governments are the last to change. This can be local, for example the Canadian social justice, environmental movements which realised that saying 'no' at places like Standing Rock over the oil pipeline was not enough. They got together to develop a Canadian Leap Manifesto, of which Naomi Klein writes that

> ...the urgency of the climate crisis might provide the catalyst for the deep transformation of our society and economy needs on so many fronts. We began to imagine that we could seize this juncture of overlapping crises to advance policies that dramatically improve lives, close the gap between rich and poor, create

> *large numbers of well paying, low carbon jobs, and reinvigorate democracy from the ground up.... so we invited leaders from across the country to dream big.*[12]

They dared to hope that their Leap Manifesto could become a springboard for similar broad-based plural alliances around the world. Such shared platforms for movements and organizations can help rebalance society, just as the World Social Forum in Porte Allegre in Brazil was a counterweight to the World Economic Forum in Davos.

Thirdly, leaders can engage with staff to develop their organization's social contribution, so as to focus on its core purpose and identity as a business, government body, or plural-sector organization. England's NHS is above all a health public service, not a business, not a government department. Running it with evermore red tape and 'more market' will be costly and corrosive. Organizations can also look outwards to their contexts, to their eco-niches, to review how productively they connect with the wider public, business and plural sectors. For example, Judy Wicks of the White Dog Café in Philadelphia enabled an organic, local, high-quality food-supply network for her suppliers as well as her restaurant competitors. She then looked outwards and co-founded BALLE Business for a Local Living Economy national network.

> *BALLE was founded in 2001 to nurture and curate the emergence of a new economy – one that will gradually displace our destructive and failing economy with a system that supports the health, prosperity, and happiness for all people and regenerates the vital ecosystems upon which our economy depends. With a focus on real change within a generation, BALLE works to identify and connect pioneering leaders, spread solutions, and attract investment toward local economies.... As an organization that is built upon relationships and that highlights solutions across economic systems, there are many leaders who have inspired our work and many more that we will continue to learn with and from.*[13]

There are extraordinary examples of organizations that have achieved a healthy business, and a mutually productive relationship with their contexts. Novo Nordisk is a large, globally successful insulin-producing company based north of Copenhagen. The founding scientists protected the business capital by putting the company into a foundation. Novo Nordisk builds partnerships with companies and suppliers to enhance resource utilization and the circular economy. It is a founding member of the Kalundborg Institute for Industrial Symbiosis where byproducts and resources (energy, water and material streams) are exchanged between other companies in the region, and heating to the city. All food waste from Danish sites is converted into biogas and, thereby, the resources are reused.[14]

Fourthly, healthy cities offer openings for rebalancing society, where people can see a real connection between their local efforts and improving well-being. Progressive cities are taking the lead around the world, for example on climate change, regenerative business and inspiring culture. But what makes for a healthy city? This question came to me when meeting Mayor Peter Clavelle at Burlington, Vermont, USA in 2003. I was researching community land trusts on a Winston Churchill Scholarship. Mayor Clavelle saw his role as mayor as being at the heart of the city, sensing what the city needed, encouraging business, developing representative and activist, participative democracy with town meetings and community organizing, and supporting the plural sector. As an example, he described how a women's group had asked for help with establishing a refuge, so he invited them to make a presentation to the councilors, and helped with funding so they could become self-supporting in providing a much-needed service.

Clavelle's predecessor was Bernie Sanders He was elected as an independent progressive, getting round the Democratic/Republican city duopoly. Sanders supported the development of both a vibrant cultural and civil-society life, and business development such as Seventh Generation, if they agreed to stay local. The city enabled an active plural sector – for example, for social housing the Champlain Community Land Trust, which is now a global exemplar. City pension money and a Credit Union invested locally, with 10 per cent of Burlington's food grown around the City.[15]

> *Thanks to the enduring influence of the progressive climate that Sanders and his allies helped to create in Burlington, the city's largest housing development is now resident-owned, its largest supermarket is a consumer-owned cooperative, one of its largest private employers is worker-owned, and most of its people-oriented waterfront is publicly owned. Its publicly owned utility, the Burlington Electric Department, recently announced that Burlington is the first American city of any decent size to run entirely on renewable electricity.*

Burlington is a good example of a 'Transition Town' before the concept was invented. Such progressive cities around the world are busy with becoming cities of well-being for people and planet.

Fifthly, establishing three-way partnerships between the public, private and plural sectors is a powerful way of tackling complex challenges such as climate change. Ros Tennyson of the Prince of Wales Business Leaders Forum developed a range of tried-and-tested tools for engaging the three sectors for development. In the early days, when it was mainly private- and public-sector people, the discovery was made that introducing plural-sector people from civil society and cultural organizations brought initiative and energy. Developing tri-sectoral dialogues for reflection, analysis and action can make more sense than top-down imposed 'initiatives'. One warm-up exercise for such a dialogue and partnership is to ask:

1. What do you see as the unique knowledge, skills, resources and strengths that (a) the business sector, (b) the public sector, and (c) the plural/civil society sector can offer?
2. How do you think the other two sectors see your sector, and your strengths and weaknesses?

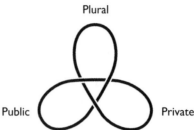

FIGURE 7.7: TRI-SECTORAL PARTNERSHIP BUILDING

So the partnership can then build on the strengths and contribution of each sector, a practical way of rebalancing. 'Common Purpose' is a leadership development charity that develops leaders to understand and work across the three sectors. Bhaskar Bhat, Managing Director of Titan Industries, Tata Group, writes that, 'Common Purpose is, above all, about collaboration – between government, NGOs and corporate sectors. This unique combination has the maximum potential to drive radical change and Common Purpose provides a platform for sharing and learning across these sectors.'[16]

Lastly, Henry Mintzberg describes how to get from current societal imbalance to balance.

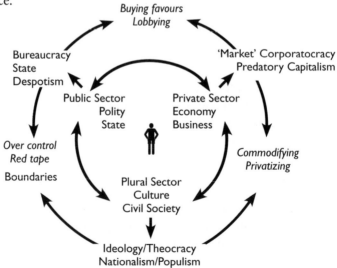

FIGURE 7.8: REBALANCING SOCIETY: IMBALANCE[17]

112 FREE, EQUAL AND MUTUAL: REBALANCING SOCIETY FOR THE COMMON GOOD

Society can be destabilized in three backward-facing ways: by state despotism, by predatory capitalism, and by exclusive populism. On a scale, these can be tendencies or extreme cases of imbalance. One sector dominates, imaged on the outer circle. On the left is state despotism dominated by government in the public sector. Predatory capitalism is on the right, dominated by exploitative enterprises in the private sector. Then there is exclusive populism with resurgent nationalism at the bottom, where a segment dominates society (like Brexit, the Muslim Brotherhood in Egypt and Trump with his racist, misogynist, white supremacist, proto fascist coalition is attempting in the USA).

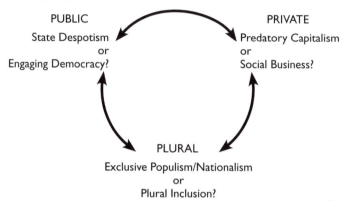

FIGURE 7.9: REBALANCING SOCIETY: BALANCE[18]

Each sector suffers a potential flaw, according to Henry Mintzberg. Governments can be crude. Just think of some European Union citizens who have lived in Britain for years who have arbitrarily been told by the Home Office at short notice to leave the country. Or the government wanting arbitrary Henry VIII powers to alter laws and regulations without parliamentary scrutiny with the proposed Great EU Repeal Bill of 2017. The private sector can be crass. Just think of the airline Ryanair's baggage policy, seemingly designed to catch you out on extra charges. All too often, it is caveat emptor – buyer beware. 'Closed' can mean ideologues exhorting people to be loyal to the faith without explaining why, like Brexit for the sake of it. Henry Mintzberg thinks balance can be achieved:

> *Crudeness, crassness, and closedness are countered when each sector takes its appropriate place in society, co-operating with the other two whilst helping to keep both – and their institutions – in check…. We just have to be careful not to mix the sectors up, by allowing the dogma of the day to carry activities away from the sector where they function most appropriately. I no more want a private company patrolling my streets than I want a government department growing my cucumbers.*[19]

Around the circle are plural inclusion based on dialogue, responsible enterprise concerned with the needs of stakeholders and engaging democracy based on active citizens being involved. You can think of healthy cities like Burlington, Vermont that engage citizens, or companies such as the global carpet company Interface, which became carbon neutral under CEO Ray Anderson, or SEKEM in Egypt which received a Right Livelihood Award for sustainable development, earthcare and social business, for greening the desert (see Chapter 10, this volume).

Concluding Thoughts

To conclude, rebalancing society starts with analysing the causes of imbalance, drawing upon threefold societal thinking. Rebalancing can be achieved by respecting the boundaries between the three sectors and analysing unhealthy boundary-crossing, such as 'what money can't buy'. The respecting of boundaries enables the private, public and plural sectors to contribute their strengths for the common good of people and planet. As individual activists, citizens and consumers or producers we can take action, as can groups and organizations. Progressive, healthy cities draw on de facto threefolding, using approaches like tri-sectoral partnerships and Common Purpose. Mintzberg suggests how society can be rebalanced by moving from state despotism to engaged democracy, from predatory capitalism to responsive business, and from exclusive populism to plural inclusion.

Rebalancing society for the common good of people and planet offers practical solutions on many levels. Seeing 'society' as the outcome of a dynamic partnership between the private, public and plural sectors, between economics, politics and culture, can help unpick the toxic mix-up of the two-legged stool of the 'free-market state'.

Finally, it's up to us to counter the excesses of the private sector. The plural sector has the power to challenge predatory business and governments which are all too often captured by the private sector, and then lead the way on the alternatives. The social threefolding map of society is a useful guide for rebalancing, rather than for revolution or breakdown, and for co-creating holistic development for people and planet. As Tom Paine wrote in 1776, 'We have it in our power to begin the world over again'. And as Margaret Mead had it, 'Never doubt that a small group of thoughtful, committed citizens can change the world. Indeed, it is the only thing that ever has.'

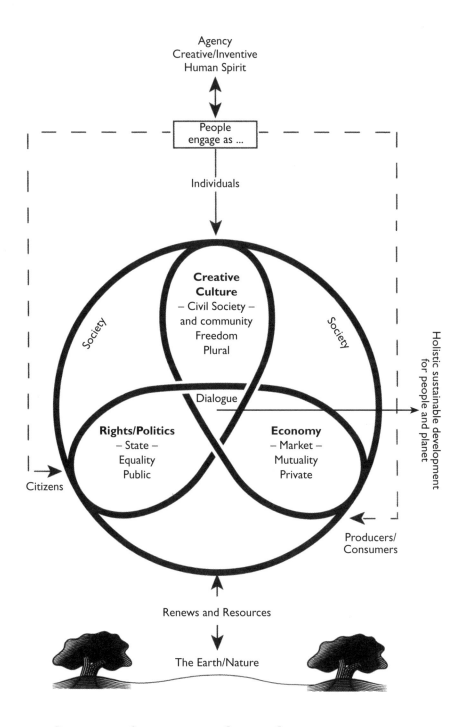

FIGURE 7.10: REBALANCING SOCIETY FOR THE COMMON GOOD

Notes and References

1. See goo.gl/9LzZYo (accessed 24 November 2017).
2. Thomas Piketty, *Capital in the 21st century*, Harvard University Press, Cambridge, MA, 2014.
3. John Perkins, *New confessions of an economic hit man: The shocking story of how America really took over the world*, Ebury Press, London, 2006.
4. Henry Mintzberg, *Rebalancing society: Radical renewal beyond left and right and center*, Berret Kohler, San Francisco, 2015.
5. Caroline Molloy, 'The billions of wasted NHS cash no-one wants to mention', 10 October 2014; see goo.gl/ppyMi3 (accessed 24 November 2017).
6. Richard M. Titmuss, *The gift relationship: From human blood to social policy*, Allen and Unwin, London, 1970.
7. Sarah Whitehead, 'Blood bikers: How volunteer motorcyclists are saving lives', *The Guardian*, 14 November 2014; accessible at goo.gl/CfRxJp (accessed 24 November 2017).
8. Michael Sandel, *What money can't buy: The moral limits to markets*, Penguin, Harmondsworth, 2012.
9. Martin Large, *Common wealth*, Hawthorn Press, Stroud, 2010.
10. Paul Hawken, *Blessed unrest: How the largest social movement in history is restoring grace, justice, and beauty to the world*, Penguin, Harmondsworth, 2008.
11. Gideon Haigh, 'The doctor who beat big tobacco', *The Guardian*, 1 August 2016; accessible at goo.gl/Mg1EFQ (accessed 24 November 2017).
12. Naomi Klein, *Saying no is not enough*, Allen Lane, London, 2017, pp. 235–6.
13. See Balle, https://bealocalist.org/about/ (accessed 24 November 2017).
14. See Marjorie Kelly, *The ownership revolution*, Berret Kohler, San Francisco, 2010.
15. Peter Dreier and Pierre Clavel, 'What kind of mayor was Bernie Sanders?, *The Nation*, 2 June 2015; accessible at goo.gl/72fnuV (accessed 24 November 2017).
16. See www.commonpurpose.org.
17. Diagram adapted from Mintzberg (note 4); cf. p. 62.
18. Cf. Mintzberg (note 4), p. 62.
19. Mintzberg (note 4), p. 42.

CHAPTER 8

The Dance of Shadows in America: Reflections on the US Presidential Election of 2016
Christopher Schaefer

Always the assumption is that we can first set demons at large and then, somehow, become smart enough to control them. Wendell Berry[1]

The election is over. Many of us are confused, dismayed and live with the questions of what actually happened? How can we make sense of it, and what can we do now?

We live in strange times when both presidential candidates had extraordinarily high negative ratings, each being loathed by close to half of the population. President Trump is described by many as having some of the ugliest character traits one can imagine: 'A hypersensitivity to criticism, a streak of viciousness, an inability to confess error and a willfull ignorance about the issues.'[2] One can easily add other unsavoury qualities – that he is a proud and unrepentant liar, a narcissist, an acknowledged tax evader, a racist, misogynist, sexual predator and woeful bigot. Clearly singularly unfit for office, and yet now President of the United States.

With Hillary Clinton the situation is more complex because she has been in the public eye for decades, as first lady, as a Senator, presidential candidate in 2008, and more recently as Secretary of State. Given her experience and background it is hard to understand the demonization and profound anger which the Republican Right has directed at her for many years: she is the feminine face of evil, the devil incarnate, the murderer who has dispatched dozens of individuals, an organizer of the Clinton Foundation as a pay to play Ponzi scheme and, listening to Donald Trump, the person most responsible for what is wrong with America and the world.

There is also another element which comes into play. Hillary Clinton is described as the symbol of the changes which our modern technocratic and more socially inclusive society represents, giving minorities, women and people of diverse sexual identities more rights and opportunities. Hillary has thereby been made into a scapegoat by many white Trump voters, who blame her for a society in which they feel increasingly disrespected, misunderstood, undervalued and unemployed.

There have been many efforts to explain the popularity of Donald Trump and his capture of the Republican Party and, in November 2016, of the Presidency itself: he is the next logical step in the evolution of the Republican Party, he represents a backlash against having our first black president; he is a charismatic sociopath, he has become the voice of the dispossessed white underclass who are fast losing control over their lives and who are suffering poverty, unemployment and alcoholism, as well as high levels of drug use.[3]

While many of these statements contain some truth, they do not explain the extreme vitriol of the election. Such intensity of feeling, of mistrust and mutual denigration is only possible, I believe, because the election, and its two main candidates, have triggered shadow elements in the American psyche that reveal the many ways in which our society and its institutions and leaders have failed to meet the real needs and the hopes of many Americans.

The Shadow in American Society

The basic concept of the shadow is that light invariably creates shadow. However we present ourselves to the world and may admire our better natures, we also know we have issues we struggle with and which we seek to hide, or deny – such as addictions, prejudices, a tendency towards violence, lying, manipulating people and many unmet cravings and secret fears.

Our culture owes its awareness of the shadow in human nature largely to the work of Carl Jung, and his impact on the field of modern psychotherapy. In popular culture, redeeming the shadow is the central drama in the story and Disney film, 'The Beauty and the Beast' (1991), in which Belle's growing interest and love of the Beast restores him to his rightful nature as a noble prince. Oscar Wilde's *Picture of Dorian Grey* is another depiction of the shadow, showing how he stays young and beautiful while his portrait gets ever uglier as it becomes a record of his crimes and debauchery.[4]

Jung describes the shadow as 'the thing one has no wish to be', and Jerimiah Abrams adds, 'we continue to know it by many names: the alter ego, the lower self, the other, the double, the dark twin, the disowned self….'[5] In religious traditions it is usually referred to as meeting our demons or working with the devil.

Shadow dimensions do not only exist in us as individuals but also in institutions and nations: think pedophilia in the Catholic Church, or the recent cheating of elderly and Latino clients by Wells Fargo Bank. If we look at the United States as a country, our shadow is visible in the discrepancy between saying that we promote democracy when we allow dark money to influence our own elections, or when we participate in the overthrow of democratically elected governments, as in Iran, Chile, Egypt and the Ukraine. It is the growing gap between who we say we are as a people, a society and a nation, and how society functions and how we often act, that creates our collective shadow. The election has activated this contrast between our better natures and our shadow, unleashing despair, anger, prejudice, fear and a longing for a simpler, kinder past.

Before describing dimensions of the American Shadow that have been aroused during the election, I want to acknowledge that there is no shadow without light, that 'America was once the hope of the world'. The historian and philosopher Jacob Needleman then added:

> *the deeper hope of America was its vision of what humanity is and can become –individually and in community. It was through that vision that all the material and social promise of America took its fire and light and its voice that called to men and woman within its own borders and throughout the world. America was once a great idea and it is such ideas that move the world, that open the possibility of human meaning in human life.*[6]

This idea and this promise were expressed in the three founding documents of the new republic, the Declaration of Independence, the Constitution and the Bill of Rights. In the preamble to the Declaration of Independence we hear the famous words, 'We hold these truths to be self-evident, that all men are created equal, that they are endowed by their creator with certain unalienable rights, that among them are Life, Liberty and the pursuit of Happiness'.[7] These words contain a promise and a dream which the new country attempted to realise, and in so doing drew millions of people to its shores, all hoping for a new opportunity, an escape from tyranny and poverty and the freedom to practise one's beliefs.

I clearly remember arriving from Europe by boat as a young immigrant aged seven, and seeing the Statue of Liberty outlined by the setting sun as we steamed into New York harbour with the skyline of the city in the distance. I was deeply touched without knowing why, but feeling that sense of arrival, of promise, of entering a new land and a new life, a feeling shared by millions of people before and after me.

Of course, from the beginning our founders did not see people without property – slaves, women, native peoples, and later Asians, Jews or Latinos – as full human beings, and much of our history has been spent attempting to transform this mighty shadow built into the very foundation of our nation.

A second significant aspect of our collective shadow, of the American double, is that our institutions and society no longer embody the American Dream. In economic life, unemployment and underemployment have undermined the hopes of many Americans. Effective unemployment is judged to be at around 11 percent and real poverty at 17 percent of the population, since many Americans never recovered from the financial crisis of 2008–10 and stopped looking for work.[8]

Central to the Neoliberal Capitalist Canon, actively promoted by economic and political elites since the time of President Ronald Reagan, is the idea that life is about material competition, and so the best strategy is to look out for 'number one'. The corollary to this message is that if you are not doing well, it must be your fault as you lack the talent and energy to succeed. Such 'shaming' is reinforced by the media through the constant marketing of the good life, of material well-being, which few can afford; and the ongoing struggle for survival shown in popular TV shows such as 'Survivor', 'The Bachelor', 'Game of Thrones', 'House of Cards', and Donald Trump's own 'Apprentice'. Selfishness, greed and manipulation become the accepted norms of our society, and justify obscene salaries and growing income inequalities. No wonder that Michael Lerner, in reviewing the psychopathology of the election, notes that 'the triumph of selfishness as common sense creates a huge psycho-spiritual crisis and a society filled with deeply scarred and lonely people'.[9]

The fact that the economy does not work for many people, and that it carries a shaming message for those who are struggling financially, is one part of the shadow of American society. Another aspect of our shadow is the breakdown of governmental institutions, and an undermining of the US Constitution by those sworn to uphold it. Garrett Epps writes in *The Atlantic*,

> *A few weeks ago I wrote that the rise of Trump is a sign that the Constitution is gravely, perhaps terminally ill. I underestimated how far the rot has spread and how hard it will be to cure. A constitution is not simply a collection of words, or even a set of rules, it is a complex focus of text, history, values and institutions. And as the nation forsakes the values, and devalues the history, the institutions – for all their marble majesty – are hollowing out. The Comey episode (in which the FBI director interfered with the election by releasing damning information on the Clinton e-mail server issue just before the voting) is but the latest symptom of a seriously ailing civic culture.*[10]

The role of hidden money in US politics, made possible by the Citizen United decision of the Supreme Court in 2010, is to my mind one of the worst attacks on our democracy, being a cynical and obvious effort to undermine the principle of 'one person, one vote'. What ever legal arguments can be made, every citizen knows in their heart that corporate money in politics is only spent to buy favours and steer legislation to one's advantage. Since mainly corporations and their owners have large amounts of money, corporate kleptocracy is officially sanctioned at the expense of the public interest. The movement of Senators and Congressmen and women from the House of Representatives and the Senate into the lobbying firms on K Street further underlines this evident corruption of our political institutions, as do declining corporate tax rates and decreases in effective taxation on the rich.

The Supreme Court and the institutions of the law are not exempt from corruption either, given their history of racism and the meddling in the Presidential election of 2000. Nor is the executive branch immune, as the widespread use of mass surveillance of American citizens and others has not been abandoned or even significantly curtailed under President Obama; while the illegal use of drones to kill both US and foreign citizens continues unabated. There can be little surprise, then, when the Pew Foundation found in 2014 that only 19 percent of voters trusted the government to do its job, and some 74 percent thought that elected officials put their own interests ahead of those of the public.[11] No wonder Trump's promise to 'drain the swamp' of Washington echoed so widely, even among some loyal Democrats.

Cultural life reveals similar weaknesses, with the media being controlled by corporate advertisers and largely owned by six families. Add to this the mass surveillance of citizens by the National Security State and the militarization of local police forces through the transfer of surplus equipment from Iraq and Afghanistan, and we have a lot to be concerned about.

As with government and the state, education in schools and universities is also increasingly driven by a corporate agenda where teachers and parents are excluded from policy decision-making and are forced to work with a mandated set of guidelines known as the Common Core. Colleges also copy the forms, thinking, objectives and procedures of well-known corporations.

We seem to have drifted a long way from the American Dream, from the promise and hope of freedom, equality and brotherhood/sisterhood, or the hope of a diverse community of striving, developing and caring human beings on a new continent full of natural blessings. In recognizing this loss we are also asked to face the fact that our very way of life, our striving for material abundance through the creation of industrial and post-industrial societies, is severely threatened. Climate change is perhaps the greatest shadow of our times, a scourge which raises questions about the continuation of life on the planet. As a critical issue for the future of humanity, it was not discussed once during the Presidential debates.

Hillary Clinton and Donald Trump each strongly represent aspects of this threefold shadow of American society. Trump embodies the shallowness, narcissism, egotism, materialism, misogyny and racism active in our culture. His victory assures us that national politics will continue to mirror the dynamics of reality-show television, as he brings his show to the national stage, with the media echoing his every tweet. For many, Hillary embodies what is wrong with our political system, which serves the well- connected and the wealthy while pursuing the interests of Wall Street and the bi-coastal elite, and not those of people living in the heartland of America. And both, in different ways, portray the self-serving, egotistical and often corrupt nature of our economic system.

Transforming Shadow in Self and World

I do believe that 'a sense for truth is the silent language of the soul' – that we are all aware, albeit semi-consciously, of these shadow elements not only in ourselves, but also in our history and in our society.[12] The election has revealed this long-developing economic, political, moral and spiritual crisis in American life. The resulting anxiety, a deep angst about our future, has led to aggression, pessimism, vitriol, fear and shame at what we have become. Unfortunately, neither candidate could address this longing for a new and moral articulation of an American future, although I think Senator Bernie Sanders, the other Democratic Presidential candidate, did try; and so instead, many chose Trump, an immoral outsider, a personification of the worst aspects of the American psyche, out of fear and in the hope that he would change the system, even if he might break it in the process. Decisions based on anxiety and fear, in which our collective shadow promotes a person who embodies the darker aspects of our nature, unfortunately seldom have good outcomes.

Perhaps, as one commentator noted, we need to add 11/09 (the election) to 9/11 as an important marker in our history. The call for 'regime change', which the 'War on Terror' led us to promote in other countries, has now come home to haunt us 15 years later, in a strongly media manipulated-election. First, there is strong evidence that the Russian state attempted to influence the election through hacking into the Democratic and possibly the Republican Party servers and producing false news to discredit the Clinton campaign. Secondly, as previously noted, the head of the FBI, James Comey, made an unwarranted and, in all likelihood, illegal, announcement 11 days before the election, re-opening the investigation into Clinton's e-mail servers.

Then there is the dimension of the media's increasing ability to manipulate people's voting directly. Roger Ailes, the long-time President of Fox News and a friend and advisor of Donald Trump, saw the potential of the media for manipulating feelings in politics as early as 1968, and is reported to have remarked, 'This is a whole new concept. This is it. This is the way they will be elected for ever more. The next guys will have to be performers.'[13] Fox News and Facebook have proved his insight true, demonstrating the power of the media to shape the thoughts, feelings and actions of large numbers of anxious Americans.[14]

I am stunned, and find it deeply ironic that part of the American electorate, being aware of and suffering most deeply from this threefold shadow of American society and clearly seeing corporate kleptocracy at work, would choose a president who represents the worst aspects of these shadow elements. And Trump's recent appointment of so many military officers and corporate CEOs to his cabinet seems to cement the military industrial complex's take-over of American society.

So what can we do? Yes, we must be watchful, and support and join groups that are concerned about the environment, about economic fairness and jobs, and above all about the state of democracy and human rights. We can also meet with friends and develop a sense of what we want to practise with others, such as a commitment to truth, increasing our giving to causes that protect democracy (for example, the American Civil Liberties Union [ACLU]), not support leaders that engage in hate speech or promote simple solutions, learn to be calm and thoughtful in times of threat, and conduct open, non-threatening conversations with people who supported Trump. Each of us can develop a list of such practices and values, and discuss their application with others in order to promote a renewed sense of civic-mindedness and democracy in our culture.

The election also offers us a deeper opportunity and a warning: either we pick up the challenge of self-development, of transforming our personal shadow and learn to become more open, less prejudiced and more caring people; or we risk a further undermining of democracy in ourselves and in society at large. As Gandhi said many years ago, 'The only devils in the world… are those running around in our hearts. That is where the battle should be fought.'[15]

This battle can be fought if we channel at least some of the anxiety and fear we feel about the election into self-reflection and inner work. Creating moments of inner quiet is a start, and regardless of our spiritual or religious orientation, developing gratitude and expressing thanks to a divine order of the universe for the life we have been given, even with its difficulties, is an important next step. The journey then requires that we pay close attention to the ways in which our life and our partners and colleagues reveal our own shadow to us. This help is often unpleasant, since our partners, colleagues and children have the unique capacity to push our buttons, and in so doing to pierce through our self-assurance, our authority or our defences. Indeed, life itself is the great school, continuously asking us, and at times demanding, that we acquire self-knowledge. Reflecting on our experience in life, seeing that which is being asked of us and that which we need to transform, is also essential for our sanity. This is what allows us to take more responsibility for our lives, thereby avoiding the externalizing of our pain through blaming others in a ritual of victimhood.

Working with the shadow asks us to explore what it is in us that we seek to deny, or hide. This is also true in our families and places of work. What are the things which cannot be talked about, that are excluded from conversation automatically, and which, if mentioned, lead to anger, aggression and blaming? I remember a family conversation many years ago between my brothers, sister and myself as well as our partners about the role that my grandfather, a retired naval officer, played during the Nazi period in Germany as the governor of a small rural county. Clearly he must have co-operated with the Gestapo. Very quickly the conversation degenerated, ending in shouting and tears. We were not yet ready to face this aspect of our family history, just as we as a country seem not yet ready to face the racism of our legal system or many of the other shadow dimensions of our society.

Facing shadow elements in ourselves, and in our relationships, and bringing some awareness to the fact that we are each capable of behavior which we deplore in the world at large, releases energy and gives us an experience of meaning and of more personal freedom. We can then begin to have a small sense of that experience which the English poet and playwright Christopher Fry expressed in a drama called 'The Sleep of Prisoners'. 'Thank God our time is now when wrong comes up to face us everywhere… Affairs are now soul size…'[16]

In doing such inner reflection we deepen the capacity for moral discernment and, I would say, truer political and social judgement. Having some awareness of our personal shadow allows us to begin acknowledging the collective shadow of American society, of the erosions to our freedom, the challenges to equality and democracy, and the gross inequities of our economic system.

As we work on ourselves and begin transforming our shadow, we can also begin practising with others the principles of a more wholesome society. When listening deeply to an adolescent child in trouble, or paying careful attention to a colleague with whom we disagree, we are acting as a guardian of the other's freedom. When we let this listening deepen, we invariably come to an experience of the other's essential humanity, and will want to safeguard their rights rather than undermining them, or wishing to marginalize them. Seeing and understanding the other in a conversation, in a family, or in groups and institutions, awakens a genuine desire to help, to serve the other in word and deed. This becomes the basis for a sharing economy, an economy that seeks to enhance life, rather than exploit other human beings and the earth.

As we begin to practise the principles of a new society in our own life, we can bring to consciousness three deep longings which I think live in all human beings: the longing for inner and outer freedom, the longing for the mutual recognition of the equality of all human beings, and the longing for meaningful work and the wish to serve others. These yearnings, while in us, are often covered over by our egotism, our fear and our prejudice. A willingness to reflect, to wake up, and to work on oneself will uncover them as a force for joy as we work towards being more caring and loving human beings. In this way we are also working with the second great commandment of the Bible, 'Love thy neighbour as Thyself'.[17]

I have described two basic steps: using the election as a spur to working on our double, and then taking a second step of practising the principles of a healthy society in our relationship with others, with our partners, in our families, with friends and colleagues and at work.[18]

The third step is that of supporting and joining the many thousands of groups who are wanting to protect what has been achieved against the ravages of the Trump administration. Many people are also busy creating a new, freer, more democratic and sustainable society in the United States and around the world. This largely hidden, new society is visible in many towns and regions of the United States and abroad, and is movingly described by Paul Hawken in his book *Blessed unrest* as a global movement of civil society seeking to undo the unholy alliance between big business and big government.[19] Some of its manifestations are sustainable food networks and CSAs (community-supported agriculture), direct-democracy initiatives, citizen councils and sociocracy efforts, co-operatives and employee-owned businesses, socially and environmentally responsible local investment networks, corporate charter groups and groups working on getting money out of politics. One can add many local, regional and national groups committed to social justice, to environmental reform, to neighbourhood education, and thousands of groups focused on physical, psychological and spiritual health.

The three steps, which are not sequential but can be practised together, are summarized in this simple chart:

Working on Self · Practice in Life · Working with Others
Transforming Shadow · Caring for the Other · Creating a New Society

THINKING > Overcoming Prejudice   Developing Interest   Mutual Freedom (CULTURE)

FEELING >   Overcoming Dislikes   Developing Empathy   Mutual Equality (STATE)

WILLING > Overcoming Egotism   Developing Service   Mutual Service (ECONOMY)

FIGURE 8.1: TRANSFORMING SELF: TRANSFORMING SOCIETY

The election of Trump I think represents an effort by an older world order, based on egotism, nationalism, materialism and exploitation, to reassert itself. It can be the spur to our practising a more open heart towards others and the world, towards transforming the shadow of empty materialism and the wanton search for power, to a resurrection of the American Dream. America could again become a beacon for the world, but only if we combine deep inner work with the disciplined desire to create a caring, sustainable society and if we remember and make real that 'America is the fact, the symbol and the promise of a new beginning'.[20]

Notes

1. Wendell Berry, *Standing by words: Essays*, North Point Press, San Francisco, CA, 1983, p. 65.
2. Quoted from the *Los Angeles Times*, Vol. 16, Issue 791.
3. These two books give a detailed and caring account of the plight of working-class people from Appalachia. Joe Bageant, *Deer hunting with Jesus: Dispatches from America's class war*, Barnes and Noble, New York, 2000; and the more recent J. D. Vance, *Hillbilly elegy: A memoir of a family and a culture in crisis*, Harper Collins, New York, 2016.
4. 'The Beauty and the Beast' was a fairy tale written by Jeanne-Marie Le Prince de Beaumont, and made into an animated film by Disney in 1991. *The picture of Dorian Gray* was a controversial novel published by Oscar Wilde in London in 1891 (Ward, Lock and Co.).
5. J. Abrams (ed.), *The shadow in America: Reclaiming the soul of a nation*, Nataray Publications, Novato, CA, 1994, p. 25.
6. J. Needleman, *The American soul: Rediscovering the wisdom of the founders*, Jeremy Tarcher/Putnam, New York, 2002, p. 3. A deeply philosophical and moving reflection on our history and society.
7. Declaration of Independence, passed by the Continental Congress on 4 July 1776.
8. The effective poverty rate was judged to be 17.9 percent in 2012, and has dropped somewhat since then. See wwwdemos.org/blog/10/20/15. The unemployment rate, counting those who are underemployed and have stopped looking for work, is at around 11 percent as I write. See Consumer News and Business Channel, Nicholas Wells, 3 June 2016.
9. Michael Lerner, 'Psychopathology in the 2016 election', in *Tikkun*, 31 October 2016; available at goo.gl/Ff6v7J (accessed 15 November 2017). A very insightful analysis by the founder of the Network of Spiritual Progressives.
10. Garrett Epps, 'Trumpism is the symptom of a gravely ill constitution', *The Atlantic*, 20 September 2016; available at goo.gl/BxcZUG (accessed 15 November 2017).
11. Pew Research Center, Research Report, *Beyond distrust: How Americans view the government*, 23 November 2015; available at goo.gl/LUVZQx (accessed 15 November 2017).
12. Rudolf Steiner, *Staying connected*, Steiner Press, Great Barrington, MA, 2009, p. 38.
13. Douglas Kellner, *Television and the crisis of democracy*, Westview Press, CA, 1990, p. 65.
14. In a report from 3D Research by K. Sokoloff it is suggested that the Trump campaign developed a highly sophisticated Facebook program to target individual Trump supporters in key battleground states, and that this effort was much more effective than TV advertising. *3D Research Report*, 'What I learned this Week', 24 November 2016 (see http://www.13d.com/research/).
15. Quoted in Abrams (ed.), *The shadow in America* (note 5), p. 41.
16. Poem contained in the play by Christopher Fry, *A sleep of prisoners*, Oxford University Press, New York, 1951.
17. Mathew, 22.36–40, *The Bible*, King James Version.
18. Paul Hawken, *Blessed unrest: How the largest movement in the world came into being and why no one saw it coming*, Viking, New York, 2007.
19. See Otto Scharmer, 'On the making of Trump, the blind spot that created him', *Huffington Post*, 11 November 2016 for an insightful perspective on the election, in which he refers to the shadow elements I have described as blind spots, as well as giving a picture of a new society. Available at goo.gl/ZszHTd (accessed 15 November 2017).
20. Needleman, *The American soul* (note 6), p. 5.

CHAPTER 9

Great Again? Thoughts about the World Situation[1]
Gerald Häfner

We are living at a turning-point. Fear and tensions are increasing everywhere in the world. How can we find a way forward?

In recent times the degree of violence and conflict in the world has increased with every passing year. Figures from 2014 and 2015 indicate that over 160,000 people have died in situations of conflict, which has not been the case for the last 25 years. Moreover, there is no sign of a lessening of terror and violence. War may as yet seem a distant prospect, but violence is not.

Even in an otherwise peaceful Germany, in 2016 alone there were more terrorist attacks than in the past 20 years taken together. Not only is the number of attacks alarming but also the very nature of terror. The focus is no longer – as, for example, at the time of the assaults by the Red Army Faction – upon specific, selected 'representatives' of the system but has become devoid of any conscious choice or purpose. Destruction awaits innocent non-participants, such as people present in a theatre, on a train or at a Christmas market. This random aspect reveals an especially evil form of violence.

Around 60 million people are implicated in this picture – people who are at present having to flee from somewhere in the world, desperate, helpless, trying to reach countries and people who will receive them. Not only is it them who have fear. Lack of orientation, fear of the future, fear of competition and of immigration, the decline and loss of what has hitherto been assured – all have also become entrenched in countries that are apparently rich and secure, and are increasingly changing the social climate. And fear makes for narrowness, rigidity and hardness, and engenders rigid, aggressive and backward-looking answers.

Alongside physical violence, persecution, suppression and terror, violence of a political and economic nature is also increasingly coming to expression through thoughts and spoken words. In the Philippines, a man is chosen as President who proudly propagates the view that drug addicts and drug-traffickers should be assassinated without trial. In Turkey, critics of the President are taken away at night, arrested and released in their thousands, newspapers and broadcasting stations are shut down, opposition members of the government are persecuted and locked up. Russia and China stir up nationalism on a massive scale and pursue power-politics without any thought of the likely consequences.

And virtually every decree of the new President of the United States contains and conveys violence, as did his election campaign: from building a wall along the frontier via the humiliation and dismissing of qualified colleagues and insulting women and minorities, to approving methods of torture, from issuing sweeping entry prohibitions for citizens of Islamic countries to making massive threats towards certain religions, countries and enterprises. Although the symptoms of breakdown may be extreme in the USA, these developments are not an exclusively American phenomenon. This movement is gaining pace around the globe. In Europe, too, the number and influence of nationalistic, chauvinistic and popular groups are growing. They simplify everything by creating scapegoats, search out people to blame and victims, encourage an exclusive, egotistical attitude and emphasize popular, national, material and racial aspects. They live by a backward-looking longing to be 'great again'. It is like an ever-louder derogatory whistling in an increasingly dark forest.

The Rising up of the Down-Trodden

Why is there this derogatory note of mockery in the forest? How could it reach such proportions? What has opened up in recent years and come to the surface has for some while been smouldering down below, and is only now becoming visible. Our world is falling apart. We know – and can apply our knowledge – more than ever before: we have ever-more-precise scientific knowledge, more refined technology and laws more complex than ever.

And we have an incredible amount of money. It seems incomprehensible, but despite this immense world-wide affluence and knowledge there is so much need – an anonymous, infinite number of poor, deprived, disappointed and downtrodden people, regions and countries. Ever-more inconceivable sums accumulate in the hands of ever-fewer people, firms, funds and trusts, while at the same time millions of people are deprived and struggle simply in order to survive. In the past week as I write, the relief organization Oxfam published its latest calculation of the world-wide distribution of income and wealth, based on the figures from *Forbes*. According to this calculation, *the richest eight individuals possess just as much as the whole of the poorer half of humanity.*

This is a degree of inequality that leaves one speechless. In a world that both through the media and in a real way is growing ever-more closely together, this obscene disparity between rich and poor is alone sufficient to evoke despair, anger and fury. People have a growing understanding that this is by no means God-given and unchangeable, and are even less prepared to put up with it. But there is more to it.

Even in the rich and developed countries there are many at present who have no prospects. I shall merely give some figures about the dramatic extent of youth unemployment. In France the figure was 24 percent, in Ireland 25 percent, in Portugal 36 percent, in Italy 42 percent, in Greece 51 percent, in Spain 54 percent.[2] Just imagine behind the bland figures of the statistics the millions of actual destinies, the disappointment, the lack of orientation, despair and anger of people with an educational qualification or training, between a quarter and a half of whom are told that they're not needed, there's no task, no appropriate role for them in our rich and complex world.

To make matters worse, one has the feeling that it is no longer possible to find anyone who is responsible for this injustice. The notion of responsibility disappears in a 'systemic responsibility'. A Swabian mechanical engineer who has been working in the same firm for decades discovers from one day to the next that he is now working for a Chinese owner of the business. There are some radical changes and the human element disappears. It often happens that the managers themselves neither wanted nor brought about the change.

Thus the feeling grows that cold, mechanistic, system-based forces are taking hold of one's own life, even though no one actually appears to be individually responsible. This seems to me to have also played a part in the background of the American election. With Hillary Clinton a woman appeared as a candidate for the office of president who in the eyes of many was an utterly typical example of this system that has lost touch, of a world that is intimately entangled with Wall Street and the establishment. Anyone who followed the speeches that Clinton made during her election campaign often received the impression that everything was as though staged and programmed, each of her gestures, every facial movement, every wave and every camera setting or adjustment were pre-calculated for their effect. This may be no different with Donald Trump, who may well be far more calculating and brutal – and yet the effect that he had as a type was so radically different, so unruly, furious, reckless and apparently so authentic, so bereft of etiquette and anti-establishment in tone and attitude.

Trump seemed to be indifferent to what Washington, the political world or the press expected of him, to what is politically correct or not, so that this appearance of genuineness, of naturalness, tipped the scales for many. Let's get rid of the old clique, otherwise nothing will ever change – this was the mood. With every further act of provocation and flouting of established norms he gave vent to the feeling that here at last someone is coming who wants to change things in a radical way, and who will drain the accursed swamp. Waking up the following morning was nevertheless a terrible experience. With bated breath we became witnesses on a daily basis of how the immaturity, arrogance, egocentricity and hatred of a single human being is capable of gradually transforming the greatest super-power and, hence, the world as a whole. There may be many who look with longing at the old system.

But that would also not have been good for humanity and the world.

Two Significant Causes

In order to understand what is going on here, one needs to delve into the very specific depths of American politics and democracy; and there is no space for this in my brief contribution. Nevertheless, the result of the anticipated break that angry citizens who have had less than their fair share have made with the hated 'elite' is a horrifying irony: a government emerged consisting of the uppermost 1 percent, a cabinet of the super-rich, millionaires and generals. It is not only disturbing who becomes a minister but, rather, who is given which job. Thus the prominent coal lobbyist Scott Pruitt becomes the leader of the Ministry for the Environment, while Rick Perry – who acquired notoriety through his denial of climate change and his demand that the Energy Ministry be abolished – is made (of course) Minister for Energy.

There are even more disturbing powerful figures behind Trump and his ministers. For example, his election campaign leader Steve Bannon, who also runs the right-wing, conservative on-line magazine *Breitbart*, has now, as I write, become the President's chief advisor: 'Darkness is good', enthuses Trump's principal advisor in an interview. 'Dick Cheney, Darth Vader, Satan: that is power!' And: 'If we deliver… we'll govern for 50 years'.[3]

How does it happen that such thinking meets with approval today? The answer to this question is decisive for our future. Without such an answer there is no hope of finding a way forward. It is, I think, essential to note that the problem has many layers. In another context it will be possible to enter further into this. Anyone who seeks to reduce a social phenomenon to just one cause will always go astray. It is indeed impossible to explain everything with one great reason, with a single formula. I often meet people – and increasingly also in anthroposophical circles – who think they know exactly how, for example, events in the Ukraine or in Syria are to be understood. They know without any doubt which side is to blame, who in any particular conflict is good and who is bad or evil. All phenomena are integrated with and subordinated to this view of the world.

Unfortunately, situations today are for the most part incomparably more complex than such supposedly clear attributions in accordance with the friend/foe pattern might suggest. So many layers play a part that one is unable to penetrate to the inner circumstances, but merely arrives at a key model of explanation. All the same, this should not prevent us from recognizing what we are able to recognize, and from acting where through such knowledge we are capable of acting and have a commitment so to do. Only now that I have emphasized this would I wish to try initially to highlight two particular areas of the social realm as they appear from my own perspective.

What Really Counts Here is Love

'Threefolding lives in the facts!' This is one of the most important indications emanating from Rudolf Steiner's Threefold Impulse. Thus the threefolding of the social organism is not an abstract system that someone has thought up and which is to be imposed upon reality. It is observable, and exerts an influence in the world, in the same way as the threefold nature of the human soul in thinking, feeling and willing. Just as one can observe in the body and the soul an actual threefold nature with its own respective functionary laws, so does one also find this in human social life.

If one considers economic life, it becomes apparent that it has a tendency towards a brotherly quality in human affairs which reaches beyond all boundaries of whatever kind. This is an observable fact. Geographical and political boundaries become of increasingly less significance in an economic sense, and instead a world-wide collaborative impulse extends beyond all boundaries. Only out of the collaboration of ever-more people across the globe can the goods and services available today be manufactured and sold on the principle of the division of labour. People make their faculties available to others, and each person lives entirely from what others do for him – this is what 'being brotherly' means. In modern society we are even directed towards this brotherly quality, because we would no longer be able to sustain ourselves in isolation. We can only live in the way we do in our time because millions of other people are active on our behalf.

This is the reality. At the same time we have forcibly subjected this brotherly worldwide fabric, woven from working for one another, to concepts and rules which have their origin in a totally opposite kind of logic. This latter claims that if everyone always pursues his or her own self-interest, then this leads to the greatest benefits for everyone. The attitude of 'I am working for myself' is, so it is thought, the engine and essential core of economic and social life.

It is worth considering this fact in all its implications. What is actually established as a worldwide endeavour of mutual exchange – what is, therefore, manifested in globalization as the power of love, as the power of true brotherliness – is not something that is experienced: it does not become conscious and, hence, cannot be lived and brought to fulfilment. Instead, a martial battle of all against all is raging in the economic world.

That boundaries are losing their validity, that everything is connected with everything else, that I am no longer able to ascertain who is responsible, is – under the underlying maxim of egotism – becoming a dramatic threat both to the individual and society, instead of the qualitative next step of humanity in the direction of world-citizenship. The rule that everyone should attend to his or her needs and think only of self is the cause of immense damage of a bodily, soul and social nature in a finite, interconnected and ever more populated world.

The contradiction between the actual realities of brotherliness and rules that are based exclusively on self-interest, profit and competition leads to ever more violent tensions. And more and more people feel unconsciously that this is not right. They experience the system in which they are living as cold, unjust, unsocial and threatening, and they long for change. Some 51 percent of young Americans and 90 percent of Germans say in opinion polls that we need a different economic structure. But where is it? Socialism in the Soviet Union and neighbouring countries has failed; and however far one looks, no credible alternative is visible. What has happened to the ideas of socialism, of social democracy? Does it have any convincing scenarios? There are no ideas to be discerned anywhere. This immense vacuum of ideas is the real tragedy. There seems to be no alternative. There is little orientation that might be able to establish trust and confidence.

Spewing Forth Residues into the Ether

Democracy has a particular commitment to there being an open and public space where people can meet and have exchanges with one another. In such a realm we are able to learn from one another, adjust our views and arrive at common convictions. This space no longer exists, for the Internet has taken its place. It is, however, organized in accordance with different rules. The spaces in the virtual world are fashioned in accordance with strict economic laws and are formed on the basis of maximizing profit.

When I communicate through Twitter or Facebook or make searches through Google, algorithms are working in the background in such a way that I always come to see the news or offer that I would most probably want to see. The calculation is made out of my past behaviour. I am always held, mirrored and confirmed within my own past. Something deeply backward-looking is at work here which encourages narcissism. However 'open' the Internet may apparently seem to be, I meet through this structure that is provided by those who are mainly similar to me, who think just as I do. Thus, bubbles and echo-chambers arise in which people with similar views communicate with those with a similar outlook, whereas different views, world-pictures and life-intentions are totally excluded. Conversation reaching beyond the boundaries of world conceptions, which is the prerequisite for learning about society and for the forming of an independent political will, is completely lost. Thus, the egocentric Internet undermines a democracy oriented towards the 'you'.

A Device for Inculcating Obscenity

Another effect of the Internet is that level-headed and measured expressions of opinion are necessarily swallowed up by its noise. Their voice is unnoticed, submerged beneath the waves of indignation and rage, of both the shrill and the trivial. We do not notice 99 percent of what is said. We never experience it, because it is not highlighted by the algorithms and shown to us. Our lesson here is that we are perceived only if we take shrillness to an extreme. This is something that Donald Trump, for example, understood very early. I have to say something extreme, express everything in excesses, flaunt rules, cause harm to people, and then this tickles interest through the brief 'teasers' which enable people to judge whether they want to see something or not. Then the profiteers take notice. And where they take notice, it goes viral. The Internet has, therefore, become a device for inculcating shrillness, obscenity, brutality, lasciviousness, arrogance and a lack of tact and respect. It necessarily involves a loss of empathy.

A big part is also played by the fact that one does not know who is actually indicating a wish to speak – and, on the other hand, that one must not see what is engendered by one's own contributions. It often happens that one does not know whether something that has been posted has been composed by a human being or by a socially programmed robot.[4] Machines have been programmed to submit opinions and contributions for discussion, while readers believe that a human being has written them. For example, after the comment made by a member of the public sympathizing with the Democrats, she was engulfed by a flood of outraged voters. Or: while the television debate between the candidates was still taking place, millions of Internet users were claiming: 'Trump has won!' But behind such phenomena there are not angry or enthusiastic members of the public but machines. In the US election campaign a fifth of the comments on social networks were generated not by human beings but by robots.

As is the case with Goethe's apprentice magician we have in both areas released a power that we are clearly unable to contain. Like that apprentice we are astonished about the buckets that are flying to and fro, and suddenly wake up in horror as we recognize that we have for the time being lost control of this technology. The same applies to the Internet as an instrument of social discourse as was said about the egotism that has been unleashed in capitalism: it seems as though we are not in control of events; they are in control of us. This helplessness in the face of forces, systems and dynamics that can no longer be controlled seems to me to be a generally valid feeling of the present day.

Where Is the Third Element?

There are three ways of reacting to the developments that have been indicated – the first being to hold on to the current modes of thought and mechanisms, muddling through and using them to one's own advantage, and hoping that in the end everything will turn out well.

This is – still – the most widespread attitude, and it is the tacit promise of the ruling parties, institutions and politicians, from Angela Merkel to Hillary Clinton. It has credence only if one is blind and deaf to the growing number of those who no longer believe in the justness and meaningfulness of this system.

The second possibility is the way back: we look for scapegoats, accuse them of being guilty, vote them out of office, chuck them out, build a wall, prevent foreigners from entering and think only of ourselves, of burning our coal, ignoring climate change, not giving a damn about the environment, re-arming, ending free trade and hiding ourselves away in our nation-state. This attitude is embodied not only by Trump but also by Farage, Wilders, Strache, Orban, Petry and many others.

The third way, on the other hand, would represent a forward step. The aim here would be that rules for the Internet would not be dictated by companies but would be developed in accordance with advice from the legal community, in order that what is now a space for egotistic self-reflection can be transformed into one of real meeting and mutual learning. A further aim would be to understand brotherliness in the context of economic life and, instead of resisting globalization for nationalistic reasons, to give it a true brotherly form. Additionally, a democracy of spectators governed by power and money would be transformed into a participatory, deliberative and direct democracy where each person can have a share in bringing about significant social decisions.

The problem of the US elections was that there was a candidate for the status quo, and there was a candidate for the march backwards to an authoritarian, nationalistic and chauvinistic community or polity. But where was the candidate for a convincing and meaningful way forwards? The third element was absent! – and it has been absent not only in the USA. It is lacking virtually everywhere, also in the heart of Europe.

This is the greatest – and the real – tragedy of our time: we are functioning far below our true potential. Amidst all the threatening weight of these developments it is worth asking what we may finally learn through these challenges. What new capacities are necessary, what future do we need to imagine in order that instead of further sacrifices, something truly constructive can arise amidst these challenges?

If we succeed in understanding the deeper forces underlying economics and actually build an economic order based on brotherhood, this would engender an immense healing power which would ray out across all boundaries. For this we need a new, transformed understanding of money and the enormous forces that lie within it. In his book *Schulden* David Graeber[5] has strikingly shown how through money and through the concept of debt in the nature of money, power enters into human relationships, and how everyone, even those who have to submit to this power, is inclined to feel this power to be legitimate. Our way of thinking about economics, money and also democracy has arrived at a dead-end. Without changing the way we think, without radically new ideas about our cultural, political and economic life, fear and violence will take hold to an ever greater extent. Democracy, too, must take a new qualitative step, because it will otherwise cease to be able to function. It is not only a matter of enabling there to be more transparency or somewhat more public participation but of a substantially new step in democratic life.

A Year of Real, Substantial Change

All the same, our modern world is primarily determined by economics. Everything is assessed and evaluated according to its price and its profitability. Hence the economy is the most important point if one is thinking about a new way of living together. When I buy something today, every product in a globalized world has an extensive biography. With every item that I purchase there is a long chain extending from me via the salesman and the manufacturer of the final product to the originator, whether this be a cotton gatherer in India, a cocoa farmer in Nicaragua or a miner in the Congo. These chains, which for the most part embrace half the globe, need to be perceived in their totality and warmed through in a human way. Our task in the coming years will be to form them in accordance with the viewpoint of brotherhood. Ultimately it means that I cannot take pleasure in rejoicing either about the product that I have acquired or the price that I paid for it until I am certain that not only I but all the people connected through this chain of value creation have been treated fairly and are able to live adequately from their work. In this way a revolution of brotherhood comes about.

In the first months of 2017 there is a sense that this will be a year of real, substantial change. The old order is increasingly unable to cope. There are rents in its fabric and it is threatened with imminent disintegration. Are we prepared for this? Will we find the way forward to a better future, or will we retreat to a narrow, threatening past? It is obvious what needs to be done. When the old is dying, what needs to happen is to work tirelessly so that something new can emerge from it. But if this does not happen, if our understanding and courage are inadequate, if credible, courageous, convincing, enduring, meaningful and essentially human images for the future are lacking, the dangerous, authoritarian (se)ducers will have free rein.

Notes

1. Published in German in *Das Goetheanum*, Volume 6, 3 February 2017. Translated by Simon Blaxland-de Lange with kind permission of the author and the publisher.
2. Statistics are from *Eurostat*, June 2014.
3. Interview in *The Hollywood Reporter*, 18 November 2016; see goo.gl/u66B9m (accessed 16 November 2017).
4. The author here uses an apparently English phrase 'social bot'. 'Bot' is an Australian and New Zealand slang word for a scrounger or freeloader, one who is a habitual borrower of money and, hence, a social parasite (see *The Historical Thesaurus of the Oxford English Dictionary*, 2009). Although this meaning is by no means irrelevant in this context, I have opted for the above phrase which, I hope, more or less conveys the author's meaning here. – Translator.
5. David Graeber, *Schulden: Die ersten 5000 Jahre*, Goldmann Verlag, Munich, 2013

PART THREE

Inspired Initiatives

CHAPTER 10

SEKEM[1] – A Model for Holistic Sustainable Development in Egypt
Christine Arlt

SEKEM tries to implement sustainable development towards a future where every human being can unfold his or her individual potential; where humankind is living together in social forms reflecting human dignity; and where all economic activity is conducted in accordance with ecological and ethical principles. Thus, its mission is the development of the individual, society and environment through a holistic concept integrating economic, societal and cultural life.

Above all, SEKEM aspires to be an impulse for continuous development in all parts of life, to be not only a model for, but also a contribution to the development of, the entire world. This can only be achieved if all aspects of life are involved.

The SEKEM vision and mission are strongly influenced by Rudolf Steiner's 'Social Threefolding' model. Its activities and organizational structure are built into the so-called 'Sustainability Flower'.

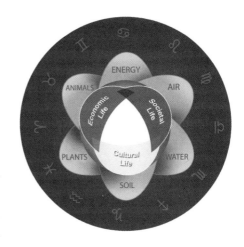

Figure 10.1: The Sustainability Flower

In essence, the Sustainability Flower represents a management, assessment and communication tool symbolizing the concept of sustainable development in its four dimensions (economic life, societal life, cultural life and ecology, with its six sub dimensions). It was developed within a network of international organizations from the Organic and Biodynamic movement co-operating under the umbrella of the International Association of Partnership for Ecology and Trade (IAP).

The Sustainability Flower therefore symbolizes the penetration of the threefold social order, representing cultural life (education, arts, belief systems, etc.), social life (civil society, human rights, legal systems, politics, etc.) and economic life (all aspects of fair trade, business interactions, etc.) – and the underlying need to reflect the cyclical eco-system with its manifold spheres in every decision that is made and in any action taken.

To understand how this is actually working, how it became alive and what it looks like today, we need to look back to the foundation and development of the SEKEM Initiative itself.

Egypt – A Challenged Country

Some 60 years ago the Egyptian Ibrahim Abouleish left his home country at the age of 20 to study in Europe. He left a country with around 18 million citizens – a country that had a flourishing economy, diverse cultural activities and an open society. But when he returned at the end of the 1970s all of the latter was gone. The population had almost doubled, and the economic and social systems were no longer able to cope. Today the situation seems to have become even worse. Current developments in Egypt give a hopeless impression. To better understand why, a short overview of the different sectors that are currently challenging for Egypt is needed.

Ecological Challenges

More than 90 percent of the country is desert land, and the only natural fertile soil is located along the River Nile. People are gathered along the precious water in the Nile Valley and Delta, which is known as the most extensive oasis on earth and covers only 6 percent of the Egyptian country. Around 60 years ago, when the population was around 20 million, living on what was in effect a desert land was already a challenge. Today the number living there has quadrupled, but the cultivated area remains the same. Additionally, climate change and lack of awareness about the consequences of certain actions, like unsustainable agriculture, poor garbage disposal, water wastage or financing short-term solutions, are all compromising the country's development.

The building of the Aswan Dam – which has supplied the country with energy ever since but which also hinders the fertile Nile River mud from refreshing Egypt's delta – supported the use of chemical fertilizers and pesticides to increase efficiency and crop yield. Today the natural ecosystem is not only becoming increasingly damaged and polluted, but it does not even bear enough water to feed the population. The country is living in water scarcity. The average water use per capita in Egypt is around 660 cubic metres per annum, while around the world it is about 1,000 cubic metres. The United Nations predicts that by 2025, Egypt's water availability will even drop to below 500 cubic metres per capita per annum. The agriculture sector alone consumes 85 percent of Egypt's available water.

Waste-water canals are awash with agricultural runoff polluted with chemical fertilizers and pesticides, which cause many diseases. The lack of waste management is another huge challenge that causes dangerous impacts on ecology and public health. According to the World Bank, in 2012 Egypt generated 89.03 million tons of solid waste. Only 60 percent is managed by formal and informal waste operations. The rest is just thrown on to the streets or left at illegal dumpsites.

Economic Challenges

The water problem also means that Egypt is dependent on food imports, which causes higher food prices and thereby increases poverty. Wheat production alone, for instance, would require a quarter of Egypt's total water supply. Hence, Egypt needs to import 40 percent of its groceries – it is the world's fourth-largest wheat importer.

Agriculture is the backbone of most of the economic activities and was for decades the mainstay of the Egyptian economy. However, its share has been reduced to roughly 13 percent of GDP. In the 1970s, agriculture used to employ more than 90 percent of the Egyptian working population, but this has now decreased to approximately 30 percent. This is one of the major economic problems that Egypt is facing, and generates yet more challenges.

The unemployment rate has reached over 13 percent, which affects mainly women and youth. The resulting poverty and income disparity is also putting a lot of pressure on the current economic and political situation. In 2011 the World Bank classified 25 percent of Egyptians as living below the national poverty line.

The high rate of subsidies for basic commodities like wheat, cooking oil and sugar makes the Egyptian government especially vulnerable to external price shocks.

Societal Challenges

The 2011 uprising against the government of President Mubarak clearly illustrated the people's dissatisfaction with the livelihood pressures they were facing.

During the past century, Egypt has been destabilized through war and conflicts, including several military revolutions, militant Islamist activity, and the intensive Arab–Israeli conflict. As a result, education of the population was chronically neglected, with many underpaid teachers and overcrowded classrooms. There is also no real incentive for children to go to school, and most of them cannot afford the expensive private lessons in order to pass their examinations. Similarly, the poor and inefficient health system also causes many problems for locals, such as inaccessibility of healthcare facilities in rural areas. Moreover, the country faces other threats like high inflation and terrorist attacks.

The number of inhabitants in Egypt has more than quadrupled in the past 50 years, from around 20 million in the 1960s to approximately 95 million today. But the area of fertile land to produce food and on which to live remained more or less the same. In particular, people from rural areas start to immigrate to Egypt's capital. The population of Cairo and its metropolitan area is estimated to be more than 22 million, which makes it one of the world's most densely populated capital cities. One third of the total population in Cairo is under 15 years of age, and nearly three-fifths is under 30. Cairo struggles with many health problems, including malnutrition, bacterial infection (Egypt has one of the highest hepatitis C rates worldwide), and serious air pollution.

Cultural Challenges

Poverty and income disparity are also putting a lot of pressure on an education system which does not even meet basic needs. Egypt is ranked last out of 148 countries surveyed in the World Economic Forum's 2012–13 Global Competitiveness Report for the quality of its primary education. Public education in Egypt is free, but it is not uncommon for there to be up to 70 students per class. Teachers are also underpaid, which forces them to take up a second job. Due to the large class sizes, children also have to take extra lessons to pass exams, and which cost their parents extra money. The public school buildings and their surroundings are often in a poor condition. Proper cleanliness and hygiene is missing, and the curriculum is mainly targeting monotonous learning rather than fostering deeper understanding or encouraging independent thinking. The overall illiteracy rate in Egypt was estimated at 25 percent in 2015. This is hardly surprising when only 3.8 percent of GDP is spent on education.

Places for cultural activities, like arts or music, as well as philosophical discourses are very rare. Hence, the preconditions for laying down a proper understanding of and awareness about the impacts of the country's developmental trajectory are not provided.

The SEKEM Vision

All of these challenges currently faced by Egypt had already been in the offing during the 1970s when Dr Ibrahim Abouleish returned from Europe. The situation did not seem any more hopeful than it is today. However, Dr Abouleish decided to create an impulse to address these many negative developments. He was full of confidence and trust despite the many obstacles he encountered. SEKEM was founded based on a different development paradigm, based on a holistic business model integrating human development, economic and ecological as well as cultural and societal development as part of its daily business operation.

In Europe, Dr Abouleish had not only studied pharmacy, chemistry and medicine but also encountered Rudolf Steiner`s anthroposophy, which he worked with for a long time and which deeply influenced the vision of the SEKEM Initiative. In anthroposophy Abouleish found answers to many questions and, at the same time, practical applications in many areas of life. Strongly influenced by this experience, his vision, the SEKEM vision, was formed:

> *In the midst of sand and desert I see myself standing before a well drawing water. Carefully I plant trees, herbs and flowers and wet their roots with the precious drops. The cool well water attracts human beings and animals to refresh and quicken themselves. (...) For me this idea of an oasis in the middle of a hostile environment is like an image of the resurrection at dawn, after a long journey through the nightly desert. I saw it in front of me like a model before the actual work in the desert started. And yet in reality I desired even more: I wanted the whole world to develop.*[2]

Against all odds, Dr Abouleish decided to leave behind his successful career in Europe, and he moved back to Egypt together with his wife and two children. He bought 70 hectares of desert land near Cairo where he wanted to realize his mission.

People, even friends, called him crazy, but he was deeply convinced that he could realise his plan – and he succeeded. Today the SEKEM Initiative is a place on former desert land where sustainable agriculture is applied, where different companies process healthy agricultural products, and people are living and learning in a community that offers space for individual potential and development. How was that possible? And how does it actually work?

Greening the Desert with Biodynamic Agriculture

When starting with nothing but infertile dry land, the first step was to reclaim the desert to vital living soil in order to create a livelihood for the community that was to be developed. Instead of using artificial fertilizers, for the very first time in Egypt Rudolf Steiner's biodynamic agricultural principles were applied. SEKEM is convinced that biodynamic agriculture is the best way, and the basis for a healthy and sustainable ecology. The aim of creating integrated, environmentally sustainable agricultural production systems is rooted in the concept of biodynamic agriculture itself. Reliance is placed upon self-regulating agro-ecosystems, renewable resources and the management of ecological and biological processes.

Biodynamic farming respects the environment's own system for controlling pests and diseases in raising crops and livestock, avoiding the use of synthetic pesticides, herbicides, chemical fertilizers, growth hormones, antibiotics or genetic manipulation. Instead, biodynamic preparations are used, and cosmic rhythms of development are adhered to in harmony with agricultural activities. By recognizing the effect of sun, moon, planets and the constellations of fixed stars on plant development and by using biodynamic preparations made from plants, minerals and animal manure for spraying and composting, farming operations can be optimized in harmony with their environment, and they have led to a proven increase in productivity and superior food quality.

Today, 40 years after the first square metres of desert were reclaimed by biodynamic methods, SEKEM has been able to support the transformation of almost 5,000 hectares of arid land to vital soil (varying between 0 and 30 cm in depth), which is rich in organic matter and contains a broad spectrum of microbiological life. The biodynamic fields of the SEKEM Farm thereby have a much higher water holding capacity. They require up to 40 percent less water than conventionally treated soils, which is a great advantage, especially when considering one of the above-mentioned challenges, Egypt's water scarcity.

Compost as a natural fertilizer and the biodynamic preparations are produced by SEKEM, and are also sold to other farmers. Meanwhile, other agricultural institutions that have gradually established themselves around the SEKEM Farm are producing compost by themselves and selling it to others. Even conventional farmers have started to appreciate the power of compost fertilization.

The nutritious soil was then first planted with medical herbs and spices, and before long, Lotus – SEKEM's first company – was founded to process and market the products both locally and internationally.

Besides applying biodynamic principles through the SEKEM Farms, SEKEM also promotes sustainable land management, and has facilitated the establishment of the Egyptian Biodynamic Association (EBDA) that has supported the transition of 400 farms, with more than 4,500 acres of land, to biodynamic farming practices. EDBA was also a global pioneer in growing and producing biodynamic cotton, which has helped to reduce 90 percent of chemical use in Egypt's textile industry by promoting sustainable agriculture practice. EBDA also provides training to farmers, and this has in turn helped to raise awareness of sustainable practice.

Through EBDA, SEKEM engages more than 800 contracted farmers and producers, and offers them a fairer income or a fixed contract with fixed prices for their produce. SEKEM pays the farmers 20 percent more than the current market price. SEKEM's ecological activities, strongly informed by the anthroposophic approach, are creating the basis for its further commitment to economy, society and cultural life.

Economy of Love

Sustainable development and land reclamation cannot be genuinely sustainable if their yields are processed and distributed through a market that does not care about those who created the value. A fair and conscious economy is crucial for the sustainable development of ecology, and societal and cultural life. This is why the SEKEM Initiative today includes different companies that employ more than 1,500 people, and which are market-competitive, although economic profit is not the primary focus.

First, the Lotus company was established to process the herbs, spices and seeds that SEKEM cultivates on its fields. The raw material then goes to the ISIS Organic company, which produces tea from it and has become the pioneer and market leader for organic products in Egypt. ISIS Organic today provides organic products for the Egyptian market, such as vegetables, juices, milk, and many others.

As people do not only need healthy food but also good medical products that combat disease in a natural way, thus sparing them from additional harm, ATOS Pharma was founded, which has pioneered phytopharmaceuticals on the Egyptian market.

In addition, the famous Egyptian cotton, which has for a long time also been a huge economic sector of the country, is processed into organic certified textiles, garments and children's wear by SEKEM's company NatureTex, mainly for the European market. However, SEKEM keeps its consolidated target of selling about 75 percent locally and exporting not more than 25 percent of its products.

Sustainable farming and economic activities for SEKEM do not only mean applying Biodynamic agricultural methods and fair working conditions. SEKEM invented the term 'Economics of Love', which can be compared to the international Fairtrade-values but with some additional benefits. Farmers and co-workers do not only receive stable contracts and prices for their products, which enable them to ensure their families' livelihood and to plan and expand their business activities; they are also supported by regular training courses and cultural activities, such as literacy courses or workshops on new agricultural approaches. Monthly, SEKEM invites them to discuss the challenges they face in their businesses and everyday working life. And two times a year, all contracted farmers join a great festival in the roman theatre at the main SEKEM farm where they celebrate and enjoy a rich cultural programme attended by all SEKEM institutions. The farmers and co-workers as well as SEKEM as employer benefit from a win–win-situation based on solidarity instead of competition and egoism.

A Closed Value Chain

By the above-mentioned activities, SEKEM ensures a closed value-chain being able to determine conditions from the field right to the final consumer. It is thereby guaranteed that the environment is not harmed, that people who create the value receive a fair income and work in safe and proper conditions, and that those who consume the product benefit from high quality and a healthy product.

Generally, over 1,500 jobs have been created through SEKEM subsidiary group and have directly benefited local communities.

Sustainability Flower

The 'Sustainability Flower', referred to earlier (see Figure 10.1, page 139), does more than create the basis for SEKEM's vision and activities. Within a network of international organizations from the organic and biodynamic movement co-operating under the umbrella of the International Association of Partnership for Ecology and Trade (IAP), the Sustainability Flower was developed as a management, assessment and communication tool symbolizing the concept of sustainable development in its four dimensions. Each dimension consists of several performance aspects, defined in detail through performance indicators. These are, wherever possible and applicable, linked to the international standard for sustainability reporting, the GRI G3.1 of the Global Reporting Initiative.

In a thorough review process SEKEM adapted the Sustainability Flower framework in accordance with its learning experiences, so that other companies can also make better use of the tool. In 2013, for the first time SEKEM used the redefined framework to assess its performance. In order to make the provided data more accessible, the detailed status and target overviews filled with hard facts from general information about SEKEM have been separated. In the operations of SEKEM companies, the Sustainability Flower is fully applied in its three functions as a management, assessment and communication tool.

Societal Life

There is a very simple – but at the same time fundamental and powerful – ritual that SEKEM includes in its daily routine. Every day in the morning managers, farmers or factory workers of each SEKEM institution gather in a circle, welcoming each other and the new day. The circle symbolizes a community in which everyone is equal. It creates an awareness of wider society, but at the same time also of the individual.

To strengthen an equal society, SEKEM's activities do not just target a specific part of society members but all people from different ages, different educational backgrounds and different beliefs. A nursery and a kindergarten are provided for the youngest community members, and different schools educate children and young adults. There is a Vocational Training Centre, but also the Heliopolis University running under the umbrella of SEKEM because a society needs academics as well as crafts people. SEKEM's companies produce healthy products for different societal needs: organic food and beverages, pharmaceuticals and textiles.

The SEKEM Code of Conduct summarizes the framework of values guiding SEKEM's operations. Based on its vision of sustainable development, the principles of the UN Global Compact and the relevant UN and ILO conventions, it formulates explicit commitments regarding legal compliance, business ethics, anti-corruption, labour standards, human rights and environmental responsibility.

Weekly Social Meetings are held in SEKEM companies that offer employees a space to discuss their personal or team-related concerns.

Sustainable societal development means not only caring about one's own enterprises and co-workers but also taking into account those people that surround you. The SEKEM Farm is located in a rural area about 60 kilometres from Cairo. Its closer neighbourhood consists of small, very traditional villages. To contribute to the health of this surrounding community and at the same time offer its employees proper healthcare SEKEM established the Medical Centree. Here, people are told about sanitation and hygiene, provided with information on health, nutrition, disease prevention and environmental issues, and are encouraged to use the services of the Medical Centree for preventive and curative treatments. Every day the hospital serves several hundred patients by a holistic and advanced approach to medicine – and also those who are not able to pay for their treatments.

Gender Equality

The Medical Centree also forms part of SEKEMs effort's to empower women. Female employees regularly attend sessions with a gynaecologist to raise awareness about women's and children's health and well-being, including clarifying information about female genital mutilation, which is still a widespread practice in Egypt.

To support women's empowerment, which contributes enormously to a sustainable society, SEKEM organizes various activities in and outside its companies. On the one hand, social workers support SEKEMs female employees in any work-related or personal issues, while on the other hand, women's positions are fostered in the outer community through microcredit and education programmes.

Due to traditional rural habits, the majority of women marry early and concentrate on family life. But of course Egyptian society needs women not only as mothers and housewives but also in economic, societal and cultural life. SEKEM therefore published a comprehensive 'Gender Strategy for a Balanced Society', which summarizes the targets and efforts of the initiative with regards to the empowerment of women, from schools to factories.

Partnership

No matter how strong is a vision and the commitment to its implementation, nobody can achieve anything alone. To strengthen a society it needs a bond of people that work and stand together for one goal. From its beginnings, SEKEM was able to build up a network of partners who support the initiative directly in Egypt but also spread its spirit to their own regions and networks. SEKEM has strong business partners but also a vast number of people who contribute with their knowledge to many activities. A worldwide network of friends, stakeholders and shareholders carries SEKEM's vision, thereby supporting the development of a sustainable society in Egypt. A huge number of them come out of the anthroposophical movement.

International Association of Partnership

One network of partners was founded in SEKEM and builds one of the main pillars in SEKEM's economic life: the International Association for Partnership in Economy and Trade (IAP). The corporation was established by several long-term European business partners in order to create a dynamic interaction between farmers, producers and traders, with the goal of providing consumers with high-quality products. The partners have co-operated since 1984 to strengthen the basis for biodynamic and organic agriculture worldwide and build a community of interest that connects East and West.

Cultural Life

Cultural and artistic activities are also included in all SEKEM employees' everyday work. SEKEM believes that art can initiate a transformation process, which enhances people's awareness, and helps them by enabling more precise observation of the environment and closer involvement in global development issues. SEKEM co-workers can regularly be found in drawing classes, working with clay or on stage performing a theatre play or music. Artistic activity and culture elevate people's sense for the beauty and values of nature as well as for fellow human beings, thereby fostering consciousness for the environment and for society.

SEKEM believes that human development is the precondition for a 'living society'. SEKEM thus builds on the concept of sustainable development as working with and through nature; it emphasizes the importance of individual human development in everyday life; and it supports human dignity and harmonious social interaction through its institutions and attitude towards all members of the community.

Through the SEKEM Development Foundation (SDF), SEKEM has established kindergartens, schools and a Vocational Training Centre to enable those who have little opportunity to receive education. In 2012 the Heliopolis University for Sustainable Development was set up to provide more opportunities for national and international students to deepen their knowledge in sustainable development technologies that integrate societal and cultural values.

All of SEKEM's educational institutions foster the individual development of children and young adults and create awareness and understanding by means of a holistic educational approach, with the latter based on Waldorf education. Although the schools are following the government curriculum, pupils receive extra lessons that strengthen their cultural and practical skills and their individual creativity. Carpentry, pottery or Eurythmy belong to their everyday school life as well as direct activities in and with nature.

The SEKEM Environmental Science Centre, for instance, offers interactive science classes on environmental topics to students from the SEKEM Community, as well as from local and international schools. SEKEMs Vocational Training Centre offers eight different technical professions, and is constantly linking to handling natural resources in a sustainable way.

Heliopolis University for Sustainable Development

Similar targets are pursued by the different departments of Heliopolis University for Sustainable Development, the first non-profit university in the Middle East that is declaring sustainable development as its overall guiding principle, and which was established under the umbrella of the SEKEM Initiative. The curriculum aims to support students to become social entrepreneurs – entrepreneurs able to face and overcome tomorrow's challenges through innovation, collaboration and technology. By a renewed understanding that integrates teaching, learning, research and practice, the (currently) more than a thousand students receive the possibility of developing holistic and critical thinking, which is the basis for realising challenges, experiencing responsibility and taking action.

Research

> SEKEM founder Dr Ibrahim Abouleish once said:
>
> *Education and science go hand in hand. Together they promote interest in the world and create awareness about the value of self-knowledge and personal ad-*

vancement. At the same time, they strengthen the trust of a society in its own abilities, which helps to understand challenges and develop solutions.[3]

Education and research need to move in the same direction: research may lay the foundation for intelligent, environmentally friendly new products, and for resource-efficient business practice and production methods. Education should not just be concerned with the acquisition of knowledge, but it should also promote the responsible use of resources and strengthen confidence in an individual's ability to independently identify problems and to cope with them for the benefit of environment and community.

Since 1999, Heliopolis Academy – and since 2012, Heliopolis University for Sustainable Development – have been conducting research in fields like phytopharmaceuticals, biodynamic agriculture, renewable energy, sustainable economics and green technologies, and in the social sciences and the humanities.

Recently, for instance, SEKEM published a study titled *The future of agriculture in Egypt*[4] that compares the full costs of organic and conventional production development for Egypt's five principal crops. By considering environmental impacts, such as the pollution of soil, air or water, the research concludes that although organic agriculture has a slightly higher direct input cost, it enables a reduction of the environmental and health-damage costs, and therefore results in better cost effectiveness and profitability in the long term for society as a whole.

SEKEM Today

Over the past 40 years SEKEM has become a living example for what is possible if one has a strong vision, the will and the involvement of like-minded people who support the idea with a similar level of awareness. On what was formerly desert land, there are today more than 1,500 people living and learning together. Around SEKEM Farm, moreover, the social conditions for a huge number of further people have constantly been improving. By co-operating with contracted farmers all over Egypt, a total of around 40,000 people benefit from the holistic SEKEM approach.

One meaningful aspect of this phenomenon is the impulses that the SEKEM community has gleaned from Rudolf Steiner's anthroposophy, especially social threefolding. Liberty, equality and solidarity function as central pillars of the SEKEM Initiative; and the strong love of people with a deep understanding of their souls and minds also plays a huge part. Hence, SEKEM always tries to consider the human soul qualities in everyday life, which Steiner once defined as 'sentient soul', 'mind (or intellectual) soul' and 'consciousness soul'. These soul qualities are, according to Steiner, part of human development – of both the whole of humanity and of every individual. These qualities stand in relationship with the physical body, the etheric body and the astral body which the human being brings together in an interrelated unity (cf. Steiner's views on nature of the human being).[5] In broad terms the sentient soul is characterized by feelings, will, passion and instincts, while the mind soul is more serene, developing understanding and putting one's own self at the centre of the inner life. The consciousness soul brings thinking and scrutinizing, which take human beings beyond their own life and soul.

In Egypt there are many people whose lives are deeply influenced by the sentient soul, some by the mind soul, and only a small number that show themselves as being in the consciousness soul. For example, the sentient soul can be seen in the belief in authority and in dependence on it. The mind soul occurs in many economic activities and in people who strive after power and money. At the same time, a growing impulse of the consciousness soul is emerging in the younger generation. From knowledge of these different stages of development, many questions and many patterns of behaviour are answered, with each stage of development having its time. Progress and change will need time, but they will surely occur.

Giving this space, time and trust to the people is another secret that helped SEKEM to become a

> *living and learning community where every human being can unfold his or her individual potential; where mankind is living together in social forms reflecting human dignity; and where all economic activity is conducted in accordance with ecological and ethical principles.*[6]

The awareness of this kind of development also offers a different perspective on all the challenges described earlier. It supports the belief, even conviction, that there is hope for Egypt. Change and progress will sooner or later come to the country, which is still strongly influenced by political, social and economic instability.

Challenges will become opportunities; this is what SEKEM believes in. Out of hopeless situations, little miracles will arise. SEKEM is confident that its community members will become part of a critical mass that will one day bring change. Every day, this confidence is supported by observing how the development of souls is possible through the creation of a conscious approach to the environment and a holistic way of working and living together. Former students of SEKEM's educational institutions, for instance, show how much potential is living in their soul life when they return to the initiative with exciting new projects and ideas. They are responsible adults who can contribute to a transition as reformers, social entrepreneurs or artists. Hence, SEKEM tries to welcome any new challenge as an opportunity for the development of potential, which then brings progress.

Resources

Website: www.sekem.com

News-Blog: http://www.sekem.com/en/news/

SEKEM Image Film and other links: http://www.sekem.com/en/media/videos/

Film: SEKEM – Aus der Kraft der Sonne (by Bertram Verhaag, DENKmal Film, Language: German)

Book: *SEKEM – A sustainable community in the Egyptian desert* by Dr Ibrahim Abouleish, Floris Books, Edinburgh, 2015.

Other publications:
SEKEM: A holistic Egyptian initiative prepared by Tarek Hatem, UN Development Programme Report, New York, 2007 (available at goo.gl/d8U4wP; accessed 13 November 2017)

'Garden in the desert: SEKEM makes comprehensive sustainable development a reality in Egypt', *Innovations* journal, Summer 2008 (available at goo.gl/ZwwXNP)

SEKEM Impact Evaluation Study, December 2014 – March 2015, Oikocredit, Centre for Development Innovation, Wageningen, The Netherlands, 2015 (available at goo.gl/Y1iQmo; accessed 13 November 2017)

'SEKEM Initiative receives UN prize in the fight against soil erosion', NNA / News Network Anthroposophy, November 2015 (available at goo.gl/z1Jfvq; accessed 13 November 2017)

Notes
1. The SEKEM Group of Companies is a part of the SEKEM Initiative founded in 1977 by Dr Ibrahim Abouleish to strengthen Sustainable Development in Egypt by producing, processing and marketing organic and biodynamic foodstuff, textiles and phyto-pharmaceuticals in Egypt, the Arab World, and on international markets. SEKEM has been widely praised as an 'Egyptian organic pioneer', and has received the 2003 Right Livelihood Award ('Alternative Nobel Prize') as a 'Business Model for the 21st Century;' and an 'economy of love'. With part of their profits the SEKEM companies co-finance the social and cultural activities of the SEKEM Development Foundation that runs, amongst others, schools and a medical centre. In 2012 the Heliopolis University for Sustainable Development was opened under the umbrella of the SEKEM Initiative.
2. Sourced from the SEKEM website at goo.gl/yHcoHX.
3. Sourced from a SEKEM press release and quoted on the SEKEM blog, at goo.gl/5uVSXZ.
4. *The future of agriculture in Egypt: Comparative full cost accounting study of organic and conventional food production systems in Egypt,* prepared by Thoraya Seada & others in co-operation with Heliopolis University; Carbon Footprint Center, Cairo, January 2016. Available at goo.gl/nahju3 (accessed 13 November 2017).
5. See, for example, Steiner's *The foundations of human experience* [original title, Study of man], Steinerbooks/Anthroposophic Press, Herndon, VA, 1996.
6. Sourced from SEKEM's website at www.sekem.com.

CHAPTER 11

A New American Revolution? Associative Economics and the Future of the Food Movement
Robert Karp

The American landscape has been witnessing a slow but promising revolution over the last six or seven decades. Clothed sometimes as a 'sustainable agriculture movement', 'organic food and farming industry', or 'good food revolution', it is really, I would suggest, the struggling emergence of a new economy in the USA, one based on a fundamentally different set of values, principles and practices from those which most of us have been raised to think of as the driving forces behind economic life.

My first taste of this revolution came back in the early 1980s when I was a sophomore at Oberlin College, Ohio, and a member of a student-owned and -run, natural food 'dining co-op'. These dining co-ops have been a steady fixture of Oberlin College life since the 1950s – which in and of itself is a remarkable achievement, given the continuous change in the student bodies and therefore co-op leadership.[1]

While working together with the other students to cook and clean and manage the co-op, which fed hundreds of us three natural-food meals each day, and which was in and of itself a revolutionary experience, my real awakening came one evening after a meal, when a student stood up and read a rather long account of the fate of chickens in modern industrial-scale poultry farms. This was the first time I had learned of those deplorable conditions, and I suspect that was true for many of us young people. I distinctly remember the silence that fell on the room that day, as waves of shock, outrage, grief and compassion poured through us.

Herein lies, I believe, one of the most fundamental yet overlooked features of this emergent economic revolution – namely, that it is based, at the deepest level, on a new and growing human capacity for profound empathy and connection with other beings. Indeed, I think it could readily be argued that the driving force behind the food movement is in fact a kind of spiritual awakening, a shift in consciousness, a change of heart that results in new ways of seeing and being in the world. This inner shift can lead one to feel the Earth and her creatures as a part of one's own essential being, and extend one's sense of responsibility to include the whole planet. You could also call it an awakening of conscience.

It is remarkable to me that though there are hundreds and thousands – and perhaps, today, millions – of stories from farmers, entrepreneurs, activists and consumers that attest to this awakening, this aspect or dimension of the food movement is often not explicitly recognized nor celebrated. But it is there, nonetheless, as a deeply felt reality and is, I would suggest, the hidden fountainhead of this movement.

This taste of a revolution at Oberlin became a full draught of new wine that summer when I attended a Prairie Festival at the Land Institute in Kansas, where I had my first encounters with the Kentucky farmer and author Wendell Berry and the pioneering biologist and plant geneticist Wes Jackson – two individuals who had recently emerged as key leaders of the food movement. Listening to Wendell, with his measured drawl and Lincolnesque bearing, peel back the layers of the dark heart of mainstream American values, and then Wes, like a fiery old-time preacher calling down the holy spirit of the soil, I felt the placeless landscape of my middle-class upbringing begin to fade far into the background. There was indeed a revolution afoot in America, but towards what end? And what did it ask of me, a young man studying theatre and creative writing with no previous experience or interest in agriculture?

The answers to these questions only began to take form in me in the late 1980s when I became a member of one of the first community-supported agriculture (CSA) farms in the USA. Though pioneering organic farms, natural food stores and co-ops like the ones I encountered at Oberlin had already carved out a small foothold in the landscape of America by that time, and though the atrocities of factory farms, together with the writings and work of individuals like Wendell Berry and Wes Jackson, had begun to awaken deep and dormant forces of empathy and conscience in thousands of Americans, it was only with the emergence of CSAs, I would suggest, that the food revolution began to really take root in American life, drawing thousands upon thousands of new people into the movement by bringing them into a new and more intimate relationship to the renewing life of agriculture.

The Radical Vision of the Early CSAs

Though many have come to think of CSA as little more than an alternative marketing strategy for farmers, it is important to realise that for the pioneers of the CSA movement, like my friends at Temple Wilton Farm in New Hampshire, CSA represented a bold attempt to embody a radical new way of thinking about agriculture based on the economic insights of Rudolf Steiner. They felt, for example, that there was no future for agriculture unless the whole community began to take as much responsibility for local farms as the farmers themselves.[2]

Thus, in many of the early CSAs began the practice of forming a core group of consumers who worked with the farmers to establish the annual budget for the farm, down to the last detail, and reach out to other possible members in the community. The vision was not one of members buying food from a local farm through an equal share price paid up front, but rather of community members committing to care for the farm as whole, in partnership with the farmers, over the long term. One could think of it as a new kind of gift economy: the members made free-will gifts of time and money to support the well-being of the farm, and the farm then offered up all its fruits as a gift to the community.

At Temple Wilton, inspired by Steiner's associative ideas, what each member could contribute to the farm had to be an individual matter. To this day, for example, there is not an evenly distributed share price at Temple Wilton. Rather, all members attend an annual meeting each year to review and discuss the farm's total budget, and then each decides what amount they feel they can contribute to that budget. Each member then writes down his or her proposed financial offering on a piece of paper, and if those sums don't add up to meet the annual budget, the members go around again and offer additional sums until the budget is met. The process, in other words, is highly participatory, communal and transparent.

While I was a member of Sunways Farm rather than Temple Wilton Farm, I nonetheless caught this spirit of the early CSA movement, and realising the powerful role that non-farmers like myself could play in this new American revolution, I decided, incongruous as it seemed at the time, that I wanted to make agriculture the focus of my life's work.

The Growth and Decline of the Food Movement

Since that time, I have had the privilege of being an active part of the food movement as a consumer activist, a community organizer of dozens of local and regional food-system projects, a facilitator of investments in organic farmland, and as a board member and Executive Director of several non-profit farm organizations. And while this movement remains somewhat on the margins of mainstream American life, the growth I have witnessed is truly astounding. Consider just a few data points:

- The number of farmers' markets across the country has nearly doubled between 2008 and 2013, from 4,685 to 8,144. In 1994, there were only about

1,755 farmers' markets in the United States;[3]
- Some have estimated that there are now as many as 6,000 community-supported agriculture projects in the United States;[4]
- Consumer demand for organic food has grown by double digits nearly every year since the 1990s. Between 1997 and 2015, for example, organic sales increased from $3.6 billion to $43.3 billion;[5]
- More than 4 million acres of US farmland are now devoted to organic agriculture, representing an 11 percent increase over two years ago. The number of certified organic farms is close to 15,000, rising just over 6 percent since 2014;[6]
- Many in the supply chain believe that non-GMO will be a product claim of growing importance to consumers. In 2016 some 49 percent of manufacturers planned to introduce products that are non-GMO.[7]

As encouraging as these statistics may seem, many challenges currently beset the further development of this movement, perhaps most notably exemplified by the recent buy out of Whole Foods supermarkets by the massive online merchandizer Amazon, not to mention the recent passage of HR 1599, The Safe and Accurate Food Labelling Act of 2015, otherwise known as the 'Dark Act', which makes it ever-more difficult to secure a genuine genetically modified organism (GMO) labelling programme in the USA.

But these are only the latest and most outstanding examples. For years now, in part through the transfer of organic certification to the federal government in 2002, we have witnessed a steady decline in the integrity of organic farming and processing practices, as articulated so clearly in Michael Pollan's book *The omnivore's dilemma*.[8] Even CSAs have for many farmers become just another marketing strategy or 'box scheme' – and for many consumers, just too much bother. In other words, the food movement seems to be bleeding integrity at every turn. What is to be done?

The Need for a Clear and Shared Vision

The thesis of this chapter is that, while the food movement gives expression to profoundly good work at many levels of society, we remain a very fragmented movement and at every turn subject to erosion and the compromising of our core values and intentions, because we lack a clear vision of the future society, and especially the future economic system towards which we are working – and flowing from this vision, a clear set of guiding principles for our work. Many academics have been saying the same thing for years, for example:

> ...we contend that the agri-food systems change community needs to develop proactive and shared visions of what 'should be' and a firm agreement on the

fundamental steps to make things right ... These shared visions are essential to produce master frames with sufficient mobilizing capacity. Their absence is due to the multiplicity of issues and groups within the food systems change area ...[9]

Or as Michael Shumann, another prominent leader in the food movement, once put it:

Too little is being invested today in answering a fundamental question: What exactly are we organizing for? Many of our pat 'answers' are obsolete. State socialism lies in ruins, and Great Society liberalism is increasingly outmoded ... Can anyone say, with confidence, what our economic program is?[10]

Rudolf Steiner and the Emergent Economy

Long before Otto Scharmer and others began to articulate the idea that human beings have the capacity to tap intuitively into emergent properties of the future and thus work consciously and co-operatively with the driving forces of history, in the early twentieth century Rudolf Steiner was already practising this methodology.[11] Steiner described it this way:

There are two ways of thinking about what ought to happen in the social sphere or in any other field. We may present a program, may form programmatical concepts; we ... think out how the world should develop in a certain field; this can be presented in beautiful words. We can swear by these words, take them as dogmas, but nothing will result from them, nothing at all! ... No statistics, no programs, however well thought out, are of any value. Only the observation of what wills to appear out of the hidden depths of the times is of value. This must be taken up into consciousness; by this the intentions of the present must be governed.[12]

One area in which Rudolf Steiner practised this art was in the realm of economics, and his ideas and suggestions in this field have come to be referred to as Associative Economics, or even Steinerian Economics.[13] It is of the utmost importance, however, to realise that Steiner's economic ideas were not a system of mental constructs to be imposed on current reality. Rather, they represent an attempt to sense into, to discern what is trying to emerge within humanity and within the economic life of our time, and from there to suggest creative forms which these emergent properties might take, or sound principles that might guide their healthy unfolding.

Using this same methodology and drawing on Steiner's economic insights, I wish to explore further the new economy that I believe is emerging within the food movement in the USA, and from there suggest ways in which these emergent properties could be given forms more capable of realising the deeper mission of this movement. While I acknowledge that today there is a whole chorus of voices calling out for and seeking to understand this new economy, I feel that Steiner's contribution is unique, and remains relevant enough and unknown enough to be worthy of the effort to add his voice to the chorus in the modest fashion I have attempted here.

For reasons of length, however, please note that in this chapter I will focus solely on questions of trade and will have to leave to a future article the important questions of the transformation of land, labour, capital and ownership which are also so essential to the emergence of this new economy. Without new forms of capitalization and ownership, for example, our best food companies will continue to be sold to the highest bidder and their long-term integrity compromised.

Towards Associative Trade

From a 10,000-feet perspective, present-day economic life already reveals itself as an immense web of collaborative, interdependent, supply chain relationships. These supply chains span the globe, producing, processing and distributing the products and services that human beings need to carry out their lives. Looked at up close, however, in the light of day-to-day realities, we can see that these supply chains are usually controlled by relatively few of the actual economic players involved. We also see that much of the genuine economic progress that could result from this global economic co-operation is undermined by self-interested goals and aims on the part of these few players, and the immense sums of the capital and governmental influence they have at their disposal.

What Steiner suggested is trying to emerge in the midst of this reality, is a method of economic co-operation or 'association' that transcends both laissez-faire capitalism and state socialism by empowering the producers, processors, distributors, retailers and consumers involved in the economic life of particular regions and products to work together to manage the economy out of shared insight. Steiner explained this need as follows:

> *Economic life is striving to structure itself according to its own nature, independent of political institutionalization and mentality. It can only do this if associations, comprised of consumers, distributors and producers, are established according to purely economic criteria ... Not laws, but human beings using their immediate insights and interest, would regulate the production, circulation and consumption of goods.*[14]

And it was an emerging capacity for altruism, rather than competition and self-interest, that Steiner saw to be the driving force of this new economy:

> *It is neither a God, nor a moral law, nor an instinct that calls for altruism in economic life – altruism in work, altruism in the production of goods. It is the modern division of labour – a purely economic category – that requires it ... The social conflicts are largely due to the fact that, as economic systems expanded into a world economy, it became more and more needful to be altruistic, to organize the various social institutions altruistically, while in their way of thinking, men had not yet been able to get beyond egoism and therefore kept on interfering with the course of things in a clumsy, selfish way.*[15]

What Steiner is seeing as a potential for economic life could be described as a kind of 'voluntary socialism' in which economic actors themselves, independent of the state, choose to work together through formal and informal associations in order to regulate supply and demand and facilitate the healthy production, distribution and consumption of the goods that human beings need to carry out their lives. But we should not let the term 'socialism' confuse us. In this vision, independent producers, distributors and retailers would not go away, nor would the kind of competition that happens when a consumer faces multiple choices on a grocery shelf. But underpinning these independent businesses and this competition would be an organized and deeply rooted network of co-operative relationships focused not on the private benefit of the players involved, but rather on shared good – for people and planet.

Altruism and Association in the Food Movement

Looking at the food movement in the US today, it is remarkable the degree to which this striving is evident, for example, in the prevalence of an altruistic, mission-based, or triple bottom-line mind-set amongst farmers, consumers and entrepreneurs. As pointed out above, I would suggest that one cannot really explain the food movement at all without recognizing that a whole new value system has emerged amongst a large percentage of the population – a value system born out of new capacities for empathy with the planet and for other beings. I believe Paul Ray and Sherry Anderson were some of the first people to begin to quantitatively study this demographic, which they estimated to be 25 percent of the population, and point to its potential significance, not only as a 'market', as most later commentators have done, but rather as a movement for social transformation.[16]

But what is also remarkable is the degree to which associations of producers, distributors and consumers have come to play such an important role in the food movement. Examples include:

- The many organic farming co-ops, small and large, such as Organic Valley, Ofarm, the Midwest Organic Famers Cooperative and the Tuscarora Organic

Growers Cooperative, to name just a few;
- The dozens of member-driven farm organizations that sustain the grassroots energy of the food movement through their conferences and programmes for farmers. Some examples of these include the Maine Organic Farming and Gardening Association, Northeast Organic Farming Association, Pennsylvania Association for Sustainable Agriculture, Practical Farmers of Iowa, California Alliance with Family Farmers and the Biodynamic Association, to name just a few.
- The hundreds of consumer-owned natural-food co-ops across the USA and the larger association, the National Coop Grocers Association, to which most of them belong;
- The Independent Natural Food Retailers Association which fosters co-operation among over 300 independently owned natural-food stores;
- The Organic Trade Association and the Sustainable Food Trade Association, which includes many of the larger organic branded-food companies, retailers and distributors amongst its members;
- The Organic Consumers Association, and a host of smaller, consumer-driven, food-activist groups, not to mention the thousands of CSA farms through which thousands of consumers have allied themselves with small, local farms;
- The growing number of regional 'food hubs' that actively manage the aggregation and distribution of source-identified food products, and the larger association that supports their work – the Good Food Network;
- The plethora of local and regional food projects like Red Tomato, Fair Food Philly and many others that work with multiple stakeholders to facilitate the distribution and sales of locally grown foods.

As encouraging as these many examples of 'association' are in the food movement, by and large, with a few exceptions, these groups and associations are not yet working together to manage supply chains from farm to plate, nor to regulate regional economies in the way I would suggest is necessary if our movement is not to be subsumed by the dominant US economic ethos.

An Alternative Strategy

Imagine, for example, how milk production, consumption and prices could be actively managed and harmonized, not by the government, nor by the invisible hand of 'market forces', nor by a few dominant companies, but rather by multi-stakeholder associations made up of representatives of farmer groups, consumer groups, traders, retailers, businesses and other logical stakeholders who would have the mandate to work together to regulate, out of economic insight and shared values, this important commodity in a fashion that benefits everyone.[17] Indeed, a vertically integrated co-op like Organic Valley already engages in a great deal of this very kind of activity with its own members and buyers; such activity simply needs to be logically extended to include the other economic actors in the organic dairy sector.[18]

Rather than seeking to influence government farm policies or programmes of one kind or another, the food movement might consider a completely different strategy: namely working to gradually transition the federal government out of the farm economy altogether by demonstrating, within the laboratory of the food movement, how associations of diverse stakeholders could independently manage the farm economy themselves on the basis of both their business savvy and the shared values they hold for the earth and human communities.[19]

Steiner is also helpful in pointing out the deeper economic reasons why we need associations to work together to manage the economy. These reasons reside in the inherent complexity and fluidity of a global economy based on the division of labour. This complexity prevents any one person, business or organization from having a total grasp of the complex conditions and factors impacting the life cycle of any product at any particular time. Only when the many players involved in the economic life of particular product categories and/or regions come together and associate can such a holistic picture emerge, along with insights on how best to work together to facilitate healthy trade. Through this coming together and the trust it engenders, decisions can emerge regarding all aspects of a product category, particularly appropriate prices, that simply would not otherwise be possible, even with the best-intentioned governmental policies or the most idealistic fair-trade agreements.

We could say that it is a new human need and capacity, stimulated by the complex conditions of modern life, to come to a real picture of the economic processes at work in particular regions and in the lifespan of particular products. This need and capacity come to expression in the concept of the food system, for example, which has had such a deep impact on the food movement in the last 30 or so years. It also comes to expression at a literary level in the plethora of books and films that trace the history of particular foods or meals.

Yet this need, as Steiner suggests, is also economic in nature, and cannot be fulfilled by food-systems research or culinary literature alone. It can only be truly fulfilled when people actively at work in the economy, including consumers, come together to learn about one another's needs, harmonize their efforts and serve the wider community. It is only in this way that the self-interest which naturally attends economic life can be transformed into interest in the other – that is, into altruism:

> …The moment the life of associations enters the economic process, it is no longer a question of immediate personal interest. The wide outlook over the economic

process will be active; the interest in the other fellow will actually be there in the economic judgment that is formed. In no other way can a true economic judgment come about. Thus we are impelled to rise from the economic processes to the mutuality, the give and take, between human and human and furthermore to that which will arise from this, namely, the objective community spirit working in the associations.[20]

For me, the beauty of CSAs and other local and regional food projects is that it has allowed just this kind of community spirit to arise in connection with economic transactions, giving consumers, farmers, chefs and retailers the opportunity to experience the joy, meaning and community that emerge when the economy brings them together, rather than separating them. The question now facing us is whether we can take this kind of work to the next level so that this heightened spirit of co-operation can be embedded in higher-volume, longer-distance supply chains and thus become the guiding principle and modus operandi of the whole food-movement.

Without a concerted effort in this direction in the coming years, I am concerned that we will increasingly betray our own ideals, and the ideals of our founding farmers and pioneering entrepreneurs, by allowing this movement to be completely industrialized –and in so doing, become a caricature of itself, with little to no semblance of economic co-operation and social justice, much less truly ecological farming, behind the growing number of brands and products spouting poetic slogans about ecology, spirituality, social justice and pure food.

The Emergence of the Value Chain Approach

Perhaps one of the most promising developments within the food movement in recent years is a trend among some food and farm businesses for managing their wholesale supply chains as collaborative ventures or as 'value chains'. Whereas traditional supply-chain relationships are characterized by competition between businesses for their share of the consumer dollar, as well as by a lack of transparency and communication across the chain, in value chains, the entire supply chain is reconceived as a co-operative venture requiring shared mission, shared decision making and a great deal of transparency.[21]

In Oregon, for example, a wheat-growers co-op has created a 'pricing formula' in partnership with their wholesale buyers that modifies prices regularly based on the farmers' costs of production as well as on impacts of inflation and volatile grain markets on both farmers and customers.[22] In the Kansas City area, an alliance of over 100 small and mid-sized farms and a regional grocery chain are working together co-operatively and transparently, through a written memorandum of understanding, to build up the market for locally grown food, support sustainable agriculture and set prices that are fair to all.[23] In the Boston area, a non-profit food broker aggregates ecologically grown apples from farms in the region and sells them to hundreds of stores, setting prices through a co-operative, ongoing process involving dialogues with both stores and farmers. These are just a few of the many examples that have begun to be carefully documented and which are proliferating.[24]

Some of the key characteristics of food-value chains have been defined by the Agricultural Marketing Service as follows:

- Using co-operative strategies to achieve competitive advantages and the capacity to adapt quickly to market changes
- Emphasis on high levels of performance, trust and responsiveness throughout the network
- Emphasis on shared vision, shared information (transparency) and shared decision-making and problem-solving among the strategic partners
- Commitment to the welfare of all participants in the value chain, including providing adequate profit margins to support the business and its owners, fair wages and business agreements of appropriate and mutually acceptable duration.

In addition, farmers, ranchers and other agricultural producers in food-value chains:

- Know their production and transaction costs and are able to negotiate prices based on acceptable profit margins above those costs;
- Perceive contracts and agreements as fair, having been freely agreed to, providing equitable treatment to all partners, and including appropriate time frames;
- Are able to own and control their own brand identity as far up the supply chain as they choose. This may involve co-branding with other strategic partners;
- Participate fully in the development of mechanisms to resolve conflicts, communicate concerns about performance, and alter directions within the value chain.[25]

What the value-chain model and these many examples suggest is that the inherent trajectory of the food movement is indeed towards a model of trade based on supply-chain collaboration, transparency and the setting of true prices that reflect the needs of all parties involved. Through this promising effort, I would suggest, we are beginning to see some of the core values of the original CSA farms embedded in longer-distance, higher-volume trading relationships. Could a new kind of domestic fair trade be emerging, not out of the ethical imperatives of third-party certifiers but simply because it makes short- and long-term economic sense? How might we ramp up such efforts? Could whole regions, for example, establish a value-chain approach to trade and economic development? Could commodity farm programmes ultimately be replaced by multi-stakeholder associations?

A Possible Pilot Project

At the Biodynamic Association (BDA), we have begun to explore different ideas for a pilot project that could advance the associative economy that is emerging in the food movement. One of these ideas would have us build on our growing connection to the Independent Natural Food Retailers Association (INFRA), whose members have begun to show a growing interest in carrying Demeter certified Biodynamic® food products in their stores.

As mentioned above, INFRA is an association of over 300 independently owned natural-food stores in the USA. INFRA supports the success of these stores in many innovative ways. For example, many INFRA members share all their sales data and other vital economic data with the other member stores, through a programme called Cometrics. Cometrics allows INFRA member stores to function like a virtual chain, so that, for example, if one INFRA member store is having great success with their produce marketing, another store can quickly see that through the Cometrics software program, and reach out to that store to learn more about how they are doing it. This is a truly wonderful example of an associative economic practice.[26]

In addition, INFRA supports their members by facilitating collective buying from vendors. INFRA staff members, each working with different regions of the country, identify product lines that the member stores in that region would all like to carry or are already carrying, and INFRA then uses this collective buying power to negotiate higher-volume, lower-cost deals from these vendors. Could we build on this existing infrastructure to foster more associative economic trading practices and support the growth of local, organic and biodynamic farmers in a given region?

What if, for example, we set up a regional, multi-stakeholder association of retailers (starting with INFRA members and perhaps food co-ops, who also, by the way, use the Cometrics system to collaborate with one another), consumers, processors, distributors and organic and biodynamic farmers in that region, along with other logical stakeholders, e.g. other non-profit food groups, University Extension Service, foundations, and so on? Focusing perhaps initially on whole products like fruits, vegetables, meat and dairy products, we could use the Cometrics system to quickly determine the current volume of purchases by these stores within these product categories.

Then we could work with these stores and their consumers to determine how much of this volume is already coming from regional sources and how much they would like to transfer to regional organic and biodynamic sources. With commitments from these stores and their consumers, we could begin to facilitate the formation of value chains across the region, from farm to consumer – value chains that would in turn be continually monitored and modified as needed by the players themselves, through the regional association we will have started. At the farm level, we would also have the opportunity to begin to explore a nagging question in the biodynamic community – namely, is it possible for the biodynamic concept of the 'farm individuality' to be extended to several farms co-operating ecologically and economically within a region?

This represents just one idea for beginning to extend the associative-economic principles within the food movement. There are certainly many other approaches possible, and I hope readers with ideas will not hesitate to contact me.

Toward Convergence

One of the most remarkable things Rudolf Steiner said about the emergence of the kind of associations I have described above is that they will only be able to succeed if those who create and participate in them feel inspired by a deeper sense of community and shared purpose:

> ... if any man works for the community, he must perceive and feel the meaning and value of this community, and what it is as a living organic whole ... It must be informed by an actual spirit in which each single person has his part ... the whole communal body must have a spiritual mission. All the vague progressive ideas, the abstract ideals, of which people talk so much, cannot present such a mission. If there be nothing but these as guiding principles, the one individual here, or one group there, will be working without any clear comprehension of what use there is in their work, except its being to the advantage of their families, or of those particular interests to which they happen to be attached. In every member, down to the least, this Spirit of the Community must be alive and active.[27]

When contemplating these ideas of Steiner's, I realised that this feeling of being a part of a community of shared purpose, in a deeply spiritual and also practical way, is what I invariably feel when attending the smaller and larger conferences that make up the food movement, when visiting local, organic and biodynamic farmers, when shopping in my local co-op. Indeed, the more I have reflected on this, the more convinced I have become that the food movement is a spiritual community of the kind Rudolf Steiner described above, a community of people who feel deeply united in the effort to bring a transforming influence upon our current civilization.

What this movement needs at this point, however, after decades of immense outer expansion, is not just a host of new strategic marketing campaigns to make the deep and profound values that inform our products more accessible to mainstream America. What we need, more importantly, is to challenge ourselves to live these values more fully and more deeply in our economic practices with one another. By beginning to practise the art of economic association at the local, regional, national and worldwide levels, we can both strengthen the core of our movement and begin to demonstrate to others, in a way no strategic marketing effort ever could, the life-affirming values and holistic worldview that inspire us, and the benefits these make possible when embedded in economic practices. In other words, we could begin to properly align or converge the values of our movement with the practices of our industry and in so doing, bring to realization the revolutionary promise that has inspired so many extraordinary farmers, entrepreneurs and activists to give their lives to this great work.

NOTES AND REFERENCES

1. For more information on Oberlin's co-ops, see the website of the Oberlin Student Cooperative Association (OSCA) at http://osca.wilder.oberlin.edu/ (accessed 14 November 2017).
2. For more information about CSA, Temple Wilton Farm and associative-economic ideas, see Trauger Groh and Steve McFadden, *Farms of tomorrow revisited: Community supported farms, farm supported communities*, Biodynamic Farming and Gardening Association, Kimberton, PA, 1998.
3. See United States Department of Agriculture (USDA), *National Farmers' Market Directory*; Agricultural Marketing Service, Washington, D.C.; available at goo.gl/P3icCk (accessed 14 November 2017).
4. See Steve McFadden, 'Unraveling the CSA number conundrum', The Call of the Land blog, 9 January 2012; available at goo.gl/9VbP2b (accessed 14 November 2017).
5. From the Organic Trade Association, State of the Industry report, Fact Sheet OTA-1600, 2016; available at goo.gl/ykJLTq (accessed 14 November 2017).
6. See Jason Best, 'Organic farming in the U.S. is now bigger than ever', *TakePart* digital magazine, Participant Media, Beverly Hills, CA, 10 November 2016; available at goo.gl/WE1wmk (accessed 14 November 2017).
7. From Ron Tanner, *The state of the specialty food industry*, 2016; available at goo.gl/PdMsuA (accessed 14 November 2017).
8. Michael Pollan, *The omnivore's dilemma: A natural history of four meals*, Penguin, New York, 2006.
9. G.W. Stevenson, Cathy Ruhf, Sharob Lezberg and Kate Clancy, 'Warrior, builder and weaver work: Strategies for changing the food system', in T. Lyson and C. Hinrichs (eds), *Remaking the North American food system*, University of Nebraska Press, Lincoln NE, 2008, pp. 33–63.
10. Michael Schumann, 'Why do progressive foundations give too little to too many?', *The Nation*, 12 January 1998; available at goo.gl/sJUvQx (accessed 14 November 2017).
11. C. Otto Sharmer, *Theory U: Leading from the future as it emerges – The social technology of presencing*, Berrett-Koehler Publishers / The Society for Organizational Learning, San Francisco, 2009.
12. Rudolf Steiner, *The mission of the Archangel Michael*, Anthroposophic Press, New York, 1961, p. 147.
13. Gary Lamb and Sarah Hearn, *Steinerian economics: A compendium*, Adonis Press, Hillsdale, NY, 2015. See also Rudolf Steiner, *World economy*, Rudolf Steiner Press, London, 1936. See also, 'As-

sociative Economics' on Wikipedia at goo.gl/bKLAsw (accessed 15 November 2017).
14. Rudolf Steiner, *Towards social renewal*, Rudolf Steiner Press, London, 1977, pp. 17–18.
15. Steiner, *World economy* (note 13), pp. 42–3.
16. Paul H. Ray and Sherry Ruth Anderson, *The cultural creatives: How 50 million people are changing the world*, Three Rivers Press, New York, 2000.
17. For a description of this approach to managing major commodities, see: Christopher Nye, 'Pulling together: A new way to think about the farm price problem', 1987; mimeo available to the author.
18. For a good description of Organic Valley's innovative supply chain practices, see Larry Lev and G. W. Stevenson, 'Values-based food supply chain case studies: Organic Valley', Center for Integrated Agricultural Systems, University of Wisconsin-Madison; available at goo.gl/CFt7bc (accessed 15 November 2017).
19. While space does not permit me to discuss this further here, transitioning the federal government out of their role as certifiers would probably be another key part of this process.
20. Steiner, *World economy* (note 13), p. 133.
21. For more background on value chains, see Adam Diamond, Debra Tropp, James Barham, Michelle Frain Muldoon, Stacia Kiraly and Patty Cantrell, 'Food value chains: Creating shared value to enhance marketing success', US Dept of Agriculture, Agricultural Marketing Service, May 2014; available at goo.gl/oRt6Yb (accessed 15 November 2017); and M. F. Muldoon, A. K. Taylor, N. Richman and J. Fisk, Innovations in local food enterprise: Fresh ideas for practitioners, investors, and policymakers for a just and profitable food system, Wallace Center at Winrock International, Arlington, VA, available at goo.gl/vM2ch6 (accessed 15 November 2017); and Levand Stevenson, 'Values-based food supply chain case studies' (note 18).
22. See Levand Stevenson, 'Values-based food supply chain case studies: Shepherds grains' (see note 18).
23. Shonna Dreier and Minoo Taheri, 'Innovative models: Small grower and retailer collaborations: Good natured family farms and balls food stores', Wallace Center at Winrock International, March 2008; available at goo.gl/kqRT3s (accessed 15 November 2017).
24. See Lev and Stevenson, 'Values-based food supply chain case studies: Red tomato' (see note 18).
25. Adam Diamond Debra Tropp, James Barham, Michelle Frain Muldoon, Stacia Kiraly and Patty Cantrell, 'Food value chains: Creating shared value to enhance marketing success', US Dept of Agriculture, Agricultural Marketing Service, May 2014; available at goo.gl/3TmE2V (accessed 15 November 2017).
26. For more information on Cometrics, go to https://www.cometrics.com/.
27. Rudolf Steiner, *Anthroposophy and the social question*, Mercury Press, New York, 1982, pp. 25–6.

CHAPTER 12

Land for People, Homes, Farms and Communities
Martin Large

> *The earth shall become a common treasury to all, as it was first made and given to us.*
> Gerard Winstanley, Digger, St Georges Hill, 1649.

> *Landlords grow rich in their sleep without working, risking or economizing. The increase in the value of land, arising as it does from the efforts of an entire community, should belong to the community and not to the individual who might hold title.*
> John Stuart Mill, 1848.

> *When we see land as a community to which we belong, we may begin to use it with love and respect.*
> Aldo Leopold, Sand County Almanac.

'Why is there so much poverty amidst so much prosperity?', asked the land reformer Henry George in the late-nineteenth century. The same burning question could be asked today amidst both market and state failure to provide decent and affordable housing for all.

Rudolf Steiner thought that one key factor in the housing crisis was treating land wrongly as a commodity to be bought and sold on the market, like, say, a chair. From a social threefolding angle, land is a right, and it is a category error to treat land

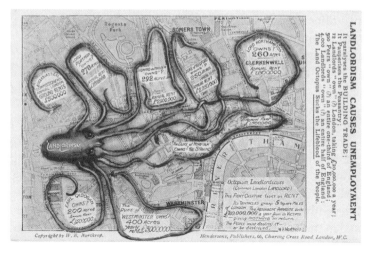

Figure 12.1: Octopus Landlordicus: Landlordism Causes Unemployment

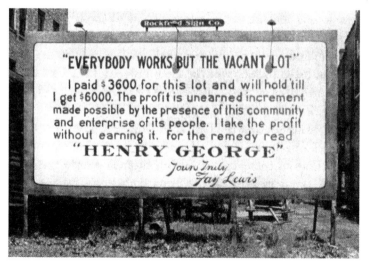

Figure 12.2: Henry George: We All Work for the Vacant Lot, but the Landlord Profits

as a finite market commodity. It has been treated as a fictional commodity, however, and this has been brought about by the enclosures, clearances, landlord-controlled laws and conquest. Furthermore, Steiner – like other thinkers such as John Ruskin – advocated that land be stewarded and owned not by the state or through markets, but by various forms of what we would call now civil society, mutual, charitable or community trusteeship bodies working in the plural or civil-society sector. The right to use land for farming, housing, industry, cultural and public facilities would be leased by land commons stewarding bodies, but not privatized.

This chapter will outline the housing crisis, Steiner's ideas about land, and how treating land, not just as a 'common pool resource' but as a commons to be stewarded by non-profit organizations in the plural sector, can provide solutions alongside the state and the market. Lastly, I will review some practical community land-trust solutions, for housing, land and farm access, as some readers may be interested in co-housing, community land trusts, co-ops and community-supported farms.

First, the UK housing crisis. The June 2017 Grenfell tower block fire killed at least 80 people in a tragedy which highlighted both market failure and state failure to provide safe, decent, well-designed and affordable social housing. The fire could have been prevented by listening to tenant concerns about safety, and not 'saving' £300,000 on cheaper cladding that was more flammable.[1] Better fire and building regulations had been recently turned down by a landlord-influenced Parliament.

Grenfell is located in the London Borough of Kensington and Chelsea, where there is a huge gap between the rich and the poor in life expectancy and in much else. The London housing free-market provides 'buy-to-leave-empty' properties for the world's wealthy 0.1 percent, offering huge untaxed speculative capital gains. UK law protects such owners yet criminalizes the homeless and squatters. Some buy-to-leave streets are largely uninhabited, with no lights on at night. Many ordinary people pay high rents, comprising much of their wages, with young people most affected. Landlords' rents and profits are heavily subsidized by state payments of housing benefits.

From a societal threefolding frame, the basic political cause of the housing crisis is that there is no recognized and implemented human right in Britain to decent, affordable, secure, warm housing. Linked with this, there is no policy that sets a maximum level of rent at 20–30 percent of income. There is a lack of fair rent control with the short one-year tenure system in Britain. 'Free housing markets' offer free rein to landlords.

However, each state constructs its own particular housing policy and rights framework. For example, 50 percent of German households rent privately in lifetime leases with rent caps. Sweden sets private-sector rent levels through regular national landlord/tenant negotiations, and as a result, the year 2014 saw Stockholm rents increase by only 1.12 per cent. The right to decent, affordable housing is thus respected and implemented in Germany and Sweden, but not in Britain. Sweden even has the right to warmth, and 'every man's right to roam' the countryside.[2]

Another cause is how bankers have exploited housing for profit, with the subprime mortgage scam nearly bringing the financial system down in 2007–8, as described in the 'The Big Short film'. The novelist Will Self explained this vividly in the *Financial Times*:

> *The current housing crisis is not so much emblematic of a transmogrification from a social market economy to a neoliberal one. It is constitutive of that pro-*

cess: the asset transfer from the state to the rich; the pump priming of the value of those assets; the forcing of the poor into more expensive private rental accommodation – all of which measures are underpinned by a financial system heavily dependent on mortgage lending. Of all British bank loans, 76% are for property, and 64% for residential property alone. Any radical reform of the system entailing a fall in land and house prices would, ipso facto, result in a fundamental destabilization on the banking system.[3]

Another root cause is the ongoing enclosure of our land commons by private buyers in the land market, who then capture land monopoly value by rents. As Rudolf Steiner and classical economists such as John Stuart Mill thought, land is not a commodity like a chair, but a bundle of rights governed by law. Karl Polanyi in *The great transformation* (1945) argued that treating land as a 'fictitious commodity', along with labour and capital, results in massive human insecurity and creates the conditions for a right-wing takeover.

Steiner thought that land belongs to all citizens as we all have an equal right to live on the earth, though in practice all cannot make an equal use of it. In modern economic terms, land is a 'common pool resource' like air or water. So a key political task is to agree democratically the rules for land governance, allocation and use, for example through the planning, regulation and taxation systems. Denmark requires non EU citizens to get permission from the Ministry of Justice before purchase, and they have to prove they will live there and pay taxes, and likewise summer houses with EU citizens. This means that housing is much cheaper in Denmark. Land use and management conditions are required if land owners are to get subsidies for environmental protection. Inheritance taxes on land and housing vary widely from state to state. Many European countries capture a much greater proportion than the UK of the land value uplift from the political decision to grant planning permission for the right to build, say on farm land.

From a societal threefolding perspective, over time land trusteeship bodies could secure more and more land through gifts or transfers from private and state ownership. Such plural-sector, community-based organizations, whilst holding land in trust for community benefit, would then lease the land for a variety of uses such as public amenities, farming, industry and housing, to competent people and bodies.

Steiner's thinking in the early 1920s was influenced by what he saw as the dangers of Bolshevik collective, top-down state ownership of land on the one hand, and on the other, unfettered private ownership in a free market. He emphasized the importance of a personal relationship, a real sense of ownership of housing and land that enabled responsible use – more of a 'conservative' approach. However, radically – like Ebenezer Howard the founder of Letchworth Garden City – Steiner also favoured trusteeship bodies that leased the land to households and to enterprises.

There are many such examples of land trusteeship in the plural sector of the land commons. Britain's National Trust is a charitable foundation with over three million members, holding over 1,500 farms and preserving many historic stately homes for public access. There are large and small charitable or mutual-housing associations; farming, wildlife and conservation trusts such as the Woodland Trust and the Canal and Rivers Trust for Britain's waterways. Communities are forming their own non-profit asset trusteeship bodies for parks, housing and public amenities as the neoliberal austerity state retreats from such provision. Scotland's Land Reform Act encourages community land buyouts across Scotland.

Locally to where I live, at the time of writing Stroud Town Council (Gloucestershire) is exploring setting up a charitable community asset body for public amenities such as its theatre, parks, lido and graveyard, as a protection and alternative to the privatization and selling of such 'family silver' by the cash-strapped local district council. Many other communities are now beginning to see that 'their' parks, housing and community facilities are not safe in the hands of the public, statutory sector.

Rudolf Steiner's ideas on land trusteeship and stewarding by plural-sector organizations anticipated the commons-governance research findings of the Nobel laureate, Elinor Ostrom. She researched the 'tragedy of the commons' thesis advocated by the land enclosers, i.e. that land is better looked after privately, as inevitably the commons are destroyed by overuse. Ostrom found that whilst some commons governance can break down in crisis situations, there are many successful examples all over the world of long-term commons governance of such common pool resources as Swiss pastures or Indian fisheries. She found that many communities managed their common pool resources and land more effectively than similar state-run schemes, and better than markets. Such bodies were self-governing, self-directing, local, long enduring and did not need expensively organizing by external bodies such as the state. However, legal-rights frameworks set up by the state did afford vitally important protection. (Compare the National Community Land Trust Demonstration Projects of 2004–10, which secured the CLT definition into UK law.) Ostrom argued that commons bodies as organizations for collective governance and action needed careful design, enabling and development to be successful.[4]

So, Stroud's Rodborough and Minchinhampton Commons comprise several hundred acres of open space grassland which are breathtakingly beautiful. The freehold is owned by the National Trust. There is a whole bundle of rights developed for usage such as the rights to roam, play golf, dog walk, commoners to graze their cattle, picnicking, sites of special scientific interest, picking fruit, and more. An association provides governance, such as deciding when cattle can graze, litter issues and car speed limits. Users are largely self-regulating and self-managing in the care of 'their' common, which can mean picking up litter, reminding dog owners of their duties, tending the Christmas dog tree and respecting rare flowers.

To summarize, then, the more land is treated as a commodity to be bought and sold on the free market, the more there will be market failure, widening social inequality, house-price inflation, accumulation of housing wealth by the rich with social exclusion and the lack of affordable homes for people. The alternative is to treat land as our common wealth. If land is understood as more than just a common pool resource, as a commons to be held in trust by plural sector, non-profit bodies for capturing enduring value for the common good, then use rights can be leased for affordable access, farming, community facilities and for permanently affordable homes. A land trusteeship sector can then develop alongside private and statutory ownership.

But how?

Community Land Trusts: Capturing Land Value for People and Communities

It is one thing to analyse the housing crisis, but quite another to engage in practical enquiry through positive action to develop working solutions. This takes time, money, skill and knowledge, prototyping and evaluating what works and what doesn't work.

Here is our own local story. Stroud was a run-down Cotswold market town in the mid-1990s. A group of us formed Stroud Common Wealth, a non-profit initiative, for the purpose of social, cultural and economic renewal, drawing very loosely on societal threefolding thinking, and on co-op thinking on social business. We developed community land trusts for housing and farming, and contributed to national demonstration projects with Bob Patterson of the University of Salford and Pat Conaty of the New Economics Foundation, which eventually resulted in a national CLT enabler and the founding of (to date) 225 community land trusts.

However, when we started in 1999, we had no idea that Stroud Common Wealth directors would variously pioneer community farm land trusts, housing projects, a communiversity, social-business development and a theatre. Or that present or former directors would be running successful businesses in their own right, such as Stroud Brewery, or become politically successful, as has Dr Molly Scott Cato as a Green Member for the European Parliament.

Steiner stressed the central importance of cultural renewal as a way of energizing people and communities for revitalizing cultural, economic and political life. Estate agents know this principle already. When they see 'pioneers' such as artists and innovative small businesses moving into a town, they know house prices will go up. We took this insight on board when our work for organizational and community renewal led us to set up successful arts and drama part-time foundation courses for adults. As a national exemplar, a generous, grateful student helped buy a pub called the Painswick Inn to successfully develop sheltered housing for vulnerable young people aged 16–25. The part-time drama courses were so successful that we secured an old church as the SPACE, Stroud Performing Arts Centre, in 1999, via a mix of gifts, interest-free loans, grants and a mortgage. Gloucestershire County Council noticed the initiative and then invited us to develop a Social Business centre, which we called The Exchange – named after Robert Owen, the co-op pioneer, and with a meeting room named after Octavia Hill, the social housing and National Trust pioneer.

However, we had the question, 'What happens if Stroud takes off and housing gets costly?'. So we held a conference in 2002 entitled, 'Land for People', which was a surprise sell-out on what proved a hot topic. This in turn led to a group of us visiting the USA in 2003, myself on a Winston Churchill Travelling Fellowship.[5] We brought the US CLT/community land trust models back to Britain, and adapted them from 2003 to 2009 with National Demonstration Projects, then establishing a CLT National Network for support, now with 225 CLTs.[6] 'Our' local CLT exemplar, Cashes Green CLT, was eventually built with the beautiful, sustainable designs of Kevin McLeod's HAB architects, which stands for happiness, architecture and beauty.

Why Community Land Trusts?

The triggers for the community land trust movement today are, on the one hand, the growing lack of affordable homes, and on the other hand, government inaction in the face of massive housing market failure and inequity. There is also the ongoing enclosure of public spaces. People in active communities wake up and then say, 'Then, we will do it (e.g. housing) ourselves!'. So community leaders, public officials and businesses from a cross-section of proactive villages, towns and city neighbourhoods see community land trusteeship bodies as one way of providing permanently affordable homes, workspace, amenities and community facilities. Secondly, as austerity has accelerated, local councils selling off 'our' assets, communities and councils see the need for charitable community bodies to protect such assets as libraries, parks, open space and public facilities and persuade councils to transfer these at nil cost.

The impetus for community land trusteeship runs deep in British social history. Basically, it is one way of reclaiming land as a commons, and for the community to democratically control the leasing-out of land rights to users. The commons tradition has deep resonance that goes back to pre-Norman times, to Anglo Saxon customary land use, and to worldwide indigenous approaches. The Maori say, 'If you look after our land as custodians, the land will look after you'.

The origins of the modern forms of community land trusteeship go back to nineteenth-century social reformers. In the 1860s John Ruskin gave his friend Octavia Hill some financial help for one of the first Housing Associations, the Marylebone Housing Society. John Stuart Mill, Ruskin and William Morris helped found the Commons Defence Association, which later became the Open Spaces Society. This successfully preserved common land that was being enclosed, such as Epping Forest, Hampstead Heath, the Malvern Hills, Wandsworth and Wimbledon Commons. John Ruskin founded the Guild of St George in the 1860s, which received gifts of land for rural renewal through smallholdings, rural crafts, the preservation of heritage and farming.

The ideas came to fruition in The National Trust, an open membership land trust founded by Octavia Hill in 1895, Canon Rawnsley and the Duke of Westminster, to preserve landed heritage. The 1907 National Trust Act made trust land inalienable, so the government cannot compulsorily purchase its land. It has 3.4 million members, owns more than 600,000 acres of land in England and Wales and Northern Ireland, including large parts of the Lake District, such as the former Beatrix Potter estates. It holds 700 miles of coastline, 1,500 tenant farms, 25 castles, 300 great houses and gardens and much else. Octavia Hill's vision of the Trust was as a way in which people could access the countryside and the beauty of Britain.

Before the First World War garden cities, colonies and villages were established using land trusteeship principles. George Cadbury set aside 6,000 acres for the mixed residential Bourneville Village Trust in Birmingham. Joseph Rowntree founded New Earswick, with the Joseph Rowntree Charitable and Housing Trusts still to this day pioneering innovative, socially just forms of housing tenure. The Quaker Joseph Rowntree was concerned about the unearned increment of rising land values, and how it could be captured to help relieve poverty. Ebenezer Howard used land trusteeship principles in purchasing the 30,000 acres of land at £40 an acre for Letchworth for the first Garden City. Ground rent and leases from the Letchworth co-operative land societies funded social, health and cultural services.

The land trusteeship ideas of Ruskin were adopted by Leo Tolstoy, and then also Gandhi in South Africa, and implemented in India in the 1950s by his follower, Vinova Bhave with the Land Gift movement, and later the village land gift of the Gramdan movement. Bob Swann picked up these ideas in the 1960s in the US civil rights movement. As a builder, Swann noticed that no matter the good quality of his work on new houses, the price was mainly determined by the land cost. His great insight was that he saw the house, the structure on the land as a commodity and that could be bought and sold to qualified buyers, whilst the underlying land was held by a community land trust, off the market. He joined with others, such as Scott King, the cousin of Martin Luther King, to set up a rural, farmland based community land trust in the US South, to combat sharecropper poverty. Today there are many housing CLT's all over the USA, alongside farm and wilderness trusts.[7]

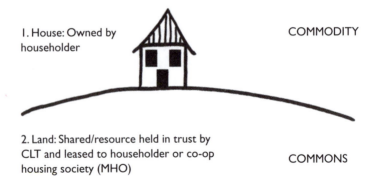

FIGURE 12.3: HOUSE AND LAND

What is a Community Land Trust?

A community land trust is a body for holding land for the benefit of people in a defined locality or community. It is a non-profit corporation that develops and stewards affordable housing, community gardens, civic buildings, commercial spaces and other community assets on behalf of a community. CLTs balance the needs of individuals to access land, and maintain security of tenure with a community's need to maintain affordability, economic diversity and local access to essential services. CLT's are not 'for' private profit, community-based organizations, constituted either as Industrial and Provident Societies for community benefit, or as a company limited by guarantee, which can be a charity. They are run by a small professional staff, directed by a board elected by members. There are directors from partner organizations and public-interest representatives as well as members and user directors. Membership is open.

A CLT, which we got defined into UK law in 2008, provides a unique way of capturing the value of public investment, philanthropic gifts, charitable endowments, legacies and private development gain for community benefit. This keeps land and property assets under the control of local people. CLTs provide a form of commons governance, 'beyond state and market', where the private sector cannot deliver, and the public sector can provide an enabling framework for local, self-directing housing solutions. The CLT model is spreading in the USA, and is used by cities such as Burlington, Vermont, Boston or Denver as partner, independent bodies for social housing.

A rough rule of thumb is that the building cost of a house today is a third of its market price, with the land cost one third, and developer profit one third. So the only way of making housing affordable is to entrust the land value, capture most of the development profit, and have it held by a public body such as a CLT on behalf of the community, a body that prevents land privatization.

Where Does the Land Come from?

As Mark Twain once said, 'Buy land, they aren't making it any more'. Acquiring low-cost or 'free' land is the basis of a CLT. CLT's can acquire land from:

- Gifts of land
- Getting land from exception site planning consents around towns and villages. This is when planning permission for affordable homes is given on land which is outside the usual boundary
- Getting a proportion of land from a planning gain agreement between developers and local planning authorities for affordable homes. In large housing schemes, this could be up to 30–50 per cent of the land
- Low-cost land provided by companies, statutory organizations or individuals to provide employment-related housing
- The transfer of publicly owned land and assets to the community, ideally at nil cost for social benefit. However, our successful Cashes Green CLT of 78 homes in Stroud, designed by Kevin McLeod of Grand Designs, had to find a considerable sum for the government-owned site, which reduced the number of social rental and part-ownership homes.

Community Farmland Trusts

Rudolf Steiner's ideas on land influence the worldwide biodynamic farming movement, as well as his philosophy of farmer competence and motivation for farm succession, rather than by inheritance. And as biodynamic farmers know that 'they can't take it with them', like spiritually minded people from many traditions they are inclined to donate their farms into trusteeship bodies to keep their farms biodynamic if family members no longer want to farm. I was therefore interested to find on my USA Churchill Travelling Scholarship in 2003 that both the two pioneer CSA/Community-Supported Agriculture farms at Indian Line and Temple Wilton were owned by land trusts so as to be leased affordably and securely to the farmers.

On return from the USA, I was approached by Greg Pilley, who was leading the pioneering CSA project for the Soil Association, and helping develop Stroud CSA as a UK pilot. As Stroud Common Wealth, we acquired funding for a Community Farmland Trust Action Research Project, which enabled the setting up of a number of Community Farmland Trusts (CFLTs), such as the Fordhall Farm community buy-out in 2006, which made international front-page news headlines.

As is 'normal' with action research, the results were extraordinary. First, we reinvented an old co-operative form called an Industrial and Provident Society for owning the farm for community benefit by individuals investing non-profit shares.

We discovered that such bodies could raise withdrawable, community shares – the original form of co-operative Crowdfunding. This IPS co-op structure was passed into law by John Stuart Mill MP for holding assets for community benefit (providence) and individual enterprise (industry). Since the successful share offer of Fordhall Farm in 2006, this IPS structure has been thoroughly updated by Co-operatives UK as a 'community benefit society' and a 2014 Act of Parliament, now used by thousands of bodies for raising 'community shares' for owning pubs, shops, renewable energy co-ops and more.

The story goes that Fordhall Farm, near Market Drayton in Shropshire, was saved for organic farming and for the community on 1 July 2006. Faced with a possible hostile buyout by multinational Mueller Dairies, the third-generation tenant farmers Charlotte Hollins, 24, and her brother Ben, 21, together with many volunteers and supporters, set up the Fordhall Community Land Initiative (FCLI). A public appeal enabled FCLI to raise £800,000 through selling non-profit shares in the farm to over 8,500 people. The success means that this pioneering 123-acre farm has now been placed into FCLI community trusteeship – safe for future generations.

FCLI was set up as an Industrial and Provident Society for community benefit, to hold Fordhall Farm in trust and lease it affordably to the young farmers. The mission of FCLI is to run Fordhall Farm as an educational, environmental and social resource, helping to reconnect people to food, farming and the countryside. It seeks to demonstrate that small-scale farming, connected to the local community, offers a viable way of life for generations to come.

Right from the start, Fordhall farmer Charlotte Hollins asked Stroud Common Wealth about practical ways of engaging people with the farm, and making it a community resource, so in early 2005 she asked us for ideas. We suggested that the farm could be safeguarded by means of a structure known as an 'Industrial Society for Community Benefit'. This means that the farmland is mutualized – a democratic, one-member-one-vote structure is set up, and shares are sold to the public at £50 each. Shares cannot be traded, but are returnable to FCLI if another buyer can be found. Members vote for a Board which runs FCLI on their behalf, developing a variety of programmes and leasing the land to the farmers.

The basic principle is a simple one: people get together and pay to take Fordhall's land off the open market, thus safeguarding it for the future. Through supporting Fordhall, people knew they were helping conservation, preserving wildlife, saving a historic organic farm and reaffirming their relationship with the land. Small gifts really mattered. Local primary school pupils contributed £7 by each giving 20p. Everything counted. People from all over the world, as well as locals, became members.

One key learning point is that a community buy-out can only work if there is considerable public support, if there are competent farmers, a viable business plan, if the purchase price is agreed with the landlord – and they give a reasonable time for the community buy-out to raise the money, and if people sign up to the values of taking land off the market by putting it into a co-op.

At the time, we perhaps over-optimistically thought that the Fordhall community buy-out might be as significant for England as the 1996 Isle of Eigg community buy-out was for Scotland. Eigg helped spark the 2003 Scottish Land Reform Act, which gave communities the right to buy their own land. At a time when current governments are busy privatizing our public land, Fordhall and CLTS show an alternative future – saving the family silver for enduring community benefit in the plural sector.

In 2011, we set up the Biodynamic Land Trust (BDLT) to serve biodynamic farms with a trusteeship body, and land for four pioneering biodynamic farms was secured. However, the price of farmland doubled in four years, and the BDLT future is likely to be receiving land bequests from farmers rather than land purchase, which is very expensive.

However, as in France with their national Terre de Liens farm land trust, there really needs to be a national farm trust in Britain for enabling farm access, not just small farm trusts with relatively high overheads. This might be a 'National Farm Trust', like the National Trust, with charitable status to steward farmland for farmer access and with sound governance. 'Brexit' (the UK's exit from the European Community), and the likely end of farm subsidies which keep many family farms just about viable, make the need for such a body greater, in the face of private investors and absentee landowners snapping up family farms.[8]

Conclusion: Plural Sector, Commons Governance and Trusteeship

The importance of CLTs, housing co-ops and co-housing bodies can be seen as ways of people learning managing and governing skills, and of learning commons governance and values. For example, Redditch Co-op Homes, the new build partner of Redditch Borough Council, is organized into large tenant co-ops, with high levels of social cohesion, human security, satisfaction with housing and public participation. The state's role can be pivotal: for example, Denmark's positive co-housing policies have enabled just over 5 percent co-housing there.

Rudolf Steiner saw land as a right, and as a commons to be stewarded by non-profit organizations in the plural sector, alongside the state and the market as equal partners. Current market and state failure to provide affordable housing highlights the need for more plural-sector housing solutions such as CLTs, housing associations, co-housing, self-build and co-ops. However, the role of the state in planning, rent-control enabling, resourcing and regulating is vitally important. For example, the Stockholm co-housing schemes were developed by the City Council as a public–plural partnership with co-housing groups. Amersfoort in Holland enables the development of co-housing for the over fifties, and Freiburg in South Germany has provided the enabling framework for the development of the green, mixed-tenure, world-famous neighbourhood of Vaubon.

FIGURE 12.4: HANDS OFF THE LAND!

In conclusion, there are many ways to share land equitably and productively. Elinor Ostrom said that there is no one best way, no panacea, for managing land well. The market, the state or the commons cannot provide an ideal model by themselves. We need distributive land design that fits the community, place, context, needs and uses, with the three sectors each playing their part in securing land access and homes for people, and for the common good.

NOTES AND REFERENCES
1. Robert Booth and Jamie Grierson, 'Grenfell cladding approved by residents was swapped for a cheaper version saving £300,000', *The Guardian*, 30 June 2017; available at goo.gl/2itE51 (accessed 16 November 2017).
2. Danny Dorling, 'The equality effect', *New Internationalist*, 19 July 2017; available at goo.gl/BuxJX5 (accessed 17 November 2017).
3. Will Self, 'A rentier nation's fading dreams of home', *Financial Times*, 16 January 2016; ; available at goo.gl/iwZwox (accessed 16 November 2017).

4. See Elinor Ostrom, *Governing the commons*, Cambridge University Press, New York, 2008; and Martin Large, *Common wealth*, Hawthorn Press, Stroud, 2010, pp. 264–5.
5. I took the 'land for people' motto from one of Winston Churchill's 1910 election speeches, in which he condemned land monopolies, campaigning for a land value tax.
6. See www.communitylandtrusts.org.uk.
7. See www.iceclt.org; a national community development organization promoting economic justice through community land trusts.
8. See www.fordhallfarm.com and www.biodynamiclandtrust.org.uk.

Follow-up Resources

Bollier, Dave (2014) *Think like a commoner: A short introduction to the life of the commons*, New Society Publishers, Gabriola Island, Canada.

Large, Martin (2010) *Common wealth*, Hawthorn Press, Stroud.

Raworth, Kate (2017) *Doughnut economics: Seven ways to think like a 21st-century economist*, Random House Business, London.

Ryan-Collins, Josh, Lloyd, Toby and Macfarlane, Laurie (2017) *Rethinking the economics of land and housing*, Zed Press, London.

www.communitylandtrusts.org.uk

CHAPTER 13

Toxic Excess: Income Inequalities and the Fundamental Social Law
Christopher Shaefer

> We can have democracy in this country, or we can have great wealth concentrated in the hands of a few, but we cannot have both.
> Louis Brandeis, Supreme Court Justice.

The Effect of Income Inequalities in the United States

For many years I have been interested in the social ideas of Rudolf Steiner, sensing that if he was able to articulate such a deep and comprehensive imagination of child development as the basis for Waldorf education, then surely what he had to say about the social issues of his time might also be important for us in the present.

In addition to proposing a new threefold imagination of the social future as an answer to the devastation of the First World War. Steiner formulated a set of social propositions which connect human consciousness and motives to social consequences. These laws are in most instances conditional, such as the Fundamental Social Law, which states,

> *In a community of human beings working together, the well-being of the community (or region or country) is the greater, the less the individual claims for himself the proceeds of the work he has himself done; i.e. the more of those pro-*

ceeds he makes over to his fellow workers, and the more his own requirements are satisfied, not out of his own work, but out of the work done by others.[1]

To this Steiner adds: 'every institution (or state and country) in a community of human beings that is contrary to this law will inevitably engender in some part of it, after some time, suffering and want'.[2]

The law points to the growth of egotism in wage-based economies in which every individual is encouraged to look out for their own interests at the expense of others, thereby producing long-term negative consequences. Steiner's law suggests that the question of motive for work is critical, and that a competitive wage-based economy will enhance the egotism of the worker and that of society by creating the illusion that we essentially work for money rather than for meaning or community well-being.

Laws are empirical propositions, and can be tested. I have attempted to do this by exploring the physical, psychological, social and economic effects of the competitive wage system in the United States based, as it is, on an unabashed neoliberal ideology, adhered to by both economic and political elites since the Reagan and Thatcher years. Neoliberalism views competition as the central characteristic of human relations and of society, and it suggests that the market is the final and best arbiter for labour, land and capital.

In the course of my research, I was frankly shocked by the deep and profoundly negative human, psychological, economic and social impacts of income inequalities in the United States. In reviewing public-health research and other studies, I found that growing income and wealth disparities in the United States since the late 1970s have decreased physical and mental health, increased prison populations and 'guard labour' (or defence, security and police) expenditures, decreased social mobility and opportunity, affected social trust and cohesion, undermined the fairness of the legal system, limited economic-growth prospects and compromised democracy.

These conclusions regarding the negative impact of large inequalities of wealth on the health and well-being of the USA and other societies are increasingly shared by health researchers and social scientists at UNICEF and the United Nations Development Programme (UNDP) as well as by many other social commentators. They were also popularized by the Occupy Movement in the United States, which made the large disparities of wealth and power between the 99 percent and the 1 percent a visible public cause in the autumn and winter of 2011. The research on income and wealth disparities unequivocally shows the truth of Martin Luther King's insight in his letter from a Birmingham Jail, 'All men are caught in an inescapable network of mutuality, tied in a single garment of destiny. Whatever affects one directly affects all indirectly'.[3] To put this slightly differently, we all suffer the consequences of stark differences in wealth and income.

The United States has the greatest wealth inequalities of any advanced Western society. The top 1 percent controlled over 40 percent of the nation's wealth, while the bottom 80 percent only had 7 percent in 2010; and more recent studies show that in 2012, the top one tenth of 1 percent, led by over 400 family fortunes, controlled close to half of the nation's wealth. Such disparities have not been seen in the United States since 1929, during the Great Depression. According to revised census figures, the effective poverty rate in the USA was close to 16 percent in 2014, with over 45 million people falling below the poverty line and spending over a third of their limited income on food.[4] In addition, the top 1 percent of income earners took home 65 percent of real income growth per family between 2002 and 2007 and it has got even more extreme since then.[5]

We have become a nation of 'Somebodys and Nobodys', to use Robert Fuller's apt phrase, with a frayed social safety net and growing social and economic hardship.[6] Little wonder that the Pew Foundation found in 2014 that 65 percent of Americans view the government in a negative light, and banks and large corporations as untrustworthy and corrupt. The election of Donald Trump can be explained in part by this growing gap between the 'haves and the have-nots'.

As public-health researcher Peter Montague has noted, 'It isn't the absolute level of poverty that matters for population health as the size of the gap between rich and poor'. This gap negatively affects physical and mental health, drug abuse, education levels, imprisonment, obesity, violence, teen pregnancy and a host of other health risk factors.[7] The greater the gap between the wealthy and the poor, the worse the range of social, psychological and physical illness in society, as Wilkinson and Pickett and other health researchers have shown.[8] This is true for countries as well as for the states and provinces of the USA and Canada.

The gap between the rich and the poor is also the primary cause of lowered longevity and increased disease in societies where per-capita income levels are in excess of $5,000 per annum. The United States spends more than twice as much on health care as other countries of the OECD, yet it ranks 48th in longevity, and does equally badly in many other health categories. Countries such as Japan, Sweden, Germany and Holland all perform considerably better. While the average spent per capita on health care in all of the OECD countries was $3,484 in 2014, it was in excess of $8,500 in the USA.[9]

Given this difference in per-capita health-care expenditures and outcomes, one would have thought that the health effects of income differentials would have played a significant role in the health-care reform debates held in the United States in 2009 as well as today. It has not, as both the mainstream media and politicians found it an inconvenient truth to deal with. More progressive taxation might have done more to improve health outcomes than changes in mandated health care, and might even be sufficient to pay for a single payer system which all other Western nations have in one form or another.

Prison Populations and Guard Labour

In addition to the psychological and physical health impact of wealth disparities, there is a second significant aspect to the impact of wealth disparities – namely, the greater the gap between the rich and the poor, the higher the prison population and the more a society spends on guard labour, meaning defence, security and police. According to researchers at the Santa Fe Institute and the University of Massachusetts, there were more prison guards in the USA in 2012 than high-school teachers.[10] The research draws a distinction between productive labour and guard labour; police, military personnel and private security guards who all protect private property and maintain public order. Guard labour, while certainly an important part of total economic activity, is not productive in the same sense as producing goods and services for public consumption.

The United States, England and Greece have the highest percentage of guard labour in their total labour force of all Western countries, with almost one in four workers in the US employed by the military, the police or security services. These countries also have some of the highest wealth and income disparities in Western societies.

According to the US Bureau of Justice statistics there were over 7 million people in the US prison system in 2009, or 3.1 percent of the population – the highest per capita reported incarceration rate in the world. Indeed, with about 5 percent of global population, the USA had 23.5 percent of the world's reported prison population at a cost of over $60 billion a year.[11] It is worthwhile noting that the number of Americans in prison grew rapidly after 1980, along with the cost of maintaining them, just as wealth inequalities were increasing during the years of the Reagan Administration. The prison population in the USA increased until 2014, when it began to decline as a result of changes in the sentencing of drug offenders.

The US Defence Budget is of course much larger than that which is spent on prisons or security. In 2010 it is estimated that total defence expenditures exceeded a trillion US dollars, when you factor in the wars in Afghanistan and Iraq.[12] While the defence budget decreased modestly in the second term of the Obama administration, it is still a huge percentage of total federal spending – and indeed of our total GDP of over 14 trillion US dollars per annum. In 2010 it was almost as much as the defence budgets of all other nations combined, and vastly in excess of what Russia and China spend together. Does a country really need over 710 military bases in 80 countries across the globe, and to equip and maintain 11 aircraft-carrier groups in all the oceans of the world?[13] Imagine the creative revolution that could occur if we devoted half of this, the people's money, to education, research, rebuilding the nation's infra-structure and alternative energy.

We have become both a Global Empire and a Garrison State, with extensive military personnel stationed abroad, as once the Roman legions were, and large prison populations and heavy security at home.

So what creates such fear and aggression, which seem to characterize American society? Is it that the country unconsciously recognizes that it uses a disproportionate amount of the world's resources to maintain lifestyle choices, and fear the poor and the dispossessed in its own communities because the growing gap between the rich and the poor seems both unfair and dangerous?

By fostering greater income equality through a more progressive tax system and cutting our military budget by 20 percent a year, the country would save more than 4 trillion US dollars over the next ten years. By fostering greater equality of wealth and reducing its defence budget, the United States would strengthen the middle class, reduce health care and prison costs, increase domestic demand and have a healthier, more robust economy.

Economic Consequences

The economic argument about income inequalities is quite straightforward, and yet amazingly, it is seldom discussed at this time of budget crises and limited growth. From 1945 until the mid 1970s, the US economy flourished. As a result of the New Deal and the lessons learned from the Great Depression, there was a broad sense of social equity as progressive tax rates, and wages increasing in line with productivity, created the basis for a shared prosperity. Marriner Eccles, the Mid West banker and Chairman of the Federal Reserve, who more than anyone else helped pull the country out of the Depression in the 1930s, understood very clearly that great inequalities of wealth undermine economic prosperity, and that wealth and income needed to be shared more equitably if there was to be sufficient consumption to support an economic recovery.

After 1975 the economic and political insights resulting from the Great Depression were lost, and working- and middle-class salaries began to diverge from increases in productivity. From 1980 to the present, median wages remained flat, when adjusted for inflation, and the government, from the Reagan years onwards, pursued policies of privatization, deregulation and lowering tax rates on the wealthy and on corporations. Further consumption and economic growth were mainly achieved through women entering the work-force in ever greater numbers, through the expansion of credit and through the granting of home equity loans. The resulting levels of indebtedness of families, corporations and the government were unsustainable when combined with the irresponsible and corrupt behaviour of the financial sector and of regulatory agencies, and the Great Recession of 2008 occurred.

The lessons of the Depression of 1929 clearly need to be relearned; great wealth disparities undermine demand, decrease consumption, increase unemployment and threaten to bankrupt the government and the nation. Robert Reich, the economist and social commentator, in his book *Aftershock: The next economy and America's future*, argues persuasively that there will be no true economic recovery unless restoring greater equity in incomes becomes a national priority.[14]

Undermining Democracy

Increasing equality of incomes and opportunity would also go a long way towards restoring US democracy. Considering the Supreme Court decision in Citizens United in 2010, which allowed corporations to give unlimited amounts of money to political parties and candidates, and the wealth disparities in the country, we have an oligarchy of wealth and special interest groups controlling the political process. 'One dollar, one vote' has increasingly replaced 'one person, one vote'. The truth of this statement is reflected in the fact that large corporations and financial interests have managed to lower effective tax rates on wealthy Americans, to decrease both capital gains and corporate taxes and to get special government subsidies for select industries under both Republican and Democratic administrations. Meanwhile, our representatives managed to help eviscerate the unions and undermine the postwar social contract between American workers and their employers. With the expense of national political campaigns today and the rapid decline of union membership and finances, there is no other source of big money today than corporations and the wealthy. The saying 'who pays the piper calls the tune' was clearly described by Simon Johnson, the chief economist at the IMF from 2007–8, when he said some years ago: 'If the I.M.F.'s staff could speak freely about the US, it would tell us what it tells all countries in this situation: recovery will fail unless we break the financial oligarchy that is blocking essential reform.'[15]

I believe that we as Americans need to face up to the reality that we live in an oligarchy of wealthy economic and political elites – a plutocracy, well described by Joseph Stiglitz, the Nobel Prize winning economist, in an article entitled, 'Of the 1%, by the 1% and for the 1%'. Stiglitz summarized his argument in his book, *The price of inequality: How today's divided society endangers our future*, by stating,

> We have created an economy and a society in which great wealth is amassed through rent seeking, sometimes through direct transfers from the public to the wealthy, more often through rules that allow the wealthy to collect 'rents' from the rest of society through monopoly power and other forms of exploitation.[16]

The Fundamental Social Law and the Nature of Capitalism

It seems clear from the evidence cited that Rudolf Steiner's insights into conditions of social health and illness are correct, and that an economy based on principles of market fundamentalism produces illness, suffering and want, not only in the

United States but to some degree around the world. Following the Great Depression and the Second World War, an effort had been made to mitigate the negative effects of unvarnished capitalism through Franklin D. Roosevelt's New Deal in the United States, and extensive social welfare and labour legislation in the social democracies of Western Europe.

These advances and the resulting amelioration of the worst aspects of capitalism have been systematically undermined in the USA and Great Britain since the late 1970s. Buttressed by the 'efficient market orientation' of the Chicago School of Economics, the Republican Right in the USA and the Conservatives in Britain have promoted a neoliberal economic ideology which one *Guardian* newspaper observer described as being 'at the root of all our problems'. In describing this ideology, he continues

> *regulation should be minimized, public services should be privatized. The organization of labour and collective bargaining by trade unions are portrayed as market distortions that impede the formation of a natural hierarchy of winners and losers. Inequality is recast as virtuous: a reward for utility and a generator of wealth, which trickles down to enrich everyone. Efforts to create a more equal society are both counterproductive and morally corrosive. The market ensures that everyone gets what they deserve.*[17]

The central values and core principles lying behind neoliberalism were well summarized by David Korten when he stated:

- *People are primarily motivated by self-interest, as expressed through the quest for financial gain and power.*
- *The actions which are taken by individuals and groups to maximize their financial gain and influence bring the greatest benefit to society.*
- *Social and economic life is primarily characterized by competition, rather than cooperation, by the struggle for existence, and society is best organized around this principle.*
- *Human progress should be measured by the consumption and production of goods and services as expressed by the Gross Domestic Product (GDP).*[18]

This is Social Darwinism all over again; the poor deserve their suffering and the rich merit their hard-earned wealth. The fact that corporations and economic elites have captured Washington, London and other capitals as well as state and local governments is conveniently ignored. The need for rethinking the social contract, and indeed the nature and structure of society, is quite clear, if we are to avoid the worst aspects of an authoritarian oligopoly. The Trump presidency adds urgency to such deliberations.

Increasing equality of incomes and wealth is therefore not only a moral imperative, but also an essential strategy for improving the health and well-being of societies. Before looking at some possible solutions to the scourge of high levels of income and wealth disparities, let me note that in no way do I want to ignore or deny the even greater injustices and inequalities which exist between the wealthy more industrial and post-industrial societies of the world, and those countries in Africa, South America and Asia who struggle with widespread famine, great poverty and violence. When 1 percent of the earth's population owns over 40 percent of the globe's wealth, as they also do in the USA, and over 40,000 people, mainly children, die of starvation every day, the balance between wealthy and poor nations is clearly of greater import, and should be of greater social concern than the growing wealth disparities in the United States.

Fixing the Existing System: Taxes and Financial Regulation

If we accept the basic tenets of capitalism, there is much that can be done to promote greater equality of income and wealth through more progressive tax rates and other measures. A study done by the *New York Times* in November 2012 found that tax rates had declined substantially for most Americans, except the poor, from 1980, during the Reagan years, to the present day. Not only have income taxes declined, but so have capital-gains taxes, a primary vehicle for the wealthy to increase their fortunes, and corporate and estate taxes. In 2000, for example, 94 percent of all US firms paid taxes of less than 5 percent on their profits.[19] Increasing top income-tax rates, raising the capital-gains taxes from 15 percent to 25 or 30 percent and lowering the estate tax exemptions from the present levels of 6 million to 1 million would do a great deal to balance the budget of the federal government, as well as producing a more equitable and healthier society. The closing of tax loopholes for businesses, increasing the effective corporate tax, as well as shutting down off-shore tax havens, would also restore more equity to the system.

Stiglitz also points to the need to fix the financial system, including improved regulation, restoring competition to the banking sector, and improving corporate governance and transparency, as well as a comprehensive reform of the bankruptcy laws.[20] He mentions other steps as also being essential to creating a healthier and more equal society, such as improving access to medical care through a single-payer system, providing equal access to higher education, and strengthening government programmes such as Social Security, Medicaid, Food Stamps and unemployment assistance.

In asking the question of whether there is a genuine hope for reform of this kind, Stiglitz suggests that there are two interconnected developments that could offer the possibility of transformation. One is that the 99 percent of the population realizes that they have been duped, or 'sold a bill of goods' by the 1 percent, and so become politically active, as happened in the Middle East during the Arab Spring. The other is that the 1 percent realizes that it is actually in their interest politically and economically to work towards a more equitable society. Yet, as Stiglitz and other observers recognize, without a reform of the political system and the public financing of elections, changes within American society are likely to be stalemated by the influence of private and corporate funds. It is as Justice Brandeis stated almost a century ago: great inequalities of wealth and true democracy are not compatible.

Improved Wages and a Guaranteed Basic Income

A more far-reaching set of solutions could be found by asking questions about the nature of work and remuneration. If work and an adequate standard for living are seen as a right, such as is articulated in the UN Universal Declaration of Human Rights and President Roosevelt's Economic Bill of Rights then quite different avenues of reform are possible.

There is a ladder of steps that could be taken to move towards a living wage as a human right. The most basic is to raise the minimum wage. Presently the federal minimum wage in the United States is $7.25 an hour, a decline of over 30 percent since 1979 when adjusted for inflation. Substantially raising the minimum wage, as some municipalities and states have done, would to some degree help reduce inequality. A more fundamental step is articulated by the Living Wage Movement, which is to establish a floor of what is required to live at a basic level in different regions of the country. The Living Wage Movement has successfully conducted campaigns to raise wages in selected cities, such as Santa Fe and New York City, and is attempting to develop state-wide and national campaigns. It has found that the argument of economic justice – namely, that a full-time worker should be able to live and support him- or herself and some dependents on the wages earned – has found substantial resonance among American voters, many of whom have at some point in their life worked for the minimum wage.

In 1969 President Richard Nixon, influenced by Daniel Patrick Moynihan, considered the question of welfare reform, and proposed a Family Assistance Plan of direct payments to families with children, in part arguing that a basic living should be a right. While this plan did not pass in Congress because of amendments to the proposed legislation, it did set a precedent that Republicans, or the political right, could be persuaded that there are alternatives to welfare reform which move in the direction of a guaranteed income.

A Guaranteed Basic Income or Citizens Income is a well-developed movement in many parts of the world, and is articulated by an international organization called the Basic Income Network. It is an idea that was expressed by Martin Luther King in his last book before being assassinated, *Where do we go from here:*

Chaos or community?, and has the support of many Nobel Prize winning economists from both the left and the right of the political spectrum, including Herbert Simon, Friedrich Hayek, James Meade, Robert Solow and Milton Friedman.[21]

The concept is quite simple: every citizen is paid a basic stipend from birth, irrespective of need. Such a stipend is seen as a right, and is financed either out of the revenues of State enterprises or State leasing revenue such as is paid by the State of Alaska to all of its citizens; or it is funded by a sales or value-added tax, which many European countries already have in place.

There are many virtues to the Guaranteed Basic Income, one of which is recognizing that work is by no means limited to paid employment when we consider the variety of human activity, from raising children to the care of the elderly, artistic activities, gardening or spending time and energy to volunteer for an environmental or social cause. Another is recognizing that developed and highly specialized and computerized economies do not need to employ more than 20 percent of the population to create the surpluses needed to support a society, as Jeremy Rifkin and others have argued.[22] An additional benefit would be to lead individuals and societies to recognize that individuals do not work mainly for money, above a certain basic level, but for meaning, contact and value, as numerous studies have shown.[23] These studies make a very convincing case that it is the challenge, contact and meaning of work which provide the real motive for labour in all of its many forms. A Guaranteed Basic Income would in addition rid us of the often demeaning and highly bureaucratic welfare system.

Providing a basic income would also lead us in the direction of seeing an adequate standard of living as a right – that is, as a rights question more than an economic question, for which Rudolf Steiner already argued almost a century ago. It would certainly enhance creativity and right livelihood, as people would be drawn to those activities which give satisfaction, meaning and joy. Coupling a Basic Income with universal healthcare, progressive taxation and free education would go a long way towards reducing income inequality and poverty, and would create much more dynamic and healthier societies.

This was shown to be the result of a four-year experiment with a Basic Income in Dauphin, Canada. Between 1974 and 1978 people received a stipend which allowed everyone to have sufficient income to cover basic living costs. Health improved and hospital visits decreased, children did better at school, there was less domestic violence and juvenile delinquency, people did not quit their jobs, and the local economy prospered.[24] Perhaps the planned basic income experiments in Finland, Scotland, Germany and Switzerland will have the same results.

Why should we be surprised that when people struggle to survive, or to have safe housing and enough to eat, that they become psychologically and physically ill, especially when living in societies that shame them by constantly promoting the images and products of the rich. Abraham Maslow, Rudolf Steiner and Martin

Luther King were quite right: mutual aid and support is a far better foundation for a healthy society and healthy people than an economy and society committed to a competitive struggle for survival. The research is there to support a different society; what we currently lack are the imagination and the political will to bring it about.

NOTES AND REFERENCES
1. Rudolf Steiner, *Anthroposophy and the social question*, Steiner Press, Great Barrington, MA, 2004.
2. Ibid., p. 34.
3. Martin Luther King, 'Letter from a Birmingham Jail', reprinted in *The Atlantic*, 16 April 2013; available at goo.gl/dtwTAE (accessed 15 November 2017).
4. Emmanuel Saez, 'Striking it richer: The evolution of top incomes in the US', 30 June 2016, available at goo.gl/GsY5Yf (accessed 14 February 2018); also quoted in Max Ehrenfried, 'Democrats internal dispute about the white working class is about to get real', *Washington Post*, 10 July 2017.
5. Saez, 'The evolution of top incomes…', (note 4).
6. Robert Fuller, *Somebody's and nobody's : Overcoming the abuse of rankism*, New Society Publishers, Gabriola Island, BC, Canada, 2003.
7. Peter Montague, 'Economic inequality and health', Environmental Research Foundation, Report No. 437; available at goo.gl/U6XuiH (accessed 15 November 2017).
8. Richard Wilkinson and Kate Pickett, *The spirit level: Why greater equality makes societies stronger*, Bloomsbury Press, New York, 2009 – in particular pp. 49–173. See also Stephen Bezruchka, 'Is globalization bad for our health?,' *Western Journal of Medicine*, 172 (May), 2000: 332–4.
9. *OECD Health Statistics*, 2010–2017.
10. Samuel Bowles and Arjun Jayadev, 'Garrison America', *Economists' Voice*, The Berkeley Electronic, March 2007; available at goo.gl/y99pzk (accessed 15 November 2017).
11. Wikipedia, 'Incarceration in the United States'; available at goo.gl/RENFHv (accessed 15 November 2017).
12. Robert Dreyfuss, 'Taking aim at the Pentagon budget', *The Nation*, 23 March 2011; available at goo.gl/KPa9qg (accessed 15 November 2017).
13. See the excellent book by Chalmers Johnson, *The sorrows of empire: Militarism, secrecy and the end of the republic*, Metropolitan Books, New York, 2004, in particular pp. 32–56, for a description of American military commitments around the globe.
14. See Robert B. Reich, *Aftershock: The next economy and America's future*, Alfred Knopf, New York, 2010, pp. 28–38. See also the insightful and colourful book by Kevin Phillips, *Wealth and democracy*, Broadway Books, New York, 2002.
15. Simon Johnson, 'The quiet coup', *The Atlantic*, May 2009; available at goo.gl/zaNffC (accessed 15 November 2017).
16. Joseph E. Stiglitz, *The price of inequality*, W.W. Norton, New York, 2012, p. 266; see also his 'Of the 1%, by the 1% and for the 1%', *Vanity Fair*, May 2011; available at goo.gl/YhgGvX (accessed 15 November 2017).
17. George Monbiot, 'Neoliberalism – The ideology at the root of all our problems', *The Guardian*, 15 April 2016; available at goo.gl/FE7yCo (accessed 15 November 2017).
18. David Korten, *When corporations rule the world*, Berrett-Koehler, San Francisco, 1995, pp. 70–1.

19. Binyamin Appelbaum and Robert Gebeloff, 'US: Tax burden for most Americans is lower than in the 1980s', *New York Times*, 29 November 2012; available at goo.gl/FSDCsK (accessed 15 November 2017).
20. Stiglitz (note 16), pp. 264–84.
21. Wikipedia, 'Basic income', available at goo.gl/QujRgz, accessed 15 November 2017; see also Martin Luther King, *Where do we go from here: Chaos or community?*, Beacon Press, New York, 2010.
22. Jeremy Rifkin, *The end of work: The decline of the global labor force and the dawn of the post market era*, Putnam, New York, 1995.
23. Daniel Pink, *Drive: The surprising truth about what motivates us*, Penguin, New York, 2009.
24. Rutger Bregman, 'Utopian thinking: The easy way to eradicate poverty', *The Guardian*, 6 March 2016; available at goo.gl/BwtpJx (accessed 15 November 2017).

CHAPTER 14

Education beyond Capital and the Neoliberal State: Challenging the 'Academizing' of England's Schools
Richard House

> *It could be high time to free education from both government and business by implementing the tripolar society concept, rather than the endless search by politicians for piecemeal, magic bullet solutions that get votes, such as academies.*
> Large, 2010, p. 234.

Introduction and Background

I would like to have subtitled this chapter 'The Economy and the State *Make Us Stupid*' (to misquote ex-US President Bill Clinton) – and I hope that what follows will make a strong case for such an alternative sub-title. What I mean by this mis-quotation is that when education and our schooling system are essentially run and controlled by either the state or by private free-market interests, the inevitable result is a dumbing-down and a narrowing of the possibilities for human potential that any education system worth its salt should be encouraging and nurturing.

Certainly, the critiques of both state-imposed and free-marketized education are devastating. Nearly a century ago now, Rudolf Steiner spoke to this issue in a way that was, typically, many decades ahead of its time. Steiner said in a lecture on 20 August 1919:

> *The state imposes terrible learning goals and terrible standards, the worst imaginable, but people will imagine them to be the best. Today's policies and political activity treat people like pawns. More than ever before, attempts will be made to use people like cogs in a wheel. People will be handled like puppets on a string. Things like institutions of learning will be created incompetently and with the greatest arrogance... We have a difficult struggle ahead of us...* (Steiner, 1996, pp. 29–30)

And from a left-Marxist position, the critique of profit-seeking private-sector schooling is equally devastating. Althusser (1971) and Bowles and Gintis (1976, 2002), for example, go into great detail about the manifold ways in which the schooling system and its organization in a capitalist society must necessarily adequately reproduce the conditions for the system's reinforcement and continuation. For example, Louis Althusser's notion of the 'Ideological State Apparatus' is very useful here. In that seminal contribution, he writes:

> *Besides techniques and knowledges, and in learning them, children at school also learn 'rules' of good behaviour, i.e. the attitudes that should be observed by every agent in the division of labour, according to the job he is 'destined' for: rules of morality, civic and professional conscience, which actually means rules of respect for the socio-technical division of labour and ultimately the rules of the order established by class domination... Reproduction of labour power requires not only a reproduction of its skills, but also, at the same time, a reproduction of its submission to the rules of the established order, i.e. a reproduction of submission to the ruling ideology for the workers... In other words, the school... teaches 'know-how', but in forms which ensure subjection to the ruling ideology...*
> (Althusser, 1971, pp. 132–3, emphasis added)

So we are left with a very disheartening situation in which whether the neoliberal state or private business interests dominate the schooling system, human creativity and potential development will be the first casualties; and the free cultural space that Rudolf Steiner urged should be the *sine qua non* of the schooling experience will be severely attenuated, if not extinguished altogether.

But it doesn't have to be like this. In his seminal book *Common Wealth*, for example, Martin Large (2010, Chapter 11) sets out very clearly the way in which England's schooling system has shifted from being one that was relatively and healthily autonomous from both the state and private business interests from 1945 until the early 1980s – to one in which, first the state (and some would say the *neoliberal capitalist* state) dramatically intruded into the education domain with its arguably brutal and highly inappropriate 'audit and accountability culture' (e.g. Power,

1997; Strathern, 2000a) and manic accountability regime (e.g. House, 2000, 2007; Strathern, 2000b), followed by the more recent drive to marketize our schools and education system more widely. It is the latter that will be the main focus of this chapter, as the audit, accountability and surveillance culture has been subjected to repeated critiques over many years, and here is not the place to rehearse those well-known criticisms.

In their contributions to the classic early book on free education, *Freeing education* (Carnie et al., 1995), Lord (Michael) Young of Dartington and Professor Richard Pring make the argument very well. According to Young, 'Twenty years ago [being 1975 as he wrote], Britain had in an important sense the most libertarian education system in the world' (p. vii), with the contrast between the 1945–79 period and what has happened to our schools since then being one of 'extraordinary change' (ibid.). So by 1995, according to Young, 'The bureaucrats [had] taken over. A [Conservative] government which claimed to be in favour of less government has in education added more to its power than at any time since 1888' (ibid.) – and that included, in 1994, the appointment as Chief Inspector of Schools that notorious scourge of teachers and of progressive holistic education, Chris Woodhead.

Pring also shows how, from the 1944 Education Act onwards, the government 'had no voice in what should be taught…; there were no state schools, only "maintained schools" within a state *system*' (1995, pp. 3–4, his italics). Moreover,

> *The government or the state did not control the curriculum. There was an underlying belief that the teachers, by reason of their experience and their training, were the experts not only in how to teach but in what to teach…. [T]hey were the custodians of an educational tradition that should not be interfered with by politicians. (p. 4)*

But it all changed in the 1980s under neoliberal Thatcherism. Pring again: 'Government felt that it could no longer trust the educational profession to deliver the goods. Much more central control over the system – over what was taught, how it was taught, and where it was taught – was seen to be required' (p. 5) – with the Secretary of State after the 1988 Act being able to determine the curriculum in detail from age 5 to 16, including attainment targets (p. 6). There was, then, little if any room for alternative approaches to education, with teachers henceforth 'delivering' a curriculum rather than teaching, learners becoming consumers, and education seen as a commodity 'to be promoted and sold like any other' (p. 7). In sum, 'The complexity of knowledge, judgement, understanding and appreciation is reduced to finite lists of competencies. Standards to be achieved… become the "performance indicators" declared by the external assessors' (p. 8).

By common consent amongst holistically minded educators, these latter changes have been catastrophic (and *unnecessary*) for the schooling experiences of both children and teachers. In the remainder of this chapter I hope to show that we could do a great deal worse than return to the pre-National Curriculum, implicitly tri-polar, threefolding approach to schooling which sees education and learning as a culturally free, relatively autonomous space that is, crucially, free from both hyperactive, anxiety-driven government intrusion and from the machinations of private capital and the market.

The Vexed Case of Academization

In 2016 and 2017, England's educational world has been consumed by a highly polarizing argument about the future of England's schooling system. This followed hot on the heels of the UK Conservative government's budget announcement by the Chancellor of the Exchequer George Osborne on 16 March 2016 (*not* by the then Education Secretary, notice) that all of England's schools were to be legally forced to become academies by the year 2022.

The academization policy was first introduced in the early days of Tony Blair's New Labour government after its election in 1997, with the first 'city academies' being established in 2002 to 'drive up' standards by replacing so-called 'failing' schools in struggling education authorities (with the government eventually dropping the word 'city' in order to allow academies to be established in rural areas, too). Essentially, academization entails the conversion of existing state-funded and local-authority administered schools to become 'academy' schools which are still state-funded, but which become directly funded by the Department for Education and are therefore independent of local-authority control. Academies are self-governing non-profit charitable trusts, and – crucially – may receive additional support from personal or corporate sponsors. Signalling at least some retreat from the centralised control of the preceeding decades, academies also do not have to follow England's National Curriculum, but are supposed to ensure that their chosen curriculum is broad and balanced.

The academization of England's schools was always highly controversial, and was (and is) seen by many left-progressive commentators as a way to move the schooling system away from government/community administration and towards the private sector (more on this later). This latter suspicion was only confirmed and reinforced as the Conservative-led coalition government of 2010–15 embraced academization with unbounded enthusiasm once it had come to power. Until recently, most newly created academies are secondary schools, with far few primary schools applying for conversion; and this was no doubt a crucial factor in the 2016 Conservative government's decision to force all of England's schools to become academies by legal statute.

In Stroud, Gloucestershire (where I live), there was a spontaneous uprising against this 'forced academization' policy immediately it was announced, with a local demonstration within days of George Osborne's budget, front-page lead reports in local and regional newspapers[1] and an open press letter signed by 125 concerned local citizens appearing in five Gloucestershire newspapers. Numerous similar uprisings occurred across the country – to the extent that some weeks later, in an extraordinary *volte-face*, the Conservative government announced that they were abandoning what was proving to be a highly unpopular and divisive policy,[2] opposed as it was even by Conservative local government leaders in key local authorities like Kent and Hampshire.

However, whilst the immediate threat of forcing all of England's schools down this path may have receded somewhat as I write (August 2017), there seems no doubt that the long-term goal of the Conservative Party is to find ways of bringing about universal academization and associated marketization of the schooling system; and in the months and years to come we can expect further strenuous, if more subtle, efforts to bring this about, just falling short of the crude bludgeon of imposed academization by force of law.

This latter view was corroborated in an open letter published in the *Guardian* newspaper on 10 June 2016 and signed by 100 educationalists (including teachers),[3] where we disconcertingly read that this supposed government U-turn on academization is

> merely a tactical retreat, and the government's reaffirmation of 'a system where all schools are academies' highlights plainly their continued stubbornness and zealousness. Although the headlines conveyed a 'U-turn' on forced academisation, the education for all bill proposes that local authorities are now coerced one at a time.

And in the *Guardian* newspaper of 14 June 2016, we find intrepid investigative journalist Warwick Mansell writing that

> The government is quietly pressing on with plans to force all English state schools into academy status by 2022, using its regional schools commissioners [RCSs] as behind-the-scenes arms-twisters…, with the powerful but shadowy RCSs seem[ingly] intent on enforcing this vision, though away from parliamentary scrutiny.[4]

Or put differently, if the Conservative government is thwarted in bringing about universal academization through the democratic process, it will endeavour to flout democracy and find underhand, by-the-back-door ways to realise its ideological ambitions.

What is arguably the parlous state of England's schooling system and teachers' ever-burgeoning workloads (with a staggering four in five teachers saying in surveys that they have contemplated leaving the profession) are the responsibility of both main political parties (Conservative and Labour), who since the late 1980s have uncritically imported 'audit culture' business practices into education, creating in the process an arid utilitarianism where narrow 'learning outcomes' invariably take precedence over the learning experience itself, and where only that which is quantifiable counts – and with the resulting statistics becoming a 'managerialist' tool that does a kind of violence to the lived experience of pupils/students and teachers alike (e.g. Block, 2000). Such alien (and alienating) managerialist values arguably have no place in our schools; and a major concern is that the academization of all the country's schools into academy chains (like chain stores) will simply make this already-dire situation (about which most politicians are seemingly in complete denial) even worse.

In this chapter I wish to cast this highly charged debate into the context of an anthroposophical approach to education and schooling that is inspired by the indications of educationalist and seer Rudolf Steiner and his 'Threefold Social Order' notion (considered below and elsewhere in this book), and within the wider cultural context of neoliberalism.[5] Certainly, an important backdrop to this discussion must be Steiner's resounding quotation from August 1919, quoted earlier.

Those sympathetic to a Steiner Waldorf approach to education (of which I am certainly one) have major and legitimate concerns about the role of what we might call 'the over-standardizing state' in its approach to children's education and learning. As political scientist James C. Scott put it in his book of the same title, governments commonly only seem capable of *'seeing like a state'* (Scott, 1999). So a simplistic, knee-jerk response to the policy of universal academization could easily be – 'At last… – all schools are to become independent of the state and government control, just as Rudolf Steiner advocated… – bravo!'.

But the argument has of necessity to be far more complex and nuanced than this. Rudolf Steiner's compelling vision was one of an education system that was administered within the *cultural* sphere of society (this being one of the three quasi-autonomous levels in his 'Threefold Social Order' framework)[6] – being a sphere that is, crucially, relatively autonomous from both the government sphere *and* from the sphere of the economy and private business. As we will see later, a central concern is that academization is merely a ruse by the neoliberal free-market Right for effectively privatizing the schooling system, *and so making schooling part of the economics/business sphere of society* and thus subject to the dynamics and logic of capitalist accumulation.

'Progressive' citizens inclined to the centre and the political left, including most advocates of Steiner education, tend to see this as a catastrophe-in-the-making – with the only thing worse than standardized state-run education being schools run for profit in a commodified corporatist world, where learning itself becomes a commodity that is subject to the market-exchange nexus (cf. Large,

2010) – to capitalist accumulation and production relations. Many believe that this would inevitably lead to 'a race to the bottom', with children's learning becoming increasingly narrow and instrumental – and with children no doubt being prepared for the Brave New World of free-market fundamentalism (cf. Bowles and Gintis, op. cit.), where everyone knows 'the price of everything but the value of nothing', and society increasingly becomes typified by 'private wealth and public squalor' (a phrase coined by J. K. Galbraith).[7]

The very idea that education can be a 'commodity' in the conventional free-market exchange sense does not stand up to the slightest scrutiny. Drawing on a useful recent *Guardian* newspaper letter[8] written by John Arnold, Assistant Dean of student recruitment at Birkbeck, University of London, education and learning can never be a 'market commodity' because you hardly ever buy it more than once, and neither is it at all practicable for an individual student to switch from one 'provider' to another. In addition, it is essentially impossible or impracticable for the 'consumer' of a given educational qualification to compare, in any meaningful sense, their learning experience with another version of the same 'product'.

At least with some 'mocked-up' markets that attempt to commodify and individualize public goods, a consumer can sometimes compare one 'product' against another offered by a different provider; but this is practically impossible for a human learning experience. This is just one reason why the attempt to apply free-market principles to educational experiences is entirely wrong-headed – and these are just the technical arguments; for when one looks at *what actually happens* to the learning experience when the attempt is made to commodify learning, the catastrophic effects are even more evident.

The ground on which this 'class war' (of a different kind!) is being fought out is between a vision of education as community-based, locally accountable and treated as a 'public good' with a public-service ethos, equally available to all irrespective of background and income; versus a vision that privileges commodified, profits-driven and corporatized schooling, with accountability to shareholders and a likely 'race to the bottom' in terms of both standards and staff working conditions.

Lest readers think these are exaggerations, there have been a number of investigative reports in the British press that have laid bare (as far as this is possible in this murky world) the commercial, profit-driven machinations lurking behind the academization process. In *The Observer* newspaper of 12 June 2016,[9] for example, the admirable investigative journalist Warwick Mansell exposed in a special investigation just how 'not-for-profit academies have been thrown open to entrepreneurial interests in an unprecedented fashion' – going into considerable detail on how the venture capitalist Mike Dwan, and his Bright Tribe Multi-Academy Trust which has ambitions to run 200 schools, has been exploiting the fact that government ministers have, at best, a tenuous hold on the billions of pounds of taxpayers' money swishing around the new academies system. As Mansell poignantly asks, 'Is the corporate world supporting the academies through sponsorship, or are we in danger of allowing state schools to become subsidiaries in business empires?'.

Several worrying occurrences have borne out these grave concerns. First, the UK's much-respected National Audit Office has long been voicing concerns about the government allowing academy chains to pay related companies on the basis that they are 'at cost' (i.e. supposedly non-profit-making) – with such a system being very difficult to audit because 'at cost' (or 'non-profit') can be a highly subjective term that is difficult to monitor and ratify with any confidence. The issue here is that academy chain 'owners'/CEOs are giving work/contracts to *their own* companies. And while the claim is that there's no profit-making involved in such incestuous transactions, there is actually no way of being at all sure that private profits are not being creamed off from the public sector in this opaque, nefarious system.

Further, in 2015 the then chief inspector of schools, Sir Michael Wilshaw, also raised concerns about the governance practices in some academy chains, seeking powers to inspect their administration. Yet incredibly, his temperate request was summarily rejected by the Department for Education. In 2016 as he left his post, Wilshaw was highly critical of the academies programme, particularly in terms of educational quality[10] – and this from someone who was usually a friend of the then Conservative administration responsible for driving through the academies programme with such intemperate speed and uncritical zealotry.

A report under the headline 'Academy chiefs "are building up empires": Ofsted chief says education suffering under bosses' ambitions' then appeared in the *Morning Star* newspaper of 16 June 2016.[11] Sir Michael Wilshaw was quoted as telling MPs that a number of multi-academy trusts 'have been allowed to grow far too quickly', with teaching trades unions saying that this was down to the government 'continuously ignoring' the 'lack of oversight' for academies. Wilshaw further warned, 'There was a lot of empire-building going on and executive headteachers who wanted to show how many schools they had, rather than whether they were any good or not'. National Union of Teachers (NUT) acting general secretary Kevin Courtney concurred, arguing that academy chiefs were often more concerned with 'paying themselves inflated salaries commensurate with the corporate sector' than they were with furthering children's education, and with there being 'a fundamental lack of oversight and accountability in the academies system which the government has continuously ignored'.

As an ex-university lecturer colleague said to me in 2016,

> *This is all very shocking, but not surprising: exactly the kind of thing we'd expected and feared. It won't be long before we see British Home Stores-style asset-*

stripping of state funds by the second and third parties involved in these dirty academy deals.

(For non-British readers, British Home Stores – or BHS – was until quite recently a large national chain of high-street department stores founded in 1928, and which recently went into receivership in very controversial circumstances.)

Another colleague even suggested to me that perhaps a Member of Parliament could use the cover of parliamentary privilege in the UK House of Commons to label Mike Dwan and his ilk 'crooks', and then call for a public investigation. Certainly, it looks as if those who oppose this academization trend might need to be even more creative than the political zealots determined to impose it without any reference to the democratic will of the populace.

As I write, yet another academies scandal has just broken, which merely confirms the aforementioned concerns. In *The Observer* newspaper of 22 October 2017 in a report titled 'Collapsing academy trust "asset-stripped its schools of millions"',[12] we read of how Wakefield City Academies Trust now stands accused of 'asset stripping' after it transferred millions of pounds of the schools' savings to its own accounts before collapsing. As I write, this report has already been shared an astonishing 22,000 times, just a few days after publication. In response, Labour shadow education secretary Angela Rayner was quoted as saying,[13] 'The government needs to come clean and tell us what they knew about this scandal.... Schools should run in the public interest, not commercial interests.'

These trends towards the marketization of England's schooling system have been familiar fare in the United States for many years now, and no one should be under any illusion that this offensive by private capital to colonize and take over public schooling systems is underway right across the Western world. A case in point is the global multinational Pearson corporation, which one commentator recently described as having a voracious 'Quest to Cover the Planet in Company-Run Schools'.[14]

Moreover, while of course it is important to recognize that the British government's importing of managerialist 'audit culture' practices into schooling since the 1990s has been a disaster, matters will almost certainly be far worse if schools *actually become* businesses, rather than merely being run according to business-like values and associated auditing practices.

I have been a prominent critic of over-standardizing state education on press letters pages and in education magazines and journals for several decades, and this is an issue that government really must start to seriously address. Although readers of this book will likely know that 'a third way' for administering education is possible and even far preferable to the polarized state/market binary, if the world of politics is still unable to see beyond a simplistic, polarized choice between an ideological vision that embraces market competition, commodification and corporatist values, or one which places a public-service ethos and community values at its core, then pretty much everyone except those on the extreme neo-conservative right will surely opt for the latter every time. In virtually all conversations I have had with people on this issue, this latter preference comes through resoundingly clearly.

It must also be emphasized that there exists no *necessary* reason why the state could not allow England's schools to have greater curricular autonomy and independence within the existing local government-administered system. This is crucial, because apologists for academization sometimes make the erroneous claim that only the academies model can give schools greater independence. If this were indeed true, it would be difficult for educators committed to Rudolf Steiner's educational vision not to support it. Yet this is a total non-sequitur; for one does not need academization and all that goes with it to give schools greater autonomy; one merely needs a more enlightened government and policy-makers to allow such autonomy within existing administrative structures. To repeat, there is no earthly reason in principle why this isn't possible. All (!) that is needed is the state/government being able to see beyond the constraining and impoverished ideology that is only capable of 'seeing like a state' (Scott, 1999).

A naïve hope, perhaps – but there are so many voices now saying similar things about the parlous state that our education and schooling system is in that we are surely moving closer to the day when a far more enlightened state *will* be able to 'see' more wisely, and make far more appropriate policy-making choices.

We also need to be aware of the erroneous arguments being proposed in relation to the notion of 'evidence', deviously deployed by its neoliberal proponents to support academization. Academy apologists are very likely to align themselves with those skilled at the duplicitous Machiavellian manipulation of statistics, fiddling and cherry-picking the data until they can claim that academization is, indeed, purely 'evidence-based'. Given the multiplicity of variables involved and the unequal resourcing playing-field between academies and non-academies, it is in reality quite impossible to reach any informed and reliable 'scientific' conclusion about the relative effectiveness of academies versus non-academies. Any such claim is entirely bogus from an informed methodological standpoint, and must be exposed as such.

On this view, then, it seems clear that *mass academization is an intrinsically ideological issue and not, as its supporters and apologists will attempt to claim, an evidential, empirical one.*

Turning now to the issue of privatization, we know from several reliable sources just what the real neo-conservative 'long-term plan' is here. First, thanks to a departmental leak, we know of former Conservative Education Secretary Michael Gove's secret memo advocating that academies become profit-making enterprises, leaked in 2013 and reported in detail in *The Independent* newspaper.[15] Grave concern has also been expressed in many circles that mass academization is nothing short of an asset-stripping exercise, where at some future date, a (right-wing) government will at a stroke sign over literally billions of pounds' worth of erstwhile public land to private-sector academies, thus essentially stealing what are the community's assets and giving them to private corporate interests, to capitalize and dispose of as they wish. In any conceivable democratic society, this would be a constitutional and democratic outrage, the scale of which it would be impossible to exaggerate.

The Wider Neoliberal Context

There is also a yet wider context to the privatization issue, which is arguably just one aspect of a longer-term neoliberal offensive that the extreme free-market political Right has been waging now for a full four decades. This neoliberal agenda has permeated all the major political parties (e.g. McCarthy, 2014), and needs to be seen in the context of United States imperialist objectives. These dogmatic ideological aims were expressed by the likes of the Austrian economist Friedrich Hayek (1899–1992) and free-marketeer Milton Friedman (1912–2006) in the 1970s, with these ideas having a profound influence on former Conservative prime minister Margaret Thatcher and, most importantly, on her close mentors, Sir Keith Joseph and Nicholas Ridley. Chilling chapter-and-verse details on these influences can be found in several documents.[16]

When one traces the links between politicians and the revolving door of senior civil servants to corporate interests (McCarthy, 2014), it soon becomes clear that corruption and the capturing of the state (Monbiot, 2000; Large, 2010) by wealthy corporate interests lie at the heart of the neoliberal agenda. It is certainly no accident that we have arrived at the point where we are today, with 'neocon' politicians looking to privatize education and health by stealth, because they know that if they were to try to do it overtly, the general populace wouldn't countenance such a privatization agenda for an instant.

Another aspect of this neoliberal agenda in relation to the hiving-off of state assets to corporate business interests is the obligation placed upon every government – a treaty of the World Trade Organization (WTO) – since 1995, when the General Agreement on Trade in Services (GATS) agreement was signed into law by then Prime Minister John Major's Conservative government. Following GATS, national governments are under international pressure from private corporate interests to refrain from excluding any service from privatization and marketization that can conceivably be provided on a commercial basis. Such a wide, all-encompassing definition makes virtually any public service that is 'provided on a commercial basis' subject to a relentless drive to privatization, save (for now!) certain areas like the police, the military, the justice system and public administration.

The privatization, or marketization, of perhaps all of what we historically consider to be public services, currently available for the whole population of a country as a social entitlement and paid for out of general taxation, is in time likely to be subject to restructuring and marketization, contracted out to for-profit providers, and ultimately fully privatized – and, *in extremis*, only available to those able to pay for such services – as with private health provision in the USA. This process is indeed already well advanced in most developed countries, and typically without properly informing or consulting the general public as to whether or not this is what the populace wants. The current desire of a right-wing Conservative government to drive forwards, by whatever means, the academization of England's schools should very much be seen in this context.

One is sometimes forced to make choices on pretty inhospitable ground that is not necessarily of one's own choosing – sometimes, indeed, having to make a choice between the lesser of two evils. It seems to this writer that the issue of mass academization reduces to one of fundamental ideological commitment, as between a schooling system rooted in and democratically administered within communities; or one which is ultimately run by corporate business interests with private profit being the overriding driving-force. Of course (as Rudolf Steiner would surely be saying today), state-administered schools certainly need to be freed up from over-bearing government control and be allowed to set their own curricula etc. without the standardizing disciplinary regime of league tables, government-imposed 'high stakes' testing, and punitive inspection regimes. But we emphatically *don't* need academies in order to bring such changes about.

As long as education remains free at the point of use, and any new owners/managers were to be either charities or co-operatives *with no private companies or corporations being allowed to make a profit from education*, there is no reason why our schooling system should not move much closer towards Steiner's vision for schools. What will be ultimately needed is politicians with the wisdom to let go of their erstwhile congenital need to control every dot and comma of the schooling system – and all those who want to see progress towards a Waldorf Threefold Social Order approach to education should join the increasing cacophony of voices that are advocating such a change.

However, there are some limited signs of light on the dark neoliberal horizon. In Britain's 2017 General Election, there was a dramatic, quite unpredicted shift of opinion away from the tired and increasingly discredited neoliberalist creed, and towards a post-austerity politics spear-headed by Britain's Labour Party under its radical new leader, Jeremy Corbyn. In a Manifesto that received widespread praise for its boldness and vision, here are some of the commitments that Labour-under-Corbyn made about education:

> *Labour will create a unified National Education Service (NES) for England to move towards cradle-to-grave learning that is free at the point of use.* (p. 35)

> *A narrow curriculum and a culture of assessment is driving away teachers, creating a recruitment and retention crisis. (p. 38)*
>
> *We will... oppose any attempt to force schools to become academies. Quality – we will drive up standards across the board. (p. 38)*
>
> *Accountability – Labour will ensure that all schools are democratically accountable, including appropriate controls to see that they serve the public interest and their local communities. (p. 39)*
>
> *We will abandon plans to reintroduce baseline assessments and launch a commission to look into curriculum and assessment, starting by reviewing Key Stage 1 and 2 SATs. The world's most successful education systems use more continuous assessment, which avoids 'teaching for the test'. (p. 39)*
>
> *...tackling rising workloads by reducing monitoring and bureaucracy (ibid.).*
> *(Labour Party, 2017)*

In relation to the vision of a third way for education that lies beyond both the intrusive state and the free-market model, these manifesto proposals warrant, at best, 6 out of 10. Their nodding towards the excesses of the toxic audit culture is welcome, but their proposals in this area are disappointingly modest (governments-in-waiting nearly always make these kinds of remarks when in opposition, but immediately *ramp up* the audit culture intrusiveness as soon as they come into government). It is almost as if politicians don't begin to understand the philosophy of 'less is more' – and they seem not to know how to *not* intervene. And while in speeches since the election, Jeremy Corbyn has made a welcome commitment to enabling every child to learn a musical instrument (Corbyn, 2017), on the other hand, their manifesto is painful to read for those who believe that our school starting age is far too early (House, 2013), with children's introduction to quasi-formal learning also beginning at an unconscionably early age (e.g. House, 2011a, 2015).

So all in all, a very mixed bag, then; and from this offering, it's not at all clear that even the Corbyn post-austerity left has *really* understood the manifold ways in which neoliberal ideology has infiltrated the schooling system and the policy-making psyche – whether in the guise of the 'Audit Culture State' or in the move towards marketized, privatized education. Moreover, an issue that I've not touched upon in this chapter is the *psychodynamics* of educational policy-making (e.g. Coren, 1997; House, 2011b), and the way in which unprocessed and unacknowledged anxiety (Salzberger-Wittenberg et al., 1983; Davou, 2002) and its accompanying low-trust culture (O'Neill, 2002) feed into and drive much of the dysfunctional policy-making to which teachers and children have been subjected since the rise of the neoliberalist ethos. Any full account would need to factor in these highly distorting psychodynamic processes.

Educationalist Jennifer Gidley has recently written a highly ambitious book (Gidley, 2016) on what she terms 'post-formal education', in which she critiques current educational Western configurations, and champions the open cultural space for learning that Steiner and other holistic educational approaches advocate. Gidley identifies four core pedagogical values that are fundamental to post-formal education – *love* (an evolutionary force); *life* (a sustaining force); *wisdom* (a creative force); and *voice* (an empowering force) – which, Gidley argues, are in 'dynamic, interrelationship with each other' (p. 182). Pedagogical features and elements of each of these core values are then outlined, including aspects of spiritual development and spiritual pedagogies. Examples of how each core value can be incorporated into professional practice are given, with sections on, inter alia, spiritual, transformative and contemplative education, social and emotional education, integral and holistic education, sustainability education, higher cognitive reasoning and creativity, and recognition of voice as an empowering factor for children in their learning milieux.

Notwithstanding the work of highly sophisticated writers like Gidley, and the exemplary practice of the worldwide Steiner Waldorf schools (amongst many others), my rather sobering conclusion is that we still have a great deal of work to do to enlighten those whose instinct is an anti-neoliberal one, persuading them that many of the statist accountability practices that they seem determined and uncritically to continue with are fundamentally antithetical to the kind of empowering, creative freeing education of which Rudolf Steiner, Sir Ken Robinson and many others are the champions.

Neoliberalism has comprehensively colonized the political psyche over many decades now, creating a Foucauldian 'regime of truth' (after the French critical theorist Michel Foucault), outside of which even those whose instinct is to be critical of neoliberalism find it very difficult to think. The threefolding approach outlined in this book, in all its richness and insight, can and will be of considerable assistance in helping to dismantle this toxic regime of truth.

Closing Thoughts

We live in turbulent times that are quite unprecedented in nature, just as was the case in the aftermath of the First World War when Rudolf Steiner tried (ultimately unsuccessfully) to introduce his threefold commonwealth notion into central Europe (Steiner, 1923; see also Steiner, 1945, 1985). And we also live in the age of Trump, Brexit, Corbyn and Sanders, which arguably brings with it great opportunities. But we urgently need a deep paradigm shift, with progressively minded politicians and policy-makers having the openness to admit that both control-fixated statist policies saturated by the audit culture, and a free-market, profit-driven approach, have abjectly failed, and need to be replaced by a third way, in which schools are collectively funded by the community out of general taxation, yet are granted radical curricular and pedagogical freedom (given certain basic minimum standards), with teachers re-professionalized and set free to teach, and our children to learn.

Those of us who have long been engaged in the struggle for a sane, child-appropriate way of educating our children have a profound conviction that the day will come when these deep changes will occur. The only remaining question concerns just how long our children and their teachers will have to suffer before the penny finally drops, and those wedded to controlling education and learning from the centre decide to withdraw from the pedagogical scene and, like the proverbial turkey, vote for an early Christmas. I regret to say that in the light of the continuing intransigence of those uncritically wedded to the tired old industrial factory-schooling paradigm (Gidley, 2016), and given the depth to which neoliberal ideology has penetrated the modern psyche, I'm not especially holding my breath.

Acknowledgements

I would like to thank Martin Large for the opportunity to extend this piece – an earlier version of which appeared in *New View* magazine, Summer 2016 – for this important new book (www.newview.org.uk), and for helpful and encouraging comments.

Footnotes

1. See, for example, goo.gl/8Ja6ME.
2. See goo.gl/b6132O.
3. Jun Bo Chan and 95 others, 'We oppose the drive to multi-academy trusts', *The Guardian* newspaper, 10 June 2016; retrievable at goo.gl/k71SjY.
4. Warwick Mansell, 'Government presses on with plan for all-academy England', *The Guardian*, 14 June 2016; retrievable at goo.gl/BxofKz.
5. 'Neoliberalism' is a term that came to prevalence in the 1970s and 1980s, referring to the resurgence of 19th-century ideas associated with free-market laissez-faire economic liberalism and privatization, and which is still very much in evidence today across the Western world. For a fuller discussion, see Harvey (2007), Large, 2010, pp. 122–6 et seq. and McCarthy (2014).
6. Rudolf Steiner's notion of the 'Threefold Social Order', developed between 1917 and 1922, refers to the three domains of human social activity: economic, legal, and cultural. Steiner proposed that the health of society depended on people understanding the characteristics of each of these three domains and 'what belonged where', such that we could consciously organize society so that each domain could enjoy independence and relative autonomy.
7. A quotation attributed to the great Irish playwright, novelist, essayist and poet, Oscar Wilde (1854–1900).

8. John Arnold, 'Marketised universities are far from utopia', Letters, *The Guardian*, Saturday 4 June 2016; retrievable at goo.gl/kv4Rk6.
9. Daniel Boffey and Warwick Mansell, 'Are England's academies becoming a cash cow for business?', *The Observer*, 12 June 2016; retrievable at goo.gl/LLGjZP.
10. Richard Adams, 'Few multi-academy trusts good enough to improve schools, says Wilshaw', *The Guardian*, 15 June 2016; retrievable at goo.gl/CH5mUU.
11. Conrad Landin, 'Academy chiefs "are building up empires"', *Morning Star*, 16 June 2016, p. 14; retrievable at goo.gl/3Vrq89.
12. Frances Perraudin, 'Collapsing academy trust "asset-stripped its schools of millions"', *The Observer*, 22 October 2017, p. 10; retrievable at goo.gl/PvoPaA.
13. Frances Perraudin, 'Labour urges ministers to "come clean" over collapsed academy trust', *The Guardian* online, 24 October 2017; retrievable at goo.gl/yKVzXH.
14. A. Kamenetz, 'Quest to cover the planet in company-run schools', *Wired*, 4 December 2016; available at: goo.gl/fw28di. See also A. Singer, 'Pearson "Education" — Who Are These People?', *Huffington Post*, 9 April 2012; available at: goo.gl/diJ8Z6; J. Reingold, 'Everybody hates Pearson', *Fortune*, 21 January 2015; available at: goo.gl/nkrXE4; V. Strauss, 'The case against Pearson – and its response', *Washington Post*, 21 April 2016; available at: goo.gl/x1PMwX; W. Mansell, 'Should Pearson, a giant multinational, be influencing our education policy?', *The Guardian*,16 July 2012; retrievable at goo.gl/kKsgvh.
15. See J. Merrick, 'Secret memo shows Michael Gove's plan for privatisation of academies', *The Independent*, 10 February 2013; retrievable at goo.gl/k7pp7l.
16. See Nicholas Ridley's Conservative Research Document from 8 July 1977, 'CONFIDENTIAL: Final Report of the Nationalised Industries Policy Group' (available at: goo.gl/iYCvHN); and Margaret Thatcher's secret 1982 cabinet papers setting out the longer-term neoliberal options for dismantling the welfare state (retrievable at goo.gl/SBUfto); see also A. Travis, 'Margaret Thatcher's role in plan to dismantle welfare state revealed', *The Guardian*, 28 December 2012; retrievable at goo.gl/HvuaSm.

REFERENCES

Althusser, L. (1971) 'Ideology and the ideological state apparatus', in his *Lenin and philosophy* (pp. 123–73), New Left Books, London.
Block, A. A. (2000) *I'm only bleeding: Education as the practice of social violence against children*, 2nd edn, Peter Lang, New York.
Bowles, S. and Gintis, H. (1976) *Schooling in capitalist America: Educational reform and the contradictions of economic life*, Basic Books, New York.
Bowles, S. and Gintis, H. (2002) 'Schooling in Capitalist America revisited', *Sociology of Education*, 75, pp. 1–18.
Carnie, F., Large, M., and Tasker, M. (eds) (1995) *Freeing education: Steps towards real choice and diversity in schools*, Hawthorn Press, Stroud.
Corbyn, J. (2017) Talk to Filton and Bradley Stoke Constituency Labour Party, 11 August, Filton, Bristol; available for viewing at goo.gl/xa8h9t.
Coren, A. (1997) *A psychodynamic approach to education*, Sheldon Press, London.
Davou, B. (2002) 'Unconscious processes influencing learning', *Psychodynamic Practice*, 8, pp. 277–94.
Gidley, J. M. (2016) *Postformal education: A philosophy for complex futures*, Springer International, Cham (ZG), Switzerland.
Harvey, D. (2007) *A brief history of neoliberalism*, Oxford University Press, Oxford.
House, R. (2000) 'Stress, surveillance and modernity: the "modernizing" assault on our education system', *Education Now: News and Review*, 30 (Winter); Feature Supplement, 4 pp.

House, R. (2007) 'Schooling, the state and children's psychological well-being: a psychosocial critique', *Journal of Psychosocial Research*, 2 (July–Dec), pp. 49–62.

House, R. (ed.) (2011a) *Too much, too soon? Early learning and the erosion of childhood*, Hawthorn Press, Stroud.

House, R. (2011b) 'Psychoanalytic ideas for early childhood', *The Mother* magazine, 45 (Mar/April), pp. 30–2.

House, R. (2013) 'What age should children start school?', *The Mother* magazine, 60 (Sept/Oct): pp. 32–4.

House, R. (2015) 'Able, but unready', *Teach Early Years*, 5.8, p. 33.

Labour Party, The (2017) *For the many, not the few; The Labour Party Manifesto*, 2017, London; available free at: goo.gl/vdw9Uu.

Large, M. (2010) *Common Wealth: For a free, equal, mutual and sustainable society*, Hawthorn Press, Stroud.

McCarthy, D. (2014) *The prostitute state: How Britain's democracy has been bought*, Acorns Publications, London.

Monbiot, G. (2000) *Captive state: The corporate takeover of Britain*, Macmillan, Basingstoke.

O'Neill, O. (2002) *A question of trust: The BBC Reith Lectures*, Cambridge University Press, Cambridge.

Power, M. (1997) *The audit society: Rituals of verification*, Oxford University Press, Oxford.

Pring, R. (1995) 'Role of the state in education', in F. Carnie et. al. (eds), *Freeing education* (pp. 3–9), Hawthorn Press, Stroud.

Salzberger-Wittenberg, I., Henry, G., and Osborne, E. (1983) *The emotional experience of learning and teaching*, Routledge, London.

Scott, J. C. (1999) *Seeing like a state: How certain schemes to improve the human condition have failed*, Yale University Press, New Haven, CT.

Steiner, R. (1923) *The threefold commonwealth*, Anthroposophical Publishing Co., London.

Steiner, R. (1945) *The social future: Public lectures, Zurich, 24–30 October 1919*, Anthroposophic Press, New York.

Steiner, R. (1985) *The renewal of the social organism*, Anthroposophic Press, Spring Valley, New York.

Steiner, R. (1996) 'Opening address given on the eve of the Teachers' Seminar, August 20 1919', in his *The foundations of human experience* (pp. 29–32), Anthroposophic Press, Great Barrington, Mass.

Strathern, M. (ed.) (2000a) *Audit cultures: Anthropological studies in accountability, ethics and the academy* (EASA series), Routledge, London.

Strathern, M. (2000b) 'The tyranny of transparency', *British Educational Research Journal*, 26, pp. 309–21.

Young, M. (Lord) (1995) 'Foreword: *Go for diversity!*', in F. Carnie et. al. (eds), *Freeing education* (pp. vii–viii), Hawthorn Press, Stroud.

CHAPTER 15

Money and the Threefold Social Order Movement
Glen Saunders

Money is essential to modern social life and to each of us individually to function effectively. We each use and understand money intuitively. We know what it means to buy something at fair value, by which we usually mean for a fair price and an amount of money. This is actually a sophisticated judgement which was uncommon in earlier times when trade, buying and selling were peripheral to how most people lived. We also know for the most part what we are doing when we save or borrow money, though we sometimes get into trouble with both, especially with borrowing; but we have a ready understanding of how that should work. We even have a feeling for what it means to give money, though this is much less developed outside of personal gifts. We handle money instinctively all the time. Given this, it is then surprising how strange and elusive money really is when one pauses to reflect on it. What is money, actually? How is it created? How does it work socially? There is no settled view on these questions, and it remains controversial.

Money is often seen to be something negative in social life. The Global Financial Crisis of 2008, when so much money was lost and much else lost with it, was essentially a problem with money, a problem in that case which started with debt and loan, and which then spread to the rest of the 'financial markets'. It was not a problem in the 'real' economy, the economy of goods and services, but its consequences have been substantial for the real economy, and will take decades to overcome fully.

Money is often seen to be harmful in people's lives, provoking greed and inhuman behaviour. St Paul is frequently misquoted as saying that 'money is the root of all evil',[1] though he actually says 'the love of money is the root of all evil'. If he is right, it is our relationship with money and what it can provoke in us which is the issue, not money as such – though there does appear to be something ubiquitous in our dealings with money which has disturbing personal effects as well as its broader social effects.

In the year 1917, when Rudolf Steiner became active with the threefold social order movement, money was not a primary issue. However, the collapse of social forms in the German-speaking world was the issue. Steiner thought this was both a tragedy and an opportunity. The opportunity was to recast social life in a new way, to achieve fundamental social change. He articulated this in many talks and essays, and especially in the book sometimes translated as *The threefold social order*.[2] This was part of a concrete programme of activity which ran till 1920 which was specific to its time. By 1920, to his considerable distress, he felt that the opportunity had passed, and that an evolved form of the old order had re-established itself. Things had crusted over. Steiner says memorably, 'Centuries have passed'. He withdrew from the practical movement, though others continued, and speaks little of social issues until the middle of 1922, when he sets out new ideas taking further some of the threefold social thinking in the 'World Economy' lecture course.

The history of the twentieth century makes obvious that the issues of 1917 had not been solved in 1920, but only postponed. And while the threefold social order movement was a specific, concrete programme, and Steiner's withdrawal from it appears to have been a pragmatic realization that nothing could be done for the time being, he believed the underlying ideas were fundamental to contemporary social life and had been so for some time.[3] Other opportunities would arise because our predominant social forms suppress the true nature of social life and will lead to chaos again. We seem to be on the cusp of that now.

Money does not figure strongly in *The threefold social order*. Steiner is at pains to make clear that it is not something in itself, but a type of coupon or cipher which finds its meaning and value in the process of exchange. This is needed because of the division of labour. He largely speaks about this in connection with economic life, which we would term today the 'real economy' of products and services. To use a well-worn example, the cobbler makes boots and the farmer grows carrots. The cobbler needs carrots and the farmer needs boots. If they are only to barter, it would be a happy coincidence indeed should they find each other, and then both would have other needs and have to begin the process again. An impossibility outside of the simplest of trading, and so something emerges which is itself useful and ubiquitous, like salt, which they will exchange for their boots or carrots because they know they will be able to exchange again for something else. Cobblers have no need for that much salt as salt, but are happy to hold it because they believe it will be readily accepted for other things they need. Something inherently useful, such as salt, has become useful because it can be readily exchanged. At that point, it has become a rudimentary form of money. Such 'innocent' money is, as Steiner says, not useful in itself but only because it can be used for further exchange. It facilitates the deepening of the division of labour, which itself creates value and allows the complex society we know today.

Steiner is writing in a period of what is sometimes now called 'industrial capitalism'. Economically, the great issues are the relationship of those doing physical work – labour – to those holding the means of production – capital. The real economy is the fulcrum; the financial and monetary economy, though even then gaining ground, is still subsidiary.

Steiner is also preoccupied by money trading on money, and the compounding of interest. He does not quote or acknowledge it, but Marx noted in *Das Kapital* that the 'innocent' process of exchange which sets up a sequence of commodity exchanged for money exchanged for another commodity contains within it a second process.[4] The first is

$$C - M - C'$$

A commodity is exchanged for money, which is exchanged for a different commodity. The point of the cobbler and the farmer was to get from boots to carrots and vice versa. Each commodity has a different use. The reason for the exchange is the exchange of uses, and the money is the means to that end. But looked at more broadly, this is part of a much longer sequence:

$$C - M - C' - M' - C'' - M'' \ldots$$

Some sharp-suited individual sees that $M - C' - M'$ lies within that – M becomes M'. But M is money as is M' too. If all is at fair value, will M not be the same as M'? Because the process of exchange does do something useful, it creates some economic value. Not much but we might agree it deserves to recoup a modest profit. But M to M' begins to peel itself away from the specifics of C to C' to C'' and endlessly on.

This is the beginning of the creation of capital, which brings speculation, money advanced at risk, money advanced in the prospect of earning greater money however used, and crucially of a financial economy separate from the real economy. The paths to that are long and complex, but this is where it starts. Steiner has a sense of that, and points to some specific issues – money becoming something in itself, money trading on money, interest or the return on money compounding – but he does not develop it further. He is preoccupied by the need to re-member the social organism.

Steiner's Later Thoughts – Threefolding Money Itself

The year 1920 comes, and Steiner decides that little can now be achieved, so he withdraws from the threefold social order movement and suggests it should stop – though, ever respectful of the freedom of others, he never instructs but only comments. He then says little about social questions until August 1922. I think this was profound for him. Social questions and the need for fundamental social change were something important to him from the beginning.[5]

Where the threefold social order movement in 1917 was a pragmatic programme for change drawing on deep social ideas which Steiner had nursed for a long time – ideas which tried to take the opportunity of the social chaos in the German-speaking world towards the end of the First World War – the World Economy lectures[6] were requested by economics students and academics. They are more contemplative and intellectual in approach, which is ironic, given Steiner's critical comments on academic economics in those lectures, and the substantial practical influence they have since had.

In *World economy*, Steiner focuses specifically on economic life which is just one of the three members of social organism within the threefold social order. So, it is narrower, but Steiner's treatment is much broader and more pragmatic. The threefold social order is predicated on a fundamental change in social life. Social life is always evolving, but fundamental change is rare. It requires many things to change in a short period of time. That means not just that I think differently but I act differently – and also that everyone else thinks and acts differently, too. Feudalism becomes capitalism.

One day, perhaps, capitalism will become the threefold social order. The Marxist idea is that fundamental social change is disruptive and often violent. It is not by consensus and agreement, and large numbers of people lose out. Marx thought it was driven by class and class interest, while Steiner was hoping for something else. But how do things change, then, other than in incidental details?

Steiner's one big push at the end of the First World War – the threefold social order movement – occurred at a time of considerable chaos, but it failed as a practical programme for change. I suspect we are at the beginning of another chaotic time – because of climate change, increasing migration, the collapsing social compact in the developed West, and many other phenomena, including our dysfunctional money system – where life will not be pleasant, but where there will be new opportunities. We will live through 'interesting times'.

Steiner's ideas about money had developed considerably by the time of his World Economy lectures. This was still 'industrial capitalism' where the predominant issues were within the real economy as they had been in 1917, but Steiner appears to have realised how much more important the 'money economy' was becoming. World Economy is an intellectually challenging lecture cycle. Those attending found it so difficult that the accompanying 'seminar' – really a series of questions and answers – were extemporized to help the audience's comprehension. A full exposition of what World Economy covers is not possible in the space available here. Even so, and as so often, Steiner's ideas are still intended as seeds for further work.

For the purposes of this chapter, two principal issues should be highlighted. The first is about how economic value is created within social life. The creation of economic value, especially surplus economic value, is essential. Every endeavour which is not creating such value is reliant on those which are. They are consuming the value. Only when economic surpluses are created above basic subsistence can the life of culture and rights flourish. Without that, people's every waking moment is focused on securing the basics of life – food, shelter and warmth. This is less apparent in the prosperous West, but distressingly, it is a fact for two billion and more people elsewhere on the planet. So in principle, surplus value, profit, is good, with the proviso that it is earned in a sustainable way, and that it is a real profit and not merely financial.

Steiner believes there to be two processes which create this economic value. The first is where 'labour transforms nature'. Manufacturing is the obvious example, but it includes all the activities needed to get some product or service to the point where it can be purchased by a consumer – transport, distribution, retailing, marketing and so on. This follows the labour theory of value which was already well established in nineteenth-century political economy. Labour transforms what nature provides 'for free' and this creates economic value.

But Steiner takes this further, describing a second, parallel process where – his words in translation – 'spirit transforms labour'. That is Steiner's shorthand for human intelligence organizing work. This is still an early twentieth century formulation from the time of industrial capitalism when it was predominantly about organizing the work of artisans more efficiently. That continues today, but now it is more about highly disruptive technologies and arrangements which create entirely new possibilities, or remove human labour completely. When Steiner was writing this was mainly about saving some labour, such as Ford's creation of organized production lines to make cars which made human work far more productive. Over the next 20 years, this will accelerate further and we will see a fundamental shift in economic life – a new, highly disruptive industrial revolution through spirit or human intelligence creating quite different economic possibilities. Organizing labour will be a part of it but it will go far further.

This application of human intelligence to labour creates economic value as well. In fact, it now swamps that created by labour. As indications, think, for example, of the valuation of companies like Alphabet (Google) and Facebook compared with General Motors.[7] This is neither good nor bad, but just a fact. However, it has substantial social consequences, and the threefold idea was to limit their destructiveness. How can the greatest permission be given to this creativity without hurting people along the way? This is something of cultural life coming into the economic process in order to reorganize it. The conduit for that is money. This is a different division from that between the cobbler and the farmer, a division of labour, but a division between those producing goods and services and those seeing economic possibilities and organizing around them.

These ideas about the creation of economic value lead to the second important development in his thinking in the World Economy lectures. Money is more than a type of coupon or cipher facilitating exchange which he described in the threefold social order, but has potentially three aspects. It is itself threefold.

The money used to facilitate trading and exchange he calls 'purchase money'. It is needed because of the division of labour, which is connected with labour transforming nature. Purchase money provides a measure of the economic value of goods and services. It is used where you pay fair value. Goods and services within this sphere are heading to the final consumer, who will pay a fair price for them and then consume them. This usually requires many intermediary steps, each of which itself takes place at fair value and is facilitated by purchase money. The goods move in one direction, acquiring value as they go, and the money moves in the opposite direction, recompensing each incremental step. At the point of consumption, the process ends, though typically the final purchase 'pulls' the next commodity into being and so this is actually part of a continuous process. Nevertheless, each purchase is complete and finished in itself.

This is different from the money used as a conduit to enable human intelligence to enter into the economic process so that spirit or human intelligence can transform labour, remembering here that transforming labour should be understood in a much wider way than simply reorganizing a work flow. This is 'loan money'. This is much broader than loans as conventionally understood, but covers any sort of investment. Its essential quality is that it is advanced to allow an intervention into economic life and stays in place over time. It carries risk, and its worth and value are uncertain until the investment has played out and a return earned. A good investment means it is worth more than the amount advanced, sometimes hugely more. A bad investment may mean it is completely lost. Only then can we tell what the loan money's value really was.

To this, Steiner adds a third sort of money. This is 'gift money', money which finances a free cultural life. To understand this, we need to understand more deeply how Steiner thinks the creativity of human intelligence comes to intervene in economic life. The circulation of goods and services in economic life depends on a number of 'free' resources such as land, material resources from the earth, the ability of plants to grow, and so on. Economic life makes use of them and until it does, they are without economic value. Human intelligence coming into economic life needs loan money to make its intervention, but that intelligence was there in the first place as a gift from cultural life. This creates an economic surplus beyond the return on loan money. This needs to be passed back to cultural life where it was nurtured as a reciprocal gift. Otherwise the financial economy and the real economy are out of balance. This is then to be used to foster the cultural life so that in future, new intelligence will come into economic life.

As an example, consider the differential calculus. This is a mathematical technique discovered in the seventeenth century. It was not pursued for practical benefit, still less any economic purpose, but to solve problems in classical physics. If now you consider anything in our modern world, it is possible only because of the differential calculus and the many practical uses found for it. It pervades everything. It was the purest of free gifts, economically speaking, coming from cultural life. It is quite different in type and scope from the organization of economic life facilitated by loan money, but it has created incalculable economic value. Steiner's idea is that this should be reciprocated by a gift of economic value to the cultural life to continue the cultural cycle. This is not a repayment but a forward-looking gift. It is not something which is valued economically. Indeed, it is something he considered would consume value which the processes of circulation and investment need to keep money in balance with the real economy. He was preoccupied by the idea that money was treated as something in itself, and which could trade on itself through the compounding of investment returns. The use of gift money to fund cultural life served an economic benefit as well as providing the means for the further development of future cultural life. Cultural life here is essentially anything which is a human developmental activity, anything where the outcome cannot be quantified in advance, such as education especially of children.

Gift money exists in some abundance. Much taxation is a type of forced gift. He believed the free gift was more productive than that forced, but both were gift money. The issue with taxation is that the thinking which accompanies it is more often akin to purchase money: government is purchasing educational outcomes. 'Investment' in education, unless meant figuratively, is another misnomer which leads to poor outcomes. There is increasing evidence that the most productive scientific research is undertaken from pure curiosity and funded completely openly, instead of the narrow advancement of money for a pre-defined outcome, as a gift, not a purchase nor an economic investment.

Is the Idea of Threefold Money Useful Today?

These ideas taken together are unique to Steiner. Forms of purchase and loan money can be found in the work of many economists, but gift money as something objective is distinctive. This could be developed to extend current thinking and address some of the monetary difficulties we face. Purchase, loan and gift are objective processes. They are in principle measurable. The failure to complement purchase and loan with gift, and the economic value-destroying process which lies behind it, contributes to our economic imbalances. There is too much money caught in circulation and in investment processes. This leads to a huge quantity of investment and debt chasing limited opportunities and the boom-and-bust instability of financial markets. This needs deflating through gift money.

How do these ideas fare today? Do they have relevance? How do they relate to current thinking?

One of the most successful social movements drawing on Steiner's social ideas, and specifically those about money, are some of the social banks. In Europe, banks like GLS in Germany and Triodos based in The Netherlands but active internationally,[8] are world leaders of the social-banking movement. They started as little more than study groups in the late 1960s, and gradually developed practical uses of money in saving and lending and in giving (and, more recently, in purchase money too). They were distinctive in mobilizing money for social ends in a more conscious way and the many social projects and social enterprises they funded. Triodos, for example, was one of the first investors in renewable energy and also investment in microfinance in the developing world. They have been distinctive in making money a tool for transparency and social choice. And they have been unusual in using Steiner's ideas about the different qualities of money in how they organized their work.

Although they are now substantial institutions themselves, they are still small against the financial markets; but even this is changing, as their ideas have been taken up by a fast-growing impact-investment movement which is being taken up by the mainstream.

But some areas of current concern are not addressed by Steiner. While purchase, loan and gift give a sense of the use of money and the archetypal types of transactions which are possible and how they should be managed, and even give a general sense of how money has a type of lifetime leading to its destruction through gift money, it does not describe the ways in which money is created in the modern economy. This is complex, but most money arises through the creation of debt within the banking system. These processes do not correspond closely to what Steiner describes. They play a large part in the processes whereby money trades on money, and they contribute to the excess of money in circulation. This in turn contributes to the instability of the financial markets, and so on. Proposals to change this, to change how money is created and by whom, to remove this from market processes – all have active followings, even by mainstream authorities such as the Bank of England. However, linking Steiner's ideas about the types of money, and especially the destruction of money through gift-money processes, could be fruitful and needs some work.

Similarly, loan money, and the way in which its value is discovered over time in the profit which good investments generate, were only developed to a certain point in Steiner's work. Today, the meaning of profit, its aggressive pursuit disregarding social and environmental factors and what reasonable levels of profit should be, are all under active debate and consideration. Steiner's monetary ideas have the germs of useful concepts which could contribute to this but have not been developed.

A key idea in World Economy, albeit not one about money as such, is that the world has now become a single economy. There is no outside, nowhere you can dump things. This anticipates the circular-economy movement which is now being strongly pursued.

There are a number of such areas clearly laid out in Steiner's work, but which remain as indications requiring further work to be made rigorous, and which need now to be updated to be relevant to today's financial and economic world. Was he then just an insightful thinker who anticipated much which has developed but is now of only historical interest? To some extent, but there are organizing ideas in Steiner's work which cannot be found elsewhere, and which could integrate many of the disparate areas of concern today – circular economy, the creation of money and management of the amount of money in circulation, the significance and place of profit, transparency in economic and monetary processes, the right way to fund cultural and developmental activity and its place in economic life. The combination of these ideas is difficult to find elsewhere. These could take on a much greater significance.

One hundred years on, the world of the next one hundred years is likely to be chaotic and alarming. This may create opportunities for Rudolf Steiner's insightful social and monetary ideas to take on greater significance. For that, they need development and bringing up to date in relation to contemporary needs.

Notes

1. Timothy, 6:10, King James version.
2. *Die Kernpunkte der Sozialen Frage*, Rudolf Steiner, published in April 1919. A number of translations exist, some of which are 'renderings' of the book. Both *The threefold social order*, a translation of the 1920 second edition by Frederick C. Heckel (Anthroposophic Press, Herndon, VA, 1966) and *Towards social renewal*, translated by Matthew Barton (Rudolf Steiner Press, London, 1999), are good.
3. Dieter Brühl, one of the four founders of what became Triodos Bank, published an extensive study of Steiner's social ideas in *Der Anthroposophische Sozial Impuls*. This is translated into English by Thomas Forman and Trauger Groh as *The mysteries of social encounters* (The Association of Waldorf Schools of North America [AWSNA] Publications, New York, 2002, ISBN 1 888365 41 2).
4. *Capital*, Karl Marx, Volume I, Chapter 4.

5. For an excellent, short exposition see *Rudolf Steiner's social intentions* by Rudi Lissau (New Economy Publications, Folkestone, 1996, ISBN 0 948229 20 9) – a slim tome of 29 pages in which Rudi summarizes his systematic and careful reading of all that Steiner wrote and spoke about social issues between October 1918 and November 1920. Rudi spent a couple of years on this and presented his conclusions at the 'Wynstones Conferences' in England in the late 1980s. What surprised Rudi was how radical Steiner's ideas were, and how much he was constrained by the necessities of those supporting him – his bourgeois 'base'.
6. *Nationalökonomischer Kurs*, 14 lectures given between 14 July and 6 August 1922, and the accompanying *Nationalökonomischer Seminar,* which are the notes of question and answer sessions from 31 July to 5 August 1922. The latter were apparently not planned, but were added as the lectures so confounded the audience for the lectures that something more was needed. For anyone interested in what Steiner was trying to say, they are very instructive. Two good English editions of translations which include the seminar notes are *Economics*, New Economy Publications, Folkestone, 1993, and *Rethinking economics*, Anthroposophic Press, Herndon, VA, 2013. Both of these are revisions of the original 1936 translation published by Owen Barfield and T. Gordon-Jones.
7. At the time of writing, the stock-market valuations are approximately Alphabet $600b, Facebook $420b, General Motors $58b. Stock market valuations are not a measure of the value the company is creating, and contain speculative elements and guesses about the future, but they are strongly influenced by the value created over time. Warren Buffet observes that stock markets are voting machines in the short term, and weighing machines in the long term. For some time now, the new economy of companies like Google have outstripped the old economy of companies like General Motors.
8. GLS stands for *Gemeinschaftsbank für Leihen und Schenken*, which translates as 'Community Bank for Lending and Giving'. The name Triodos comes from Trio Hodos, meaning threefold way or method.

PART FOUR

Openings for Co-creating our Social Future

CHAPTER 16

Three Conversations: Human Encounter in Threefold Society
Steve Briault

The Dynamics of Human Interaction

Being social creatures, human beings constantly communicate with each other. We narrate, request, argue, exclaim, command, enquire, inform and now project vast amounts of electronic data at each other every second. As described in Chapter 1, according to Rudolf Steiner[1] the process of interacting involves a tendency to 'put each other to sleep' and, conversely, to try to keep ourselves awake, through a process that involves the psychological polarity of *sympathy* and *antipathy*. In this chapter I will explore this mystery of human encounter a little more deeply, focusing especially on the different qualities of human communication which are most fruitful and appropriate in the three distinct dimensions of society.

Between sleeping and waking there lies a 'threshold' – the term is used here to indicate the boundary between different states of consciousness. Such a boundary also exists between the 'outer' world perceived by the physical senses and the 'inner' world of the mind or soul; and Steiner describes another threshold, between these worlds and the fundamental spiritual realities which underlie both of them. His description – and our everyday experience – of the 'archetypal social phenomenon' mean that a threshold also stands between one human being and another. Truly meeting another person involves crossing this threshold – allowing ourselves to be inwardly 'put to sleep' – with the force of sympathy. It means letting the other person occupy our awareness – for an instant, or longer – whilst our own inner processes and sense of self recede into the background of consciousness, as they do in sleep. This however calls up an automatic reaction of antipathy, the re-assertion of self-consciousness, which prevents us from literally falling asleep (or becoming hypnotized by the other person).

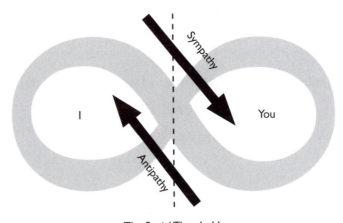

FIGURE 16.1: DYNAMICS OF SOCIAL INTERACTION

Free Cultural Dialogue

The relative strength of these two forces varies between situations and relationships. Steiner suggests that the ideal of *Liberty* in cultural life is essential in order to overcome 'old antipathies'[2] which recur in human society due to historical differences, tensions and often violent conflicts between different religious and philosophical traditions. Liberty means supporting the freedom of others to think, believe and develop differently from oneself. The principle of liberty allows different beliefs to coexist and interact, promoting mutual appreciation, exchange and discovery and thus healthy cultural development. It is the antithesis of dogma and the antidote to sectarianism.

When differing ideologies meet – if they do not fall into direct conflict – the primary mode of interaction, from the ancient Greek Sophists to contemporary Neo-Darwinists, has been *debate* – the attempt to persuade or 'win over' opponents through competitive argument. Such an approach clearly draws heavily on our antipathy forces: to be successful in debate, I must hold tightly to my own position and reject every proposition that contradicts it. However, the more we adopt this mode, the less we are likely to learn: we will focus on reinforcing what we believe we already know, and reject anything which could challenge, change or extend our understanding.

The debating mode was of course already notably modified by Socrates in

Plato's *Dialogues*, by the use of questions rather than assertions as the primary method of enquiry. In that context it appeared to be spectacularly successful in inducing his collocutors to change their ideas and perceptions, and has therefore been much emulated ever since, including in modern contexts. However, it is all too tempting to lapse from the genuinely inquisitive to the rhetorical mode of questioning, and the Socratic Method now tends quickly to arouse suspicion in those subjected to it. Indeed, it is questionable (!) whether the great man himself was genuinely expressing his 'ignorance of everything except his own ignorance' in using the technique, or whether the device was always bound to lead to conclusions of which he already had, at the very least, strong inklings.

How can the uncreative aspects of competitive debate be replaced by a more constructive mode of dialogue, without inhibiting the freedom of participants? The poet, playwright and scientist J.W. von Goethe described 'conversation' as 'more quickening than light'.[3] Clearly he was referring to something more significant and profound than everyday chatting, or indeed than academic or political debate; also to something involving a deeper encounter between human beings, as Marjorie Spock describes in her essay *The art of Goethean conversation*:[4] '... discussions base themselves on intellect, and intellectual thinking tends naturally to separateness' (p. 5).

More recently, the physicist David Bohm (1917–1992) developed a distinctive approach to *dialogue*, which he described as follows:

> *dialogue can be considered as a free flow of meaning between people in communication, in the sense of a stream that flows between banks. These 'banks' are understood as representing the various points of view of the participants ...it may turn out that such a form of free exchange of ideas and information is of fundamental relevance for transforming culture and freeing it of destructive misinformation, so that creativity can be liberated.*[5]

Bohm described the 'Principles of Dialogue' as follows:

- **The group agrees that no group-level decisions will be made in the conversation.** '...In the dialogue group we are not going to decide what to do about anything. This is crucial. Otherwise we are not free. We must have an empty space where we are not obliged to decide anything, nor to come to any conclusions, nor to say anything or not say anything. It's open and free.' (Bohm, *On dialogue*, pp. 18–19)[6]
- **Each individual agrees to suspend judgement in the conversation.** (Specifically, if the individual hears an idea s/he doesn't like, s/he does not attack that idea.) '...People in any group will bring to it assumptions, and as the group continues meeting, those assumptions will come up.

What is called for is to suspend those assumptions, so that you neither carry them out nor suppress them. You don't believe them, nor do you disbelieve them; you don't judge them as good or bad....' (ibid., p. 22)

- **As these individuals 'suspend judgement', they are also simultaneously as honest and transparent as possible.** (Specifically, if the individual has a 'good idea' that s/he might otherwise hold back from the group because it is too controversial, s/he will share that idea in this conversation.)
- **Individuals in the conversation try to build on other individuals' ideas in the conversation.** (The group often comes up with ideas that are far beyond what any of the individuals thought possible before the conversation began.)

This modern discipline of dialogue was developed and described further by Bill Isaacs,[7] Peter Senge[8] and others, often under the description of 'collaborative enquiry'. It is a demanding and quite challenging approach, often requiring repeated practice before a group can experience its full benefits – but in my experience it rewards the effort required. This effort mainly involves *taming our antipathy forces* – for example, hearing and reflecting on views and perceptions which contrast with our own, and resisting the urge to counter or replace them. When we are genuinely able to achieve this, we discover that our own perspectives broaden and deepen, and we can participate in communal learning. This is the fruit of Liberty in social life: its principles and practice extend beyond verbal conversation to all intellectual, artistic and inter-cultural exchange.

Dialogue vs Debate

- **Dialogue is collaborative: two or more sides work together towards common understanding.** Debate is oppositional: two sides oppose each other and attempt to prove each other wrong.
- **In dialogue, finding common ground is the goal.** In debate, winning is the goal.
- **In dialogue, one listens to the other side(s) in order to understand, find meaning, and find agreement.** In debate, one listens to the other side in order to find flaws and to counter its arguments.
- **Dialogue enlarges and possibly changes a participant's point of view.** Debate affirms a participant's own point of view.
- **Dialogue reveals assumptions for re-evaluation.** Debate defends assumptions as truth.
- **Dialogue causes introspection on one's own position.** Debate causes critique of the other position.
- **Dialogue opens the possibility of reaching a better solution than any of the

original solutions. Debate defends one's own positions as the best solution and excludes other solutions.
- **Dialogue creates an open-minded attitude: an openness to being wrong and an openness to change.** Debate creates a closed-minded attitude, a determination to be right.
- **In dialogue, one submits one's best thinking, knowing that other people's reflections will help improve it rather than destroy it.** In debate, one submits one's best thinking and defends it against challenge to show that it is right.
- **Dialogue calls for temporarily suspending one's beliefs.** Debate calls for investing wholeheartedly in one's beliefs.
- **In dialogue, one searches for basic agreements.** In debate, one searches for glaring differences.
- **In dialogue, one searches for strengths in the other positions.** In debate, one searches for flaws and weaknesses in the other positions.
- **Dialogue involves a real concern for the other person and seeks to not alienate or offend.** Debate involves a countering of the other position without focusing on feelings or relationship, and often belittles or deprecates the other person.
- **Dialogue assumes that many people have pieces of the answer and that together they can put them into a workable solution.** Debate assumes that there is a right answer and that someone has it.
- **Dialogue remains open-ended.** Debate implies a conclusion.

FIGURE 16.2: 'DIALOGUE' CONTRASTED WITH 'DEBATE'
Note: Adapted by the Study Circle Resource Center from a paper prepared by Shelley Berman, which in turn was based on discussions of the Dialogue Group of the Boston Chapter of Educators for Social Responsibility.

The Sympathetic Economy

In cultural life, we need to recognize and respect the freedom of others: the key questions are, 'How do you see / understand this? What do you appreciate, what inspires you?' As economic producers, we need to reach beyond ourselves in an even more radical way, to serve the choices made by others. This involves the development of what Rudolf Steiner called 'new sympathies' – asking the questions, 'What do you need, want, prefer?' It may seem banal that the most apparently material processes – cutting someone's hair, or manufacturing a lawn-mower – are potentially significant moral educators; but they require a very practical, operational ethic – sacrificing one's own immediate needs, preferences and judgements in order to serve those of the consumer.

In cultural life, we develop and express our own individual values: in economic life, we create value for others; and that economic value is assessed primarily by *their* criteria, not our own. Developing the skill of hair-dressing, for example, with its accompanying aesthetic sense, is a cultural process involving a degree of self-expression; but when the hair-dresser engages with his or her client, the aim is to serve their wishes and aspirations for their appearance – not just to shorten the hair, but to enhance the customer's self-image.

In the productive economy, value is added to nature by human activity, often involving global supply chains with hundreds of contributing businesses and millions of individual workers. In the age of mass production – still the predominant mode for many industrial sectors – goods are produced in bulk and 'pushed' on to the market where they are to be bought by anonymous consumers whose choices are driven by price and advertising (which of course invisibly increases prices). Since the 1980s, however, many manufacturing and service sectors have tried to move to systems based on 'pull' – where production is designed and managed according to 'single-piece flow' and in principle geared to meeting actual demand – 'sell one, make one' – rather than creating large amounts of stock which then has to be pushed on to the market. Such systems substitute *economies of flow* for the mass production *economies of scale*. This transition, often known as Lean Production or Lean Service, is challenging both intellectually and operationally, and is still in its early phases in many sectors.

In principle, the lean business model is both more profitable and more ethical, because it involves less waste (and therefore is also ecologically better) and is more precisely geared to the expressed wishes of consumers. It involves close co-operation and ongoing dialogue between customer and supplier organizations up and down the value streams, overcoming some of the adversarial attitudes and behaviour which have often hindered overall effectiveness. This requires a new approach to commercial negotiation in which the representatives of separate but interdependent groups and organizations develop a genuine concern for each other's needs and interests, asking each other, 'What do you need from us, so that together we can serve the final customers better?'.

An excellent starting point for this is the 'principled negotiation' approach first articulated by Roger Fisher and Bill Ury in their seminal book *Getting to yes*.[9] Fisher and Ury define the aim of negotiation as 'a wise outcome reached amicably and effectively'; and a 'wise agreement' as one which:

- meets the legitimate interests of both sides to the fullest extent possible;
- resolves conflicting interests fairly;
- is durable; and
- takes community interests into account.

Their book, and a range of follow-up writings from each of the authors, describes principles, techniques and behaviours which support this constructive approach to the central human process of making agreements (both within and well beyond formal negotiation contexts) in which we are all involved on a daily basis.

Truly 'fraternal' – or in Steiner's terminology, 'associative' – economics would go further than principled negotiation or lean supply chains, however. It would include the collaborative design of products, and the planning and operation of production systems, guided by consultation and agreements between all the relevant stakeholder groups, taking account of the legitimate needs and interests of customers and suppliers – and of the environment – at each stage of production and consumption. The conversations required for this would effectively replace abstract market forces driven by persuasive, manipulative advertising by conscious human choices based on mutual understanding. Whereas in cultural life the sovereign individual takes centre stage, in the economy sound judgements and decisions can only be reached collaboratively. This is how 'new sympathies' can be developed.

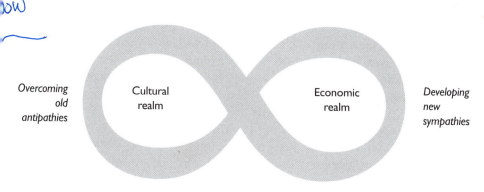

FIGURE 16.3: SYMPATHY AND ANTIPATHY IN CULTURAL AND ECONOMIC LIFE

Equality and Empathy

Equality, I spoke that word, as if a wedding vow...
Bob Dylan, 1964

It is easy to forget how young the ideal of universal, equal human rights is. For most of history, differentiation of status, power and privilege based on race, gender and class has been taken for granted. Only since the Second World War has the right of all human beings to be treated equally under the law gained a degree of global recognition – and of course it is still far from being universally respected.

Nevertheless, the last century – and even just the period of Bob Dylan's career – has seen a remarkable acceleration in the acknowledgement of equal rights and the patchy but undeniable progress towards elimination of structural injustices. Slavery, apartheid, segregation, disenfranchisement, discrimination, sectarianism have all been pushed back – in spite of their tendency to reappear in new forms and new contexts, requiring constant vigilance and insistence to contain them.

In Chapter 1 it was suggested that the subjective feeling for human rights – which ultimately leads to the objective formulation of rules, laws and policies – is derived from the experience of human encounter, across the social threshold, in which we recognize the unique and ultimately equal value of each individual, irrespective of their background or characteristics. Human encounter is not new, however, so we must presume that the growth of individualism, the sense of self – also described previously – has in parallel led to an increase in the depth of our ability to sense the other person, and to perceive the universal humanity beneath all the superficial differences.

This evolution of human consciousness underlies many of the differences between modern society and ancient practices which we would today find unacceptable, even 'barbaric', but which were a natural part of earlier cultures. It is reflected in Rudolf Steiner's insistence – well before the civil rights movements of the 1960s – that:

> *someone who nowadays speaks of the ideal of races and nations and belonging to a clan, speaks of decaying impulses of humanity. And if he believes that these so-called ideals constitute progressive ideals, when speaking of them, he is saying something that is untrue. Because through nothing will humanity bring itself more into decay than if the ideals of races, nations and blood were to continue. Nothing will be a greater hindrance for the further development of mankind than the conservation of the ideals held by earlier centuries, preserved [...] in declarations about the ideals based on nations. The true ideals for the future must be, not what is based on 'blood', but what we find solely in the spiritual world.*[10]

This was the kind of statement that caused Adolf Hitler to declare Steiner 'my greatest enemy'.

On 10 December 1948 the Universal Declaration of Human Rights was adopted by the United Nations General Assembly. Since then, organizations such as the International Federation for Human Rights and Amnesty International have campaigned continuously for global compliance with the Declaration's provisions. This has brought them into conflict with authoritarian states, ruthless corporations, and also traditional sects and cultures. Is it legitimate, for example, to require patriarchal, theocratic societies to embrace full gender equality – or is this just one dominant (Western) culture imposing itself on others that have different values? What are the limits to diversity (the liberty principle) that should be set by the striving for equal rights? Who should make such judgements – and how?

The simple-sounding concept of equality is in practice highly complex. It involves constantly creating and re-creating a dynamic balance with the other two dimensions of society, and creating and managing the boundaries between cultural, rights and economic principles. For example, if the state guarantees the equal right of all children to education, what degree of control – if any – should government exercise over the form and quality of the education which it funds? (See Chapter 14). Current debate over faith-based schools reveals how delicate and controversial such issues can be. A somewhat similar problematic exists at the boundary between political and economic questions, for instance in relation to workers' rights (parental leave, minimum wage, sick pay, redundancy….). In such areas and many others, the political process has the task of translating *the general feeling for what is fair and just* (often filtered through the preconceptions held by politicians) into coherent and enforceable legislation.

The rights realm, sometimes referred to as 'the middle sphere', sits within the polarity of culture and economy, but (true to the threefold archetype) itself manifests in further polarities – between subjective and objective, individual and community, rights and responsibilities. Rudolf Steiner insightfully points to the psychological reality that we tend to be emotionally attached to what we perceive as our rights, but rather cool and detached about our responsibilities.[11] On the road, for example, I can find myself becoming quite indignant if another driver infringes my 'right of way'; but may not always engage seriously (enough) with the legal speed limit on a stretch that seems empty and safe. In the housing community where I live, permission is required to keep a cat or dog – but my little daughter passionately desires a kitten; and suddenly it is much easier to argue for my family being a special case than it is to tolerate the barking of our neighbour's terrier.

Steiner suggests a simple but challenging path of self-development in relation to this phenomenon – to balance our attitude by bringing the quality of enthusiasm to our responsibilities, and detachment to our own rights. Can I, for example, bring a degree of warmth to the obligation to buy a vehicle licence, and some objectivity to the process of claiming a reduction for driving a low-emissions car, for which I may or may not qualify?

A healthy rights life requires an ongoing, inclusive conversation in society focused around the central questions of what is fair, reasonable and equitable in every aspect of life, based on common agreements and regulated by representative authorities. The feeling for justice lives in individuals, and thus originates in cultural life; the more such conversation can create (not impose) consensus out of the diversity of individual views, the more harmonious the society will be. The central quality required is therefore the cultivation of *empathy*. Empathy is the ability to imagine another person's experience, without necessarily sharing or endorsing it. It involves crossing and re-crossing the social threshold, managing our own sympathy and antipathy forces without submitting one-sidedly to either of them. One could describe this as a kind of 'collective dreaming' process, between the 'sleep' of sympathy and the awakeness of antipathy.

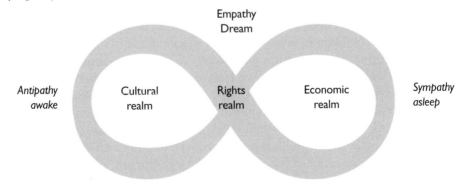

FIGURE 16.4: EMPATHY IN THE REALM OF CIVIL RIGHTS

Human and civil rights are a kind of promise, an undertaking – 'as if a wedding vow' – given by the community to its individual members. Their preservation, cultivation and evolution require ongoing, empathetic conversations at all levels and in all groupings, from neighbourhood to work-place to region, nation and global society. They are constantly under threat from both cultural and economic forces which overstep their 'right-ful' boundaries, and need to be upheld and protected not just by powers and authorities but by every self-conscious citizen.

Cultivating the Three Conversations

It would of course be absurd to suggest that only one kind of interaction is appropriate for each of the social dimensions. Artists need to negotiate their contracts, businesses need to find socially inclusive ways of involving their employees, and governments must allow free exploration of policy options before legislating. Nevertheless, this chapter has attempted to characterize a certain differentiation of human interactions which can be helpful in allowing the ideals of liberty, equality and mutuality to express themselves most fully in the different realms. A summary is given below.

Social dimension	Cultural	Economic	Political
Social ideal	Liberty	Mutuality	Equality
Conversation mode	Dialogue, exchange, collaborative enquiry	Constructive negotiation within value streams	Inclusive consensus-building
Primary aims	Discovery, creativity, development	Associative agreements that benefit all stakeholders	Equitable laws and arrangements that uphold human rights
Capabilities required	Overcoming old antipathies	Developing new sympathies	Non-discriminatory empathy

TABLE 16.5: LIBERTY, EQUALITY AND MUTUALITY IN DIFFERENT REALMS

As individuals, we continuously inhabit all three aspects of the social organism: we are participants in culture – from websites to classrooms to opera. We are all consumers, if not always necessarily producers; and we are citizens and members of communities of various kinds. The more we can develop the social skills and qualities, and practise the essential communication processes which support the healthy manifestation of the threefold nature of social life, the more we can contribute to the rebalancing of society which is so urgently required.

NOTES AND REFERENCES
1. Rudolf Steiner, 'Social and anti-social forces in the human being', revised trans. Christopher Schaefer, lecture, Bern, 12 December 1918, Mercury Press, Chestnut Ridge, NY, 1982.
2. *The inner aspect of the social question*, Three lectures given in Zürich, 4, 11 February, and 9 March 1919, SteinerBooks, Herndon, VA, 1950.
3. *The green snake and the beautiful lily*, Steinerbooks, Herndon, VA, 2006.
4. Marjorie Spock, *The art of Goethean conversation*, St George Publications, Spring Valley, New York, 1983.
5. David Bohm and J. Krishnamurti, *The ending of time*, Victor Gollanez, London 1985; cited by Arleta Griffor, 'Mind and its wholeness', ANPA West Journal, 7, (1), 1997, pp. 25–6; available at goo.gl/uo1X6x (accessed 15 November 2017).
6. David Bohm, *On dialogue*, Routledge, New York, 1996.
7. William Isaacs, *Dialogue and the art of thinking together: A pioneering approach to communicating in business and in life*, Bantam Doubleday Dell Publishing Group, New York, 1999.
8. Peter M. Senge, *The fifth discipline: The art and practice of the learning organization*, Doubleday, New York, 2006.

9. Roger Fisher and William L. Ury, *Getting to yes: Negotiating agreement without giving in*, Penguin Books, Harmondsworth, 1981.
10. Rudolf Steiner, 26 October 1917, in *The spiritual background of the external world: The fall of the spirits of darkness* (GA 177).
11. Rudolf Steiner, *The influences of Lucifer and Ahriman: Human responsibility for the Earth*, SteinerBooks, Herndon, VA, 1976.

CHAPTER 17

How Threefolding Fits – or Not – with Current Political Ideologies, and Dialogue in Threefolding Developments: An Interview
Christoph Strawe with Martin Large

I

Martin Large: **Our first main question is: What are the most frequently asked questions about, and objections to, the Threefold Social Order notion by Left-leaning thinkers, activists and politicians? And similarly, what are the main questions and objections raised by Right-leaning thinkers, activists and politicians?**

Christoph Strawe: This is a rather complex question. We need to begin with the extent to which the right–left scheme is still appropriate to the political world of the present day. One should also, I think, attempt to locate who from the above-mentioned people – social scientists, civil-society activists, members of the 'political class' – could be willing to enter into a dialogue about threefolding. Who would deal with all the relevant issues and arguments, or at least see them as being important?

    I would also propose to include among the target groups the representatives of the business world. The economy has become a 'superpower' in society. Nicanor Perlas, the threefolding activist from the Philippines and recipient of the alternative Nobel Prize, holds the view that a tri-sectoral partnership between civil society (a cultural power), politics and political administration, and the business world is today the most essential entry-point for authentic threefolding developments.

Perlas also refers to Paul Ray's and Ruth Anderson's discovery of 'cultural creatives' (Ray and Anderson, 2000), a third of the people in the countries where their research was carried out. These are people who are open to impulses towards social renewal. They are found especially in civil society, but also in politics and in the business world. Progressive people in economic and political institutions need the support of civil society, and vice versa. The more civil society becomes conscious of itself, the more the potential for threefolding emerges. If that does not happen, threefolding threatens to be sidelined by political and economic interests. This can also lead, of course, to the fact that there are objections to threefolding amongst progressive people.

In the social sciences, at least in Germany, threefold concepts hardly play a part – they are usually simply ignored. On the other hand, today's anthroposophical social science is not yet sufficiently dynamic to anchor itself sustainably in the academic world, and the resistance to something new is still too strong. Thus, in many countries the representatives of 'neoclassical' thinking or neoliberals hold many of the key roles in the economic sphere, and neoliberal thinking holds professorships in economics in most universities. There are, however, counter-currents. Critical scientists are challenging existing paradigms, and are beginning to approach threefold thinking.

Martin Large: **Can you give an example?**

Christoph Strawe: I am thinking of Ferdinand Laloux's much-respected book *Reinventing organizations*, which contains many elements of the idea of self-management of the economy. This is wonderful, because the self-organization idea is at the core of social threefolding: liberation of the cultural life by self-management, self-management of the economic life, the deepening of democracy, so that the state finally becomes an aspect of the self-administration of society. However, the self-management idea gets different colours in these three areas.

Martin Large: **What are the most important experiences that you've personally had in discussions about social threefolding?**

Christoph Strawe: The question most frequently raised with me, when I am asked questions at all, is: 'Just what does the term "threefolding" mean?' This question isn't surprising in view of the silence which still surrounds the whole issue. To answer the question one first has to provide brief basic information. In the course of such a dialogue, some people may discover that they're already threefolders, though they didn't even know of the term until that moment! Others may be skeptical, and begin to ask more questions, or to develop objections. My experience is that such questions are most frequently asked when there are real points of contact when actively participating in, for example, civil society activities. In such situations, real interest between people can best develop.

I personally have participated, for example, in discussions about the European Constitution and the World Trade Organization (WTO) Agreements, participated in three World Social Forums, and acted as a civil-society observer in Cancun at a WTO summit. In face-to-face-encounters one wants to know what is the background of the one with whom he or she is co-operating. This often requires only brief factual information, in which one above all tries to show what the threefolding impulse has to do with the corresponding joint activity.

Martin Large: My initial question you have answered with the remark that you first have to query the right–left schema. Do you think it doesn't matter any more?

Christoph Strawe: I stick to the fact that the terms 'left-oriented' and 'right-oriented' today say much less than was previously the case. In the time of Steiner, and also up to the 'turn' in 1989, there were clearer 'fronts' than today: e.g. capitalist private property and socialist state property were opposed, in a more radical or a more moderate manner. Against this background, threefolding is recognizable as a search for a 'third way' between capitalism and socialism. In our example threefolding develops the idea of a property 'in social flow'. This is also referred to as 'operational property', 'property limited in time' or 'capital neutralization'.

Today, things are less easy distinguishable. China calls itself a socialist country, yet at the same time it is a supreme power for a kind of capitalism that's promoted by an authoritarian state. China makes itself an advocate of free trade, while protectionist tendencies are strengthening in the USA, which has championed free trade for decades. But the need for development between culture, economy and the state is still growing. The term 'third way' has become ambiguous because very different forces have referred to it in recent times, from Schröder and Blair to proto-fascist actors.

Right and left were always terms of struggle. Today, political actors try to push the enemy into left or right corners in order to occupy what they call the middle. The resulting indistinguishability of the political profiles – I think of large coalitions, e.g. in Germany or Austria – then leads, on the other hand, to attempts to seize the fringes again. Think of the current boom of right-wing 'populists'.

I think it's also important for our question to distinguish between political or social concepts and ideas on the one hand, and social *ideologies*, on the other. One can represent different social conceptions ideologically, in the sense of dogmatic, fundamentalist, seeing things only in terms of 'black and white', or openly, critically, solution- and dialogue-oriented.

As far as ideologies are concerned, the extremes overlap. In my opinion Stalinism and National Socialism cannot be fully equated, but it can hardly be denied that they have essential similarities. Am I a leftist? If left is 'emancipatory', I can say 'yes'. If it is to be tutelage and totalitarian oppression, I will fight against it. So I am still not a 'rightist'. As far as it concerns the 'thinkers' and the 'activists', the 'left–right-schema' is not really purposeful. And another point of view is that in fact, we also are dealing, incidentally, with the eclectic blending of different ideological offsets. One could extend it all at will: does 'left' mean left-socialist, social democratic, social liberal, communist? 'Links' is at least always a whole spectrum.

The Greens are often seen as 'left', but the German Greens once came up with the slogan: 'Not left, not right, but front'. Where do liberals belong? You have to clarify first what you mean by the term at all. Not only is the meaning of this and other terms very different in different countries —in the US, 'liberal' means something quite different from, for example, in Germany, because it is more 'left' than there. Can we equate classical political liberalism, libertarians, economic neoclassicism, ordo-liberalism and neoliberalism?

Further developments of materialistic paradigms, such as transhumanism with its view of artificial intelligence and its cyborg visions, play almost a greater role today for the motives of the actions of certain elites than the classical socialist, liberalist or conservative concepts.

II

Martin Large: **What objections and questions did you or other people in the German-speaking countries have to deal with? – i.e. questions and objections that are representative?**

Christoph Strawe: I myself was a Marxist and a communist, and then became an anthroposophist, and as such I was trying to establish a dialogue with Marxism (Strawe, 1986). This was at once a working-through of the objections which emerged from Marxism towards anthroposophy and threefolding, and also an attempt to find out where the real strengths of Marxism lie, where points of contact with threefolding arise.

To this day, from the Marxist side we commonly meet the same arguments with which I tried to deal at the time. Those arguments go something like this:

Social threefolding misunderstands that the basis of social life lies in the economy, and that the cultural life is merely superstructural (to use Marx's own terminology), that being determines consciousness, and that the real social being is the economy. It's naive as far as the role of social power is concerned, it's idealist (assuming 'good humankind'); its emphasis on the individual is ultimately petty-bourgeois individualism; and the role of the working class and socialist revolution is denied.

Moreover, from undogmatic people in civil society including more open-minded Marxists, I often experience a question or reproach – sometimes a silent reproach – that threefolding followers isolate themselves too much, that they speak a special language which appears strange to others.

The objection that social threefolding is too idealistic is raised not only by Marxists and parts of the political left, but also by others: they think that people working with threefolding are detached, and don't really understand practical life and the human character. So threefolding is seen as being a utopian vision, nothing but a beautiful dream.

From the right-wing perspective, one often hears the objection that the critique of the capitalist economy by threefolding proponents is aimed at the elimination of the market. The associative economy is viewed from this perspective as a relapse into the 'planned economy'. On the contrary, in economic matters fraternity ceases. I have also heard this argument from Social Democrats, contending that only the welfare state can promote fraternity.

In addition, among threefolding activists some people think that the idea of associations is now outmoded, and that we should fight for a 'market economy without capitalism'. The reform of land law and that of money regulation, also a threefolding issue, is sufficient; with these changes market forces could be fully effective without causing harm. The associations are thus seen as a hindrance to the market.

With regard to the state, you find people who believe in a strong state on the political right *and* on the political left. One also finds anti-state notions held by right-wing people, e.g. the libertarian wing of the Tea Party Movement in the USA. At the time when he formulated the Basic Sociological Law, Steiner described himself as an individualist anarchist. This basic law deals with history as the emancipation of the individual from the tutelage of the collectives. But at the time, i.e. 1898, Steiner doesn't speak of the abolition of the state, but of a new role for the state. Now that the individual enters the centre of the community, the individual must no longer be subordinate to the state and society, but the state must be there for the individual. It is the image of a state of law that is a protection of, and a developmental arena for, the individual. Individual human rights come above everything. With reference to cultural life, these rights appear as liberties; in the state as equal democratic participation rights; and with reference to the economy they arise as social rights.

III

Martin Large: **Can one work out a common core in the various objections?**

Christoph Strawe: Again and again the motive of distrust in the free human being comes to light. In political elites of different provenances, the view that people are not ripe for comprehensive freedom and self-administration is widespread. This seems to me to be a key main argument, explicitly or implicitly, against threefolding. According to this view, humans need guardians who have to protect them and thus boss them around. However, there are great differences concerning the extent of domination. It extends from the stark totalitarianism of North Korea, across dictatorships and plutocracies and authoritarian forms of government, to countries in which freedom, equality and social rights are respected to a limited extent.

Tutelage has already begun where democracy is reduced merely to the majority principle. Individual initiative is then slowed down, prevented or even repressed. In many areas, of course, majority judgement is needed – what would happen if everyone were to decide individually whether he or she drives on the left or the right? This does not apply, however, where today individual abilities have to be introduced into the social life so that it can thrive. Human rights also protect the individual against the state and against majorities! Certainly there must be protective rights, but they must not lead to the emergence of a 'nanny state' in which a bureaucracy which suffers from addiction to regulation wants to protect the people from themselves. And it should not be forgotten that many of these protective rights only alleviate symptoms that result from fundamentally unresolved questions concerning property rights.

Human rights protect activity stemming from individual insights, and the possibility of coming together based on such insights into common actions and the building of task-oriented responsibility communities. We must have a general regulation for left-hand driving and right-hand driving. But in a pluralist society we do not need uniform state schooling for everyone. First, both in the UN General Declaration of Human Rights as well in the European Union Charter of Fundamental Rights, it is stated *mutatis mutandis* that parents should be able to choose the school for their children according to their pedagogical, philosophical and religious convictions. Accordingly, it would have to follow from this that education must be free: i.e. a free choice of school and freedom of teaching, with state schools not as a regular school but as an offer, (see Chapter 14) especially where there are not sufficient schools managed by teachers and parents. Who could be more competent than teachers and parents to do this?

In fact, in schools the state is not responsible for the control of the contents of pedagogy, but for the legal system, peace and security, for the safeguarding of fundamental rights, which is its genuine task. At all events, there is a transitional area where the state *should* arguably have a say in terms of competences such as reading and writing, without which a person cannot be equal amongst equals in the legal community. He or she must not therefore be deprived of these competencies. We are speaking at this point about knowledge transfer as such, not its method. State supervision under these conditions would be no problem at all. The state has to enforce fundamental rights – and the right to education is a fundamental right. In order to ensure this, the state must ensure that parents' lack of money cannot hinder them in exercising this right. It is therefore a task of the state to ensure public funding. This can happen in different ways, but always in a way that does not restrain the freedom of education. An education voucher (or school voucher) can be one way, as long as it is designed correctly.

As early as 1919, Steiner proposed an educational income (by which he meant that parents would receive an additional income for paying the school they choose) which was to be regulated by the co-operation of the economy, the cultural life and the state. In most countries, an equal right to education is not yet fully guaranteed, with differing levels of implementation. This same right also implies for everyone the choice of school, including being able to choose a free school. Free schools make their contribution to the realization of the right to education. They are therefore public schools in free administration, as long as they are not profit making. In Germany they are still referred to as private and substitute schools, but as early as 1987 the Constitutional Court ruled that for the goal of equality, free schools have to be financed by the state, but not at the same level as the state schools. This is also discriminatory for the parents, who have to pay the rest, but in other countries free schools are discriminated against to a far greater extent.

When talking with Social Democrats or Christian Democrats in Germany, the objection is often made that free schools are an enrichment of the educational landscape, but they are not a model for education as a whole. This could only be done with particularly committed parents, such as Waldorf parents, but most parents would be unable to choose such a school themselves. This can be seen as a self-fulfilling prophecy: i.e. how to develop interest and commitment if you're not faced with the choice?

Martin Large: Does this view of the human being also exist in the economy?

Christoph Strawe: It turns out that many objections are based on fundamental anthropological ideas. Let's look at the concept of 'homo economicus', which maintains that rational self-interest is the decisive motive of people, at least in economic life. That man is both a social and an anti-social being is misunderstood. The father of the modern economy, Adam Smith, assumed the balancing mechanisms of the market to be invisible to people, which should then ultimately transform self-interest into common welfare. Smith called this the 'invisible hand' of the market. From this, the demand for more 'laissez faire' arises regarding the relationship between state and economy. Thomas Hobbes, on the contrary, argued that only an authoritarian state can channel and tame the struggle of all against all.

Economic liberalism has an ambiguous approach to freedom. It advocates free enterprise , yet the law of competition is no less coercive than is subordination to a custodial state. We live in a world in which the division of labour objectively leads us to working for each other. But we still think in categories of self-sufficiency. Economic liberalism therefore denies people's ability to shape economic life in a holistic and conscious way. The invisible hand thus saves the economic actors from having to develop their social skills. The message is: 'you are not duty-bound to change yourself, your only duty is to follow your self-interest and to avoid violating the rules of competition'. An economy based on the co-operation of production, circulation and consumption in 'associations', as it is envisaged by threefolding, is of course a case for the anti-competition office. Since agreements between groups in the economy can only be conceived of as a bundling of self-interest to fleece a third party, agreements are also being pursued which are aimed at balancing interests and co-operating for the good of all sides involved.

Martin Large: **What methodological aspects do you consider essential for responding to questions and objections?**

Christoph Strawe: I would always try to relate threefolding ideas to the position of the respective conversation partner, so that he or she feels that you're interested in his thoughts and sentiments. And it makes sense to present threefolding as something alive, as a way of understanding and shaping social processes, as a contribution to the struggle for social progress in our time.

I remember a public discussion with two representatives of the International Forum on Globalization on threefolding and the Forum's alternatives to the dominant form of globalization. During the preliminary talk there was at first a certain reserve, with one of the speakers saying: 'We have a programme of our own'. The ice thawed when a colleague and me explained what results come up when this programme is seen in the light of threefolding, how threefolding can help to justify and develop this programme. On the other hand, the threefolding activist can learn a lot by studying and understanding the notions of dialoguing partners (cf. Chapter 16, this volume).

Threefolding deals with all the topics of the left, liberal, conservative, ecological and green discourses. It has something to say about the liberals' theme of freedom, the equality theme of all democrats, the topic of solidarity and social justice of the socialists and social democrats, and the genuinely green theme of sustainability, which is at the same time a theme of the preservation of the natural heritage and thus a 'conservative' theme.

Threefolding deals with all these themes, not in the form of a programme but in the sense of describing a social organism in which the role of these topics is to be correctly located: i.e. freedom questions are crucial in the sphere of culture, equality questions in the legal sphere, and fraternity issues in the economic sphere. An intrinsically correct guiding principle that is applied in the wrong social 'place' has a socially negative – and in an extreme case a destructive – effect. Under modern conditions, social subsystems must be relatively independent but at the same time live together and co-operate with each other. They are not parts, but members of the social whole, that therefore forms an organism and not a mechanism.

Threefolding is not a programme that could be codified. It is not a sample of notions which say how everything should be organized socially. Rather, the structures are researched and described that enable people to regulate their social affairs themselves, to shape their social life themselves. The muddling of politics, economics and culture cements in place vertical power structures that are no longer appropriate today, and which hinder self-organization. Threefolding is intended to create structures that make it possible to look for solutions to social problems in new and appropriate dialogical forms. It is therefore not a universal solution which is to be superimposed on reality.

It was logical, therefore, that the union for social threefolding founded in 1919 was open to all those who wanted to engage in the unbundling of power structures, independent of political party, and ideological or philosophical orientation. Threefolding can make it possible to overcome the logic of a narrow standpoint. If one thinks of the idea of human rights or the idea of subsidiarity, one ends not very far from threefolding, and ultimately the impulses converge.

Threefolding is not an ideology: it takes effect in the context of the facts, as Steiner once said. Individualization and globalization are developments that are taking place before our eyes. They do not leave the state untouched, which is less and less able to act in the traditional way, and must therefore find a new role. The social impulses of human beings demand a new form. Many institutions in social life are no longer contemporary. Where a kind of social instinct had previously existed, the social questions must now be more and more penetrated with consciousness; otherwise, chaos will arise – as Rudolf Steiner had already declared in his appeal for threefolding in 1919. Conscious shaping is therefore the order of the day, and the facts alone are not sufficient. Steiner also says that it is precisely the problem that one is to orient oneself too much to facts, instead of modifying the facts in the sense of the guiding social 'ideals'. The social organism requires its threefolding in actuality, but necessary organs cannot be formed without consciousness. They work in the wrong place, as if one were thinking with the lungs or digesting with the head, or they are completely missing. For example: we have no organs in the economic sphere, where questions of fair and balanced pricing can be handled in a practical way.

Martin Large: **Sometimes it seems that people who support social threefolding lean towards the political left. But should three-folders not be beyond left and right? Steiner was critical of both sides in his time. In the USA, from a threefolding perspective arguably, neither left nor right necessarily seems better.**

For example, the left politician Bernie Sanders' track record suggests that had he been elected he might have helped advance an economic life that is co-operative yet outside the state, thus aiding social threefolding. But on education he – and the Democrats too – wanted for the most part only to support state-run schooling, and were generally not as active as Republicans were on behalf of expanding educational freedom. Thus, in the USA at least, neither the left nor the right today lines up that well with social threefolding. What are your thoughts about this?

Christoph Strawe: We've already started to discuss schools – so I can start there. I share your observations. As far as Sanders is concerned, one can see clearly how the lack of threefold differentiation distorts judgements. The idea of fraternity is present, but it's not clear where the place for its realization resides. Compare, for example, Ron Paul, also a critical spirit, leading thinker of the libertarian wing of the Tea Party Movement. For Paul, everything is to be located within a concept of freedom, but one that is not balanced with solidarity and equality. So there is no public funding of schools, healthcare and so on, and Obama-Care is viewed as being 'from the devil'. On the other hand, the funding of schools by the state causes the misconception that the latter, so to speak, buys a right to dictate the content of children's education (cf. Chapter 14). Funding by the state, however, means to make something accessible for everybody, regardless of his or her financial situation.

If you are confronted with a specific social-design problem, it is a great methodological aid to ask which 'axial principle' is at the forefront, and how freedom and fraternity should be balanced on the basis of legal equality. The latter forms a middle, a heart, not a centre, but a mediating and process-enhancing one. For example, for the health system we have to ask how the therapeutic freedom and discretion of the medical doctor has to be balanced with the safeguarding of equal access to health services and what follows from there, and from the demand for solidarity for the form of financing.

Another example of the fertility of the threefold system as a methodological approach is the question of 'factors of production markets'. Labour, land and capital are the three factors that must interact in the production of economic goods and services. In the dominant neoliberal theory, however, they not only enable the production of commodities, but are themselves commodities which are traded on the land, labour and capital markets. In this way elements of the cultural sphere and the rights sphere are controlled by the economic sphere. In the latter therefore exist 'pseudo markets' (cf. Udo Herrmannstorfer) which create social dislocations.

Martin Large: **What helps and hinders the understanding of social threefolding both in theory and in practice at this time of 'conjunctional crisis' (Cf. ongoing financial crisis, global warming, war on terror and blowback, rising inequality, refugees etc.)?**

Christoph Strawe: The understanding of the social requires a more agile and lively way of thinking than in the natural sciences: we don't confront the object of observation, but are conscious participants who co-create social reality. Our ideas, our way of thinking becomes part of social reality. Conceptual and self-reflective work is, therefore, essential. We have to try from the beginning to build social judgements in associative working. A lack of social understanding and social feeling is a serious hindrance, as it is in practical crisis management.

The methodical approach of threefolding can help to obtain a deeper understanding of the causes of the problems. The financial crisis has to do with the fact that money is treated as a commodity, rather than as a commons. The crisis in the Middle East is connected with the primacy of the self-determination right of nations, and the subordination of individual human rights to this right of nations. The situation in Syria shows that we are still far from transforming state policy into humanity-centred policy-making. Growing social inequality has to do with the continuing coupling of labour and income, the latter with the pseudo-market economy concept. And the impact of society on global warming has to do with economic-growth fetishism, with how we think about nature, and with the imperfections of blunt legal instruments due to the selfish interests of countries like the USA.

Schools have an important task for developing empathy, social understanding and initiative. The Waldorf schools could play a pioneering role: after all, Waldorf education is a child of the threefolding movement itself. Many indications and suggestions for the Waldorf 'curriculum' from the founding period have still hardly been implemented, let alone developed.

It is helpful that there are people who create and develop institutions in the 'meso-social', organizational sphere, which prefigure another world and thus create trust in the fact that this world is possible. A company like SEKEM (see Chapter 10, this volume) produces immediate services for its customers and co-workers, but it also radiates something that changes the very atmosphere of society.

The barriers to understanding and practice seem, on the one hand, to be hidden fear; and on the other hand, they are linked to the 'shadow' of power obsession, profit, greed and intolerance. This is the fear that many people develop of their own responsibility. It is a lack of a deeper understanding of freedom that has to do with the prevailing image of human beings, as stated earlier.

IV

Martin Large: **I would like to add a few more specific questions, which focus on the role of economics: A possible objection might be that setting limits to corporate freedom will reduce profits, productivity, wages and customer service. To what extent might this be a valid objection?**

Christoph Strawe: Well, I would first like to question the term 'corporate freedom'. The freedom to buy and sell companies for the profit of shareholders is something different than entrepreneurial free disposition to use the capital entrusted to him or her for the benefit of all stakeholders – above all for consumers, and also for society. The latter is a common interest. 'A common social economy' is to be striven for; and this also leads, as already mentioned, to a distinction between legitimate private ownership of objects of personal use and the ownership of enterprises 'on a trusteeship basis'.

A second remark concerns the category of 'profit'. Profit is not an end in itself: it should be a means, a real benefit for real people. Profit as such is not in itself a problem, but rather that it sticks to the capital, as on a glue rod. Those who provide the capital own all earnings. The surplus is not regarded as something which has to be shared or given away partially for donations, e.g. for the cultural life. The income of the co-workers doesn't appear as a fair share, but as a cost factor. The workers themselves are not treated as co-entrepreneurs but as 'employees'.

A legitimate objection might be made to the bureaucratic over-regulation of companies that hinders the self-shaping of the economy. In this way, the consequences mentioned in the question would certainly occur. It is also true that to abolish the market would lead to prices which are no longer a benchmark. However, both notions have nothing to do with a properly understood associative economy.

The associative economy is not intended to abolish markets, but rather to arrange them, via their observation by representatives of economic partners including consumers, with agreements geared towards eliminating or preventing erroneous developments. Such consultations and agreements can be centred upon a part or, better, the whole of an industry or economic region – and ultimately on the whole of the global economy. The individual business view is then not the final one, even if it remains important. An associative economy is an economy of unsentimentally understood fraternity. It is thus somewhere between a planned and a market economy. A command economy destroys the price structure, and the market economy refuses interventions in price formation. In the associative economy, self-governing bodies would be analysing the markets and agreeing on measures that should lead to price improvements.

Thus, associations are contracting bodies; and contracts create a right freely agreed by the parties. How much competition and how much co-operation obtains is a matter of contract design. Attempts to allow only competitive relations to exist between the business partners are, in effect, a serious interference with the freedom to contract. The state would merely have to ensure that no contractual agreements are made at the expense of third parties. This is the only way to get a cartel law which is conformable with the freedom of contract.

***Martin Large:* A further question about the economy: Is brotherhood as a guiding principle in economic life weak compared with the so-called**

'invisible (guiding) hand' of self-interest and greed? Is market competition between people for jobs, companies for profit, and between investors the main engine driving the economy?

Christoph Strawe: If associations were confined to the mere observation of economic activity, they would be too weak to carry out fraternity. And as I said previously, one must not underestimate the market; indeed, it is in some respects very efficient, but unfortunately it is also very 'custodial'. One can say that the market plays the role of a last instance against which no objection is possible. It is not only greed that is so powerful, but also the fear of ruin through competition.

However, I strongly dispute that competition is the real driving force behind the economy. The economy arises through people having human needs that can only be satisfied by the economy. It is the pull of human needs that activates the economy. Under the conditions of the division of labour, we can only satisfy needs when we work for each other. It is only our thinking and social institutions that have not kept pace with this development. We are still thinking in categories of self-sufficiency.

Antisocial and social impulses live in human beings. To deny or destroy the former would make no sense. The worst feature of the market fundamentalist idea is that it emphasizes antisocial impulses. Egoism is rewarded, and selflessness is ridiculed. The associative economy does not presuppose perfect people; it is only through its dialogical principle that it is possible to grasp the interests of the one in those of the other, and to initiate a self-correction of egoism.

Martin Large: **Steiner's threefolding ideas pre-date the modern welfare state, and seem to argue for a 'small state'. How can people get the rights and protections they need from corporate power if not through a strong state?**

Christoph Strawe: Wilhelm von Humboldt wrote that there is no freedom without security. From the viewpoint of threefolding, ensuring internal and external security and the fundamental rights of the people is also the task of the state.

I think the alternative 'weak state' or 'strong state' is too simple. On the contrary, we must ask where the state of today is too strong, and where it is too weak. What is the appropriate level of state activity and intervention in certain social problems? And here one has to say in general that in relation to the cultural sphere, the state is still much too powerful today; and against the economy the state is too weak. In its own sphere, the state should be more democratic and more oriented to human rights.

One might counter that in relation to the economy, there is still too much micro regulation. Such a view is not completely wrong, but it doesn't apply to the 'big issues' like property rights. These issues are the field where the excesses of regulation are often a consequence of the under-developed self-management of the economy. The democratic state will not disappear in the future, but it will have to play a decisive role when it comes to questions of the economy's limits: property law, environmental law, and so on. The image of the state that emerges from threefolding is not that of the 'night-watchman state'. According to Steiner, the economy has to accept the laws agreed in legal/political life, just as agriculture has to accept the weather. However, the extent to which the state has to deal with the economy will probably diminish, as kinds of 'solidarity economy' develop.

The democratic state is responsible for protecting and safeguarding fundamental and human rights. This includes the guarantee of access to education, medical care, to water and many other phenomena. This is about public goods – the so-called 'commons'. However, the fact that the state has to guarantee their existence and access to them doesn't mean that the state is also responsible for their delivery. Increasingly, forms of social organizations will have to emerge which are active in these areas on the basis of a public contract, but which are not part of the state, but rather are situated between economic life and the state, and cultural life and state. The public sector cannot be surrendered to commerce; but it is also not, as a whole, part of the state, and is not subordinated to the state's sovereign power.

V

Martin Large: I have a final question, Christoph. Are there any successful examples of social threefolding in human history?

Christoph Strawe: A few years ago I was asked to write about 'the conditions of origin and the history of the impact of the threefolding approach' for an anthology *Anthroposophy in history and presence* (Strawe, 2011). I myself was amazed at the abundance of initiatives, institutions etc. which are due to people who have worked with the concept of threefolding, e.g. initiatives which are going in new directions concerning land, or concerning the ownership of enterprises (e.g. through transferring them into foundations). There we find social banking initiatives and a movement for regional money, self-governing schools, hospitals and therapeutic institutions, which have been created and run with the help of people from the threefolding movement.

The movement for more direct democracy, the basic income movement and the environmental movement are inconceivable without the participation of exponents of threefolding. Threefolding followers have made concrete proposals for European constitutional development and for social security financing, as well as theoretical and practical contributions to organizational development and quality management, and the improvement of the framework conditions for organic agriculture, for which the Demeter movement played a pioneering role.

We find threefolding motifs in the demands of the Prague Spring and those of the revolutionary movement in 1989 – and also in the movement for a more just globalization from 1999 onwards. The year 1989 was a matter of the overcoming of the custodial state: democracy, a self-developing economy and the liberation of culture. In 1999, the civil society movement which opposed the attacks of finance capital on democracy and diversity of culture was launched. The more conscious these motifs become, the sooner that basic social transformations will become possible.

In addition, the threefolding movement has hitherto only existed for its first 100 years. Seen in historical context, this is a short time. In the future, it will hopefully play an increasingly important role in the struggle for a society with a human face.

References

Herrmannstorfer, U. (1997) *Scheinmarktwirtschaft. Arbeit, Boden, Kapital und die Globalisierung der Wirtschaft* [Pseudo market economy. Labour, land, capital and the globalization of the economy], Verlag Freies Geistesleben, Stuttgart. (English translation at: goo.gl/RBrrJh.)

Laloux, F. (2014) *Reinventing organizations: A guide to creating organizations inspired by the next stage in human consciousness*, Nelson Parker, Brussels.

Perlas, N. (2003) *Shaping globalization: Civil society, cultural power and threefolding*, New Society Publishers, Gabriola Island, BC, Canada.

Ray, P.H. and Anderson, S.R. (2000) *The cultural creatives: How 50 million people are changing the world*, Three Rivers Press, New York.

Strawe, C. (1986) *Marxismus und Anthroposophie* [Marxism and anthroposophy], Klett-Cotta, Stuttgart (2002 edn).

Strawe, C. (2011) 'Sozialimpulse…' [Social impulses], in R. Uhlenhoff (ed.), *Anthroposophie in Geschichte und Gegenwart Gebundene, Ausgabe* [Anthroposophy in history and presence] (pp. 649–704), Berliner Wissenschafts-Verlag, Stuttgart.

CONCLUSION

Telling a New Free, Equal, Mutual and Earth-caring Story
Martin Large

Rudolf Steiner introduced societal threefolding in 1917 at a time when imperial war-torn Europe was falling apart with nationalism, Fascism and Bolshevism. Steiner first tried a 'top-down' approach, when he was invited to engage with senior figures in the German and Austrian governments. He then became an activist, but the threefold social order movement failed to take root. One cause of failure was the error of seeing societal threefolding as a utopia or as an ideology, rather than as a way of understanding the profoundly different dynamics of culture, politics and economics, of the plural, public and private sectors – and how these interact. Another cause of failure was people taking Steiner's ideas as 'gospel' – as a blueprint to be implemented, rather than as developmental principles for a healthy society. Many also did not locate his ideas as a part of the whole ferment of progressive thinking at that time. Lastly, the language of Steiner's original social and economic thinking is now hard to grasp. However, as the contributions to this book show, people who draw on these ideas have both been able to rethink them and develop innovative solutions for current burning questions, even in unusual places.

SEKEM in Egypt is a fascinating example of social threefolding in practice, which is recognized by the United Nations as a global sustainability exemplar, and by a 2003 'alternative Nobel' Right Livelihood Award. Here are biodynamic farms that have greened the desert, social businesses that create jobs and wealth for then investing in creative education, a technical college and a university, as well as cultural and health facilities. SEKEM is about creating a more peaceful, creative, sustainable world. When, as a student, Dr Ibrahim Abouleish, the SEKEM founder, was invited with other students to meet President Nasser, they were asked what to do about Israel. Instead of agreeing that the Israelis be pushed into the sea like many other students there, he said that war was not the answer but, rather, both sides should find common ground in investing in education and farming, and in building peace.

Tackling what economist Joseph Stiglitz calls 'market fundamentalism' is a burning challenge. This pernicious ideological narrative fails to grasp how good business actually works. Most businesses are based on mutuality and good working relationships rather than the dog-eat-dog world of Social Darwinism. Take the story of a new US head of Honda Purchasing. He was carpeted by head office in Japan for allowing a long-standing but obscure small-parts supplier to go bust. He was told that Honda values its business partners, and it was his job to enable partners to be successful, as these were 'shared destiny' relationships. Or take the story of community-supported agriculture (CSA) where consumers partner with farmers and commit to not just buying a monthly food share, but to supporting the farmers for the whole year, once the budget and farm plan have been agreed.

Robert Karp, director of the US Biodynamic Association, develops this associative, fraternal thinking in his chapter on the 'New American Revolution: Associative Economics and the Future of the Food Movement'. This builds a food supply chain that works fairly for consumers, distributors and farmers in a regenerative, circular economy. New co-op digital sharing platforms have helped make this possible, as have apps which tell consumers about a product's provenance, so they can make more ethical and ecological choices.

The ongoing financial and banking crisis is another burning question, inviting the reinvention of money and banking for enabling a better world, rather than the extractive bankocracy that currently dominates. Glen Saunders, a former CEO of Triodos Bank, in his 'Threefold Money' chapter, develops Steiner's creative ideas about the dynamics of gift, loan and purchase money. He shows how ethical, sustainable banking can work with a growing network of exemplar social banks. One of the key ideas is of directed investment, so that savers can specify what kinds of enterprises they want to invest in, such as renewable energy, co-op housing, microfinance, education and social business. We can forget that banking and capitalism were originally underpinned by moral values, and banks like Triodos or the German GLS bank are showing how to reinvent social banking for a better world.

Hope in the Dark: Telling Stories for a More Mutual, Free, Sustainable and Equal World

Signs of hope for a better world are emerging everywhere, despite Brexit, Trump, the relentless marketizing of our way of life, the often-negative mass media lens on the world, and the old order crumbling. Who, back in the early 1980s, would have imagined Nelson Mandela being released from prison, or the Berlin Wall coming down? As Rebecca Solnit writes, 'there is hope in the dark', with far more positive changes happening than we recognize in the face of media gloom. The neoliberal market state is a bit like an asphalt road cracking up. The more it cracks up, the more green shoots grow, pre-figuring the emerging social future. 'There is a crack in everything, that's how the light gets in.'[1]

Whether it is people running social businesses, social initiatives, environmental activists, politicians like London mayor Sadiq Khan standing up to Uber by supporting the regulator Transport for London's red light, cultural initiatives, or the greening of New York by guerrilla gardeners, it can be hard to keep up with the green shoots. Learning from and encouraging these is what Otto Scharmer of the Massachusetts Institute of Technology and the Presencing Institute calls 'leading from the social future as it emerges'. So, we need to start telling new inspiring stories that can help recognize, understand and support the green shoots of the emerging social future, joining the dots of an emerging 'common wealth' society.

We live by stories: they explain who we are and our values, and how we live. The social democratic story tells how the 1930s Great Depression resulted from the greed of a gilded elite which had captured the state and business for private gain. People – by joining together to secure common interests such as health, good public services, rights and fair incomes – limited the owning class's power and restored order, prosperity and security for all through a paternalistic state. But then, the 'neoliberal market' story tells how the world fell into crisis caused by social democratic state despotism, which allegedly crushed initiative, freedom and enterprise by means of state planning, regulation and control. Think of Ronald Reagan saying that 'The most terrifying words in the English language are: "I'm from the government and I'm here to help"'. Hero entrepreneurs are supposed to activate the free market through privatization and deregulation and free us from the over-mighty state. This results in the trickle down of more wealth and opportunity for everyone, delivered by the invisible hand of self-interest. 'Greed is good', says Gordon Gecko.

These are both 'restoration stories'. The land fares ill. It is 'always Winter and never Christmas', as with both the Narnia and the Austerity stories. The heroes rebel, fight against great odds and restore order, prosperity and peace. But currently, there is no story to replace the neoliberal story. 'TINA' – there is no alternative, as Mrs Thatcher bleakly said. Yet another world *is* possible – but what world is that? As a young friend despairingly asked, 'Is the market all there is to life?'.

So, the two unbalanced social democratic and neoliberal narratives, with their crude, one-legged solutions of 'more state' or 'more market', need balancing with the plural, creative civil society story. We need inspiring, guiding stories that offer a better future, and as ways of answering current burning questions. Social renewal depends on finding a new narrative, telling new stories. These need to be simple, vivid, profound, encourage inquiry, lead to action, draw on deeply held human values, and be both grounded and offer desirable futures.

My own personal quest for a new, alternative societal narrative first surfaced in the 1990s when working with peace-building teams in civil war-torn former Yugoslavia. They asked me their burning question, 'So what is the alternative to communism and capitalism?'.

It took a while to realise that the answer to this question had already been offered to colleagues and myself by many organizations, companies and communities with whom we had been working to help co-create their future. We noticed that when people plan for their future, the next chapter in their organization's story, they often distilled four or five 'how' questions. First, they scan what's happening in the world at large, and in their organizational context, with the question, 'What's happening in the world that strikes you as significant?'. Then, they crystallize what they see happening into three or four questions to consider when planning for the future. These are the 'seed questions' that groups often come up with:

- How are we developing a regenerative, circular, mutual economy that works for all?
- How are we caring for the earth?
- How are we engaging politically for human rights, a more participative democracy, social justice, social inclusion, equity and peace?
- How are we enabling a creative, dynamic cultural life (e.g. education, health, media, arts, science) where every person can develop and maintain their whole human potential, so that they can freely contribute?

When reflecting on these questions, people come alive when they connect with the guiding ideal or principle informing each question: mutuality, or the old word 'fraternity', for the economy; equality; and for the political (rights) life, freedom for cultural life and sustainability for planet earth care. Such reflections then lead to people sharing personal stories where they experienced the guiding inspiration of these four ideals at work, so these are embedded rather than just 'empty phrases'.

The four seed questions help to focus Steiner's societal threefolding process into action-research questions with which we can work practically. We can choose to reformulate one of the questions, and then answer the question in our own way, in our own context. These questions need not be off-putting or Olympian, for example the earthcare question can be answered in all kinds of small ways, such as using a refillable water bottle rather than plastic throwaways. So, instead of feeling powerless and confused, we can take constructive action, one challenge at a time.

These four seed questions are also embedded in our progressive political movements. These movements and political parties may focus on one seed question and ideal more than the others, although all are important strands. Typically but not exclusively, liberals are passionate about individual cultural freedom, greens about the environment, labour about co-operation, social justice and mutuality, and conservatives about respect for tradition, heritage, law and human rights.

The four questions lead to stories that, taken together, weave an emerging societal narrative. For example, some Swedes see their country's future as a 'green folkhemhet' – a green people's home – to succeed the social democratic, folkhemhet narrative. There are many good stories that illustrates this vision, such as green Kristianstad, an aspiring healthy city developing a regenerative economy and renewable energy. BERAS is a tri-sectoral, circum-Baltic partnership project with local government, biodynamic and organic farmers, universities and businesses trying to develop regenerative agriculture so as to save the Baltic.

SEKEM is a story that weaves culture, rights, economy and ecology together, with a vision for a sustainable Nile river basin economy that conserves water through regenerative agriculture. George Monbiot describes the restoration of community, participative democracy, social business, reclaiming the commons and releasing our 'extraordinary nature – our altruism, empathy and deep connection' in what he calls the new story of the 'Politics of Belonging'.[2] He argues that because we have failed, 'to replace our tired political stories with a compelling narrative of transformation and restoration', we have failed to realise the potential of what change is possible. As we rekindle our imagination, we discover our power to act. Monbiot's story is illustrated by the Burlington, Vermont journey – or indeed with all the green shoots emerging where he lives in Oxford, UK, and many other places.

Conclusion: Rebalancing Society for the Common Good and Well-being of People and Planet

Steiner's societal threefolding can be summarized thus: 'The more that freedom informs cultural life and the plural sector, the more that equality guides political life, human rights and the public sector, and the more fraternity or mutuality guides business and economic life, the more creative, socially just, democratic, healthier, prosperous and sustainable will be our society or "commonwealth"'.

Steiner's high-level advocacy of these societal guiding principles is one thing. However, some authoritative contemporary research backs them up, such as Danny Dorling's research into 'the equality effect'.[3] Kate Pickett and Richard Wilkinson's book *The spirit level* (2010)[4] shows that the more equal a society, the less there are phenomena such as unwanted teenage pregnancies, the fewer people in prison, and the more health and well-being exists across whole range of indicators. Similarly, peace and conflict researchers have found that the more a state respects and implements human rights, the less violent and the less the likelihood of that state going to war. Caroline Molloy shows there is – astonishingly – no research evidence whatsoever for the health, cost and efficiency benefits of the Labour and

Tory governments' marketization of the NHS. In fact, quite the opposite is the case: marketizing the NHS has increased costs by 14 percent overall, according to University of York (2010) research hushed up for five years by the government.[5]

The contributions in this anthology show how people have taken steps in drawing on societal threefolding ideas practically, for example with land for people and affordable homes, or social banking. However, how does one get started, and find the resilience to keep going? As our structures crumble, there is the opportunity for a bottom-up, cultural, plural sector-led transformation in consciousness and values. Some social movements, like Transition Towns in Britain, bring about learning and change through 'just doing stuff'. However, spiritual and social activists recognize that lasting systemic, structural change results from changes in consciousness, as social structures reflect our thinking, relationships and actions. Human intelligence, creativity, initiative and agency result in developing structures, which then become social habits or structures, set ways of doing things and patterns of relating. We can change these structures as we change. However, some old social structures like the theocratic 'command and control' pyramid still endure, but only with our compliance if we choose to support, say, a police *force* instead of a police *service*, for example.

To engage agency and awareness, one can start with reflecting on what is truly important in our life. What is meaningful and brings life? What are my deepest aspirations, and to what extent does my life align with my aspirations and values? Then there is the question of what keeps you awake at night, what itches, what concerns, what questions do you keep coming back to? Recall Dr Bronwyn King, the Melbourne oncologist who couldn't keep her lung cancer patients out of her mind in connection with her pension fund investing in tobacco companies. This was a wake-up call that resulted in her campaigning for hundreds of millions being divested. Such personal life inquiries can lead to what you want to do with your life, work and community. Such changes in awareness lead to personal, group, community, organizational, even societal transformation, to changes in structures in a circular reinforcing process as society changes. Just think of the cultural transformative power of the happiness, well-being and mindfulness movement, now spreading worldwide from Bhutan, and the fact that we want 'less stuff' as a result. This may increase Gross National Happiness, but decreases Gross National Product. Such social and emotional learning that can come from spiritual practices and mindfulness can help develop the compassion, care, relationships, trust and love which are central to human flourishing.

So, to conclude, imagine you have a child or grandchild: what inspiring story might you tell that you are proud about of your earth care, of restoring nature and looking after our planet? A story about bringing about a more creative world? A social regenerative business? Realising human rights? And where are the stories of working to rebalance society by restoring and respecting healthy boundaries, like getting the money out of politics, campaigning for a commercial-free childhood, and treating land as a commons? There is hope in the dark, as Rebecca Solnit writes so movingly. Preferring not to react to the challenges that beset us by becoming an alcoholic or committing suicide, I choose to remain hopeful. We live at an extraordinarily creative time of opportunities, with significant capabilities and resources with which to address the spiritual, cultural, political, environmental and economic questions coming our way.

We have it in our power to rebalance and renew our society for the common good of people and planet.

Notes and References

1. Rebecca Solnit, *Hope in the dark*, Canongate, Edinburgh, 2010.
2. George Monbiot, *Out of the wreckage: A new politics for an age of crisis*, Verso, London, 2015
3. Danny Dorling, 'The equality effect', *New Internationalist*, 19 July 2017; available at goo.gl/BuxJX5 (accessed 17 November 2017).
4. Richard Wilkinson and Kate Pickett, *The spirit level: Why more equal societies almost always do better*, Allen Lane, London, 2009.
5. Caroline Molloy, 'The billions of wasted NHS cash no-one wants to mention', 10 October 2014; see goo.gl/ppyMi3 (accessed 24 November 2017).

ABOUT THE CONTRIBUTORS

MARTIN LARGE works in organizational, social business, community and individual development as a facilitator. He has been a publisher with Hawthorn Press (Stroud) since 1981, and lectured in organizational psychology and behavioural science at Cheltenham and Gloucester College of Higher Education (1980–1997). The chair of Stroud Common Wealth Ltd, Martin has enabled community land trust, co-op and social business development since 1999. Projects include the Fordhall Farm community buy-out (2005–6), helping re-invent community shares and co-op charitable ways of holding land, setting up the Biodynamic Land Trust (2011–15). His books include *Social ecology* (1981), *Who's bringing them up?* (1981), *Futures that work*, with Robert Rehm, Nancy Cebula and Fran Ryan (2003), *Common wealth for a more equal, free, mutual and sustainable society* (2010); with Pat Conaty, *Commons sense: 21st century garden cities* (2013). *Free, Equal and Mutual* is dedicated to his wife Judith, four children and granddaughter Hedda – for a better world for all our children and grandchildren.

STEVE BRIAULT is now Director of Development at Emerson College in Sussex, UK, after 35 years in organization consulting. His early working life was in social care and refugee resettlement, and his consultancy practice has taken him to many countries and client sectors, including manufacturing and service businesses, government departments, NHS Trusts and voluntary organizations. Steve is currently Chair of Trustees at The Mount Camphill Community, and a founder of the Alliance for Camphill. At Emerson, his work includes education, and site and community development, as well as teaching on a number of programmes, especially the courses for Chinese students being run both at the College and in two cities in China. Steve is a founder member of the Association for Social Development and author of a number of books including *The mystery of meeting: Relationships as a path of discovery* and *Liquidity: flowing forms in water and money*. He lives in Forest Row, East Sussex with his family.

CHRISTINE ARLT was born in 1986 in Germany, near Cologne. After attending Waldorf School Christine studied Languages and Cultures of the Islamic World and Africa at the University of Cologne. Since school days she has worked as a freelancer for various German newspapers and magazines, with different visits abroad, for instance to Burkina Faso, Palestine and Egypt. In 2015 Christine went to Egypt to work with public relations for the SEKEM Initiative – founded in 1977 to strengthen Egypt's sustainable development by producing, processing and marketing organic and biodynamic foodstuff, textiles and phyto-pharmaceuticals. In 2017 Christine returned to Germany and now works again as freelancer for different institutions, among them the Anthroposophic Society Germany and still for SEKEM.

JOHN BLOOM is Vice President, Organizational Culture at RSF Social Finance in San Francisco (www.rsfsocialfinance.org). As part of his work at RSF he has been developing and facilitating conversations and programmes that address the intersection of money and spirit in personal and social transformation. John frequently writes for RSF's Reimagine Money blog, and has fostered collaborative dialogues on the challenging social aspects of money. As part of his work he has helped develop awareness of issues of land and biodynamic agriculture across the USA. In October 2016 John was appointed as General Secretary of the Anthroposophical Society in America. He has written two books, *The genius of money*, and *Inhabiting interdependence*, both published by SteinerBooks. He lives in San Francisco.

GERALD HÄFNER helped found Democracy International as a registered association in June 2011, and he also established Democracy International's partner organization Mehr Demokratie e.V. (Germany). He was a Member of the German Parliament for ten years and served as Chairman and CEO of the Green Party in Bavaria. Gerald is the co-founder of several foundations, including the 'Bundesstiftung zur Aufarbeitung der SED-Diktatur' and 'Petra-Kelly-Stiftung'. He was a Member of the European Parliament between 2009 and 2014, and now works for the Social Science Section of the Anthroposophical Society.

RICHARD HOUSE, Ph.D. is a Stroud-based chartered psychologist, a former senior university lecturer in psychotherapy and education (Roehampton and Winchester respectively) and a trained Steiner Waldorf Class and Kindergarten teacher who helped to found the new Norwich Steiner School. A graduate of the London Waldorf Teacher Training Seminar and a trustee of the London Waldorf Trust, Richard has been writing critically on education for several decades. His many books include *Childhood, well-being and a therapeutic ethos* (co-ed. Del Loewenthal, Karnac, 2009), and *Too much, too soon? Early learning and the erosion of childhood* (Hawthorn Press, 2011). Correspondence: richardahouse@hotmail.com

ROBERT KARP is a long-time leader and social entrepreneur in the food movement in the United States. Robert is the former executive director of Practical Farmers of Iowa and the Biodynamic Association in North America, and founder of New Spirit Farmland Partnerships, which helps organic and other conservation-minded farmers gain long-term access to farmland by linking them with social investors. You can learn more about Robert's work and find his other writings on his website at www.robertkarp.net.

NICANOR PERLAS is an author, consultant and global resource speaker on integral sustainable development, the new and more spiritual sciences, artificial intelligence, societal threefolding and self-mastery. He has been a plenary speaker on a diverse range of topics in over 100 global conferences and 130 national conferences in the Philippines. He has advised UN agencies, government departments, local chief executives, social enterprises and large businesses. He headed several global and national civil society networks, educating citizens worldwide on their inherent power to create a better world. He has written over 500 articles, monographs, and books including *Shaping Globalization: Civil Society, Cultural Power and Threefolding*, which is an international bestseller translated into 9 languages. Perlas was a presidential candidate of the Philippines in 2010 and worked as Undersecretary (Deputy Minister) for the Department of Environment and Natural Resources of the country in 2016. He is currently writing three books on artificial intelligence and its implications for the future of humanity. For the national and global impact of his work, he has been awarded the Outstanding Filipino Award (TOFIL), UNEP'S Global 500 Award and the Right Livelihood Award (Alternative Nobel Prize).

Glen Saunders is an investment banker, company director and chairman with extensive experience in banking, investment, financial and strategic planning. A main board director of the Dutch Triodos Bank until 2001, he has served as a director of numerous other financial social investment initiatives, including the Western Partnership for Sustainable Development and the Local Investment Fund. Glen also served as a director of the New Zealand Superannuation Fund, chairing its responsible investment committee. Currently a director of a number of companies and trusts emphasizing responsible investment, Glen has a long interest in how to put Rudolf Steiner's social and economic ideas to practical use. He is currently working with Triodos on the bank's history.

Christopher Schaefer has taught at Tufts University, the Massachusetts Institute of Technology and at Emerson and Sunbridge Colleges. He has been a teacher, organization development consultant and social activist since the mid-1970s and a co-founder of the Waldorf School in Lexington, the Center for Social Development at Emerson College (England) and of Social Ecology Associates, an international consultancy group. He is the co-author of *Vision in action: Working with soul and spirit in small organizations* (Steiner Press), and the author of *Partnerships of hope: Building Waldorf school communities*, (AWSNA, 2013). Christopher lives in the Berkshires, Massachusetts with his wife Signe, and has two grown children, two grandchildren and two great grandchildren.

Andrew Scott is the Great Britain co-ordinator for the Social Sciences section of the School of Spiritual Science within the Anthroposophical Society. His professional specialization is whole-organization development, including the strategic application of information and communication technologies. Andrew is a co-owner of and practitioner within two businesses, and serves as a Trustee in several cultural institutions, including as Chair of Trustees of a Steiner Waldorf School. He holds an MBA (Technology Management), is a member of the Association for Social Development and a Fellow of the Royal Society of Arts. Andrew is married with three grown-up children and lives in Lewes, East Sussex.

PROFESSOR DR CHRISTOPH STRAWE was born in Bonn in 1948. He studied Philosophy and Social Sciences, with involvement in the student movement and a dissertation and habilitation treatise on Marxism and Anthroposophy. Employed in a publishing house and an Anti-Nazi-organization, he studied Waldorfpedagogics and lectured at Stuttgart Free University. In 1989 he founded 'Initiative Netzwerk Dreigliederung', a network for social threefolding, and became editor of the quarterly journal *Sozialimpulse* (Social Impulses). Since 1991 Christoph has been secretary of the Institut für soziale Gegenwartsfragen (Institute for Social Present-Day Questions) in Stuttgart, in which context he organizes seminars and colloquia. He is the author of numerous articles and books; see www.sozialimpulse.de and www.threefolding.net.

EDWARD UDELL is originally from New York City. He has worked as a Waldorf high-school teacher and at the Fellowship Community in Chestnut Ridge, NY. He has an MS in Waldorf Education and an MA in history, and recently completed an English translation of an important work on social threefolding, Albert Schmelzer's *Die Dreigliederungsbewegung 1919*. The translation, *The Threefolding Movement, 1919: A history*, has been published by Rudolf Steiner Press.

INDEX

A
Abouleish, Dr Ibrahim, 143, 149–50, 250–1
Abrams, Jerimiah, 118
academies programme (UK), 107, 194–210
   Bright Tribe Multi-Academy Trust, 200
   lack of oversight on the, 201
   Wakefield City Academies Trust, 202
advertising, 63
afterimage, 71
Aftershock (Reich), 187
aid: *see* international aid
Ailes, Roger, 122
Alphabet (company), 215, 220n
Althusser, Louis, 195
altruism, 161–2
   in the food movement, 159–60
America: see United States
American Civil Liberties Union, 122
Amnesty International, 230
Anderson, Ray, 114
Anderson, Ruth, 236
Anderson, Sherry, 159
Anthropocene Age, 109
anthroposophy, 143, 150
   anthroposophical social science, 236
   and Marxism, 238–9
Anthroposophy in history and presence (Strawe), 248
antipathy, 30, 223–4, 229, 232
anti-social forces, 30, 49–50
Antonopoulos, Anton, 42
Appeal to the German People… (Steiner), 82
Apple, 6
Arab Spring, 190
Arendt, Hannah, 57n
Arlt, Christine, 18, 139–62, 259
Arnold, John, 200
art, 148
Art of Goethean conversation, The (Spock), 225
artificial intelligence
   artificial super intelligence (ASI), 6,9
   negative effects of, 6
assets
   concentration of, 36
   see also inequality
associative collaboration, 31, 245
   economy, 90–2 *passim*, 242
   voluntary associations, 109
   see also associative economics
associative economics, 153–67 *passim*, 229, 239, 246, 247
   associative trade, 158–9
   see also associative collaborations
ATOS Pharma, 145
audit (and accountability) culture, 195–6, 199
austerity, 252

B
Baden, Prince/Chancellor Max von, 80–2, 86
BALLE Business for a Local Living Economy, 110
banking, 41
   exploiting housing, 170
   reinvention of, 251
   see also bankocracy, banks, sub-prime mortgage scam
bankocracy, 100, 251
banks
   Goldman Sachs, 102
   social, 218, 251
   Wells Fargo Bank, 118
   see also banking, bankocracy, GLS, Triodos
Bannon, Steve, 130
baseline assessment (England), 206
Basic Guaranteed Income: *see* Guaranteed Basic Income
basic income: *see* Guaranteed Basic Income
Basic Sociological Law (Steiner), 28, 53, 239
   see also Fundamental Sociological Law
Battle of the Marne, 83–4
Battle of Seattle (1999), 15
Bayawan City, 7
'Beauty and the Beast' film, 118
behaviourism, 35
Beck, Martha, 52
Beck, Walter, 75
BERAS, 254
Berger, Peter, 57n
Berlin Wall, 252
Berman, Shelley, 227
Berry, Wendell, 154

Bhat, Bhaskar, 112
Bhave, Vinova, 175
'Big Short Film, The', 170–1
biodynamic agriculture/farming, 143–5
   Egyptian Association, 144
   Steiner on, 177
Biodynamic Association (US), 164, 251
Biodynamic Land Trust, 179
Bitter Lake Conference (1946), 37
'Bitter Lake' film (Curtis), 37
Blair, Tony, 12, 13, 197
Blessed unrest (Hawken), 109, 125
Blockchain, 41
Bloom, John, 17, 67–74, 259
Bohm, David, 225–6
boom-and-bust financial markets, 218
Boos, Roman, 82
boundaries
   between consciousness states, 223
   respecting, 33, 102–4, 255–6
   unhealthy crossing of, 104–8
Bourneville Village Trust, 175
Bowles, Samuel, 195
Brandeis, Louis, 182
Brescacin, Fabio, 62
Brexit referendum (UK), 12, 109, 179
Briault, Steve, 12–20, 23–33, 59–66, 223–34, 258
Bright Tribe Multi-Academy Trust, 200
British Home Stores, 201–2
brotherhood, 135
Brühl, Dieter, 219n
built environment, 37
Burlington (Vermont), 176, 254
   Mayor Peter Clavelle, 111

C
Cadbury, George, 175
Cairo, 142
Cameron, David, 13
Campbell, Alastair, 108
Canal and Rivers Trust, 171
capital
   creation of, 213
   liberation of, 31–2
   new kind of ownership, 87–8
   see also capitalism

capitalism
   co-operative, 83
   egotism and, 133
   feudalism to, 214
   Fundamental Social Law and nature of, 187
   fundamentalist, 109
   industrial, 213–16 *passim*
   and inequality, 101
   market economy without, 239
   'neutralization', 237
   predatory, 113
   socially responsible, 94
   see also capital, Capitalocene Age, neoliberalism, markets
Capitalocene Age, 109
car-and-ride sharing, 41
Cashes Green CLT, 174, 177
celebrity culture, 37
Champlain Community Land Trust, 111
charity, 43
Chicago School of Economics, 188
childhood: *see* commercialization of childhood
China, 237
Church of England, 108
circular-economy movement, 219, 251
Citizens Income: *see* Guaranteed Basic Income
Citizens United (2010), 187
class system: dysfunctional, 36
Clavelle, Mayor Peter (Burlington, VT), 111
climate change, 121
   see also environmental degradation, global warming
Clinton, Bill, 12
Clinton, Hillary, 117, 121–2, 129
Clinton Foundation, 117
collaborative enquiry, 226
colour
   afterimage, 71
   experience, 70–1
   integration with threefolding, 73–4
   theory, 69–70
   see also Goethe's colour theory
Cometrics, 164
Comey, James, 122
Coming Day Stock Corporation, 92–3
command economy, 246
commercialization

of childhood, 99, 105–6
of personal life, 105
commodification
   of education, 107, 196, 199
   money and, 245
   of nature, 107
   see also marketization, privatization
Common Core (the), 121
'Common Purpose' charity, 112
Common wealth (Large), 195
       see also commonwealth
commons (the), 104, 248
   governance, 172, 179–80
   tragedy of (Ostrom), 172
   see also Commons Defence Association, Minchinhampton Common, Rodborough Common
Commons Defence Association, 175
commonwealth, 37, 87, 252, 254
       see also Common wealth
community-benefit society, 178
Community Farmland Trusts, 177–9
   Action Research Project, 177
   Fordhall Farm community buy-out, 177–9 *passim*
Community Land Trust
   defined, 176
   National Demonstration Projects, 16, 172, 174
   see also Community Farmland Trusts, land
community-supported agriculture (CSA), 125, 154, 156, 162, 166n, 251
    radical vision of early, 154–5
Conaty, Pat, 173
consciousness
   evolution of human, 230
   shifting, 74
consumerism, 37
continuous assessment, 206
co-ops, 178
   co-operative capitalism, 83
   dining-, 153
   housing, 179
   Oberlin's, 166n
   Phone Co-op, 109
core pedagogical values, 207
corporatocracy/corporations, 99, 100, 102, 187
   limits to corporate freedom, 245–6

Pearson corporation, 202
Courtney, Kevin, 201
crowd funding, 41
crypto-currencies, 41
'cultural creatives' (Ray and Anderson), 236
cultural life/sphere, 72
   free, 216, 217, 227
   liberty in, 224
   of organizations, 60–1
   Steiner on renewal, 173
   as superstructure, 238
   sympathy and antipathy in, 229
Curtis, Adam, 37

D
debate, 224–5
   dialogue vs, 226–7
debt, 39
   creation of, 218
Declaration of Independence, 119
Defence Budget (USA), 185
   see also military-industrial complex
Demeter, 248
democracy, 135, 236
   deepening of, 236
   undermining US, 187
development
   stages of, 45–6, 151
   sustainable, 139–52
dialogue, 48–9
   Bohm on, 225–6
   debate vs, 226–7
   free cultural, 224
   Principles of, 225–6
differential calculus, 217
distributed-ledger technologies, 40–2
division of labour, 242
Dommes, Gen. von, 86
Dorling, Danny, 254
drones: illegal use of, 121
duality, 35, 72
   dualistic imagination, 68
   mind–body thinking, 68
   moving beyond, 71
Dwan, Mike, 200, 202

E

Eccles, Marriner, 186
ecodical practices, 12
economic life, 72, 135, 227–8
   driving force behind, 247
   economy of love, 145–6
   emergent economy, 157–8
   financial economy, 213
   fundamental shift in, 215
   gift economy, 155
   intelligence entering the, 216
   money and the, 212
   of organizations, 60
   self-management of, 236
   socialization of, 89
   Steiner's World Economy lectures and, 214–15
   as superpower, 235
   sympathetic economy, 227–9
   sympathy and antipathy in, 229
   threefolding and, 86–90 *passim*
   value chain approach, 162–4
   wage-based, 183
   see also associative economics, circular-economy movement, economic man, economic thinking, markets, 'solidarity economy', surplus value, trade
economic man, 35
   see also economic life, 'homo economicus'
economic surpluses: *see* surplus value
economic thinking
   Chicago School, 188
   liberalism, 241–2
   neoliberal, 54
   renewal of, 30–1
   see also economic life, 'homo economicus'
economies of flow, 228
economies of scale, 228
EcorNaturaSi, 62
ecosystems framework, 8
education, 74
   academization (UK), 194–210
   accountability in, 206
   baseline assessment, 206
   commodifying, 107, 196
   corporate agenda in US, 121
   curricular freedom in, 208
   in Egypt, 142
   faith-based schools, 231
   freedom in, 97, 240, 244
   as fundamental right, 240–1
   'investment' in, 217
   National Education Service (UK), 205
   post-formal, 207
   recruitment/retention crisis, 206
   rising workloads in, 206
   'teaching for the test', 206
   threefold social order in, 199, 205
   utilitarian, 37, 199
   vouchers, 241
   see also academies programme, free schools, learning, school starting age, schooling system, Waldorf education
egotism, 37, 50, 54, 131–2
   and capitalism, 133, 247
   growth of, 183
Egypt, 139–52
   education in, 142
   Egyptian Biodynamic Association, 144
   greening the desert, 143–5
   Heliopolis University, 147
   Medical Centre, 147
empathy, 30, 50, 52, 231–2
   and civil rights, 232
   developing, 245
   equality and, 229–32
   loss of, 133
enclosure of land, 171
Encode, 40
encounter: *see* human encounter
energy management, 41
environmental degradation/destruction, 36, 48, 102
   see also climate change
Epps, Garrett, 120
equality, 27
   complex nature of, 231
   and empathy, 229–32
   'equality effect' (Dorling), 254
   see also income/wealth inequality
Erikson, Erik, 46
ethical banking: *see* banks (social)
evolution of consciousness, 230
Exchange, The (Stroud), 174
Expecting Adam (Beck), 52

F

Facebook, 6, 122, 215, 220n
Fairphone, 109
Family Assistance Plan (USA), 190
farmers' markets, 155-6
fear, 127-8
financial crisis (2008): *see* Global Financial Crisis
Fisher, Roger, 228
food movement (the), 153-67
    altruism in the, 159-60
    driving force behind, 154
    growth and decline of, 155-6
    lack of clear vision, 156
    see also community-supported agriculture
Fordhall Farm community buy-out, 177-9 *passim*
    Community Land Initiative, 178
Foucault, Michel, 207
Fox News, 122
fraternity, 27, 239, 246
free schools, 241
freedom
    economic liberalism and, 241-2
    lack of deeper understanding, 245
    limits to corporate, 245-6
    see also liberty
Freeing Education (Carnie et al.), 196
Friedman, Milton, 204
Fry, Christopher, 124
Fundamental Social Law (Steiner), 53-4
    and capitalism, 187
    defined, 182-3
    income inequalities and, 182-93 *passim*
    see also Basic Sociological Law

G

Gandhi, Mahatma, 123, 175
Gecko, Gordon, 252
General Agreement on Trade in Services (1995), 204
General Motors, 215, 220n
Generation Declaration of Human Rights, 230, 236
genetically modified organisms, 156
George, Henry, 168, 169
Getting to yes (Fisher and Ury), 228
Gidley, Jennifer, 207
gift economy, 155

gift money (Steiner), 32, 216-19 *passim*
    taxation as forced, 217
Gintis, Herbert, 195
Glass-Steagall Act (USA), 105
Global Financial Crisis (2008), 211, 245
global warming, 245
    see also climate change
globalization, 29, 242
    brotherly form of, 134
    elite, 100, 101
    individualization and, 243
    International Forum on, 242
    movement for just, 249
Gloucestershire (UK), 102-3
    incinerator, 102-3
    see also Stroud
GLS bank (Germany), 218, 220n, 251
GMO, 156
Goethe, J.W. von, 69, 225
    see also Goethe's colour theory, Goethean conversation
Goethe's colour theory, 67
    colour wheel, 70
Goethean conversation, 225
Goetheanum: the first, 24
Goldman Sachs, 102
Good Food Network, 160
Google, 6, 215, 220n
Gove, Michael, 203
governmental operational systems, 41
Graeber, David, 135
Gramdan movement, 175
Great Depression (USA), 186, 252
Great EU Repeal Bill (2017), 113
Great transformation, The (Polanyi), 171
Green Party, 238
Grenfell disaster, 170
Gross National Happiness, 255
growth fetishism, 245
Guaranteed Basic Income, 54, 190-2, 248
guard labour spending (US), 183, 185-6

H

Habermas, Jürgen, 57n
Haeften, Liet. Corp. Hans von, 80
Häfner, Gerald, 17, 127-36, 259

Hawken, Paul, 109, 125
healthcare, 41
  health marketization, 106–7
  Obama-care, 244
  spending in the USA, 184
  see also medicine, National Health Service
Heliopolis University for Sustainable Development, 147, 150, 152n
Herrmannstorfer, Udo, 244
Hill, Octavia, 170–6 *passim*
Hinckley Point power station, 103
Hippocratic oath, 65
Hitler, Adolf, 75, 86
Hobbes, Thomas, 241
holacracy, 40
Hollins, Charlotte, 178
homes
  permanently affordable, 174
  see also housing, Marylebone Housing Society, Redditch Co-op Homes, Stockholm co-housing schemes
'homo economicus', 241
Honda Purchasing, 251
House, Richard, 18, 194–210, 260
housing
  bankers exploiting, 170
  benefit, 170
  co-ops, 179
  crisis, 170–1
  in Denmark, 171
  'free' market in, 170
  German, 170
  right to decent, 170
  Swedish, 170
  see also homes, Marylebone Housing Society, Redditch Co-op Homes, Stockholm co-housing schemes
Howard, Ebenezer, 171, 175
human being
  images of the, 34–43
  see also threefold human being
human encounter, 29–30
  dynamics of interaction, 223–4
  in threefold society, 223–34 *passim*
human rights: *see* rights
Humboldt, Wilhelm von, 247

I
Ideological State Apparatus (Althusser), 195
images of the human being, 34–43
income/wealth inequality
  effect of (US), 182–4
  global, 128–9
  price of inequality, The (Stiglitz), 187
  in the USA, 54, 120, 182–93 *passim*
impact investing, 8
impact investment movement, 218
Independent Natural Food Retailers Association, 160, 164
individual consciousness: emergence of, 53
individualism: growth of, 230
individualization, 28–30 *passim*
  globalization and, 243
Industrial and Provident Society, 177
Industrial Society for Community Benefit, 178
inequality
  capitalism and, 101
  growing, 245
  see also income inequality
international aid, 43
International Association of Partnership for Ecology and Trade, 146, 148
International Federation for Human Rights, 230
International Forum on Globalization, 242
Internet
  rules for the, 134
  shrillness of, 133
  socially programmed robots and the, 133
'invisible hand', 241, 242, 246–7
Isaacs, Bill, 226
ISIS Organic company, 145
Isle of Eigg community buy-out, 179

J
Jackson, Wes, 154
Jefferson, Thomas, 108
Johnson, Simon, 187

K
Kaiser Karl I (Austria), 79–80
Kaiser Wilhelm II (Germany), 80
Kalundborg Institute for Industrial Symbiosis,

110
karma, 50–2
Karp, Robert, 18, 153–67, 251, 260
Khan, Sadiq, 252
King, Dr Bronwyn, 109, 255
King, Martin Luther, 190–1
    letter from a Birmingham jail, 183
King, Scott, 175
Klein, Naomi, 109–10
kleptocracy, 120
Korten, David, 188
Kristianstad, 253
Kühn, Hans, 80–1

L
labour, 39
    guard labour spending (US), 183
    reproduction of labour power, 195
    'spirit transforming', 215
    theory of value, 215
Labour Party manifesto (2017), 205–6
laissez-faire economy: *see* markets, neoliberalism
Laloux, Ferdinand, 236
land, 39, 168–81
    enclosure of, 171
    as finite commodity, 168–9
    as a right, 168, 179
    Steiner's ideas on, 170, 172, 179
    trading of, 31
    trusteeship bodies, 171
    see also Community Land Trust, Land Gift Movement, Land For People conference, Land Reform Act, land trusteeship
Land Gift Movement, 175
Land For People conference (2002), 174
Land Reform Act (Scotland), 172, 179
land trusteeship: Steiner on, 172
language, 47
Large, Martin, 12–20, 99–116, 168–81, 194, 195, 208, 235–56, 258
lean thinking (Jones and Womack), 63
'lean' process/business approach, 66, 228
Leap Manifesto (Canada), 109
learning
    as a commodity, 199
    core pedagogical values, 207
    spiritual pedagogies, 207
    see also education
left–right schema, 235–8 *passim*
Leopold, Aldo, 168
Lerchenfeld, Count Otto von, 77
Lerner, Michael, 120
Letchworth Garden City, 171, 175
LGBT rights 48
liberty, 27
    see also freedom
Lievegoed, Bernard, 46
Lindenau, Christof, 55
Lissau, Rudi, 220n
listening, 49–50
    deep, 49
Living Wage Movement, 54, 190
loan money, 216–19 *passim*
Lotus company, 145
love, 131–2, 207
    economy of, 145–6
low-trust culture, 206
Ludendorff, Gen Erich, 81–2

M
MacArthur, Ellen, 13–14
McLeod, Kevin, 174, 177
Mandela, Nelson, 252
Mansell, Warwick, 198, 200–1
Marcuse, Herbert, 57n
marketization of health, 106–7
markets
    boom-and-bust financial, 218
    without capitalism, 239
    as 'custodial', 247
    factors of production-, 244
    fundamentalism of, 109, 187–8, 200, 247, 251
    'invisible hand', 241, 242
    moral limits to, 107
    and price formation, 246
    triumphalism, 107
    see also capitalism, 'invisible hand'
Marx, Karl, 213, 214
    dialogue with Marxism, 238–9
Marylebone Housing Society, 175
Mead, Margaret, 114
media manipulation, 122

medicine, 65
  see also healthcare
Mehta, JoJo, 103
Middle East crisis, 245
military conflicts, 36
military-industrial complex, 107–8, 123
Mill, John Stewart, 168, 171, 175, 178
Minchinhampton Common (Stroud), 172
mindfulness, 255
Mintzberg, Henry, 104, 112–14 *passim*
Molloy, Caroline, 106, 254–5
Molt, Emil, 82–3
Moltke, Gen. Helmuth von: memoir of, 83–6 *passim*
monarchism, 26, 40
Monbiot, George, 254
money, 39
  in American politics, 120
  creation, 218
  destruction of, 218
  dysfunctional system of, 214
  excess in circulation, 218
  instinctive handling of, 211
  nature of, 216
  new understanding of, 135
  overwhelming power of, 63
  reinvention of, 251
  and the threefolding movement, 211–20
  treated as a commodity, 245
  see also gift money, loan money, purchase money
Montague, Peter, 184
Morris, William, 175
Motto of the Social Ethic (Steiner), 54
Moynihan, Daniel Patrick, 190
mutual aid, 192

N
narcissism: encouragement of, 132
National Community Land Trust (UK): *see* Community Land Trust
National Coop Grocers Association, 160
National Education Service (UK), 205
National Curriculum (UK), 197
National Demonstration Projects: see Community Land Trust

National Health Service (UK), 106–7, 110
  as institutional threefolding, 65–6
  marketization of, 255
National Socialism, 237–8
National Trust (UK), 172, 175
  Act (1907), 175
nationalism, 24, 113
NatureTex, 145
Needleman, Jacob, 119
negotiation: aim of, 228
neoliberalism, 12, 183, 199, 203–7 *passim*, 236, 244
  defined, 208n
  economic orthodoxy, 54, 188
  story of, 252
New confessions of an economic hit man (Perkins), 103
New Deal (USA), 188
New Economics Foundation, 173
news manipulation, 37
NHS: *see* National Health Service
Nixon, Richard, 190
Novo Nordisk, 110

O
Obama-care, 244
Oberlin College (OH), 153
Occupy movement, 48, 183
Old souls (Schroder), 52
omnivore's dilemma, The (Pollan), 156
Open Spaces Society, 175
'operational property', 237
Organic Consumers Association, 160
organic food/agriculture, 156, 159, 248
Organic Trade Association, 160
organizations
  cultural life of, 60–1
  design of, 61–2
  economic life of, 60
  organizational development cycle, 64
  rights life of, 60
  social dimension of an, 61
Osborne, George, 197
Ostrom, Elinor, 172, 180
Owen, Wilfred, 23
Oxfam, 128–9

P
Paine, Tom, 114
Painswick Inn, 173–4
'Parable of the old man and the young' (Owen), 23
Patterson, Bob, 173
Paul, Ron, 244
Perkins, John, 103
Perlas, Nicanor, 6–10, 235–6, 260
Perry, Rick, 130
personal choice, 28
Philippines, 7–8
  Development Plan, 8
Pickett, Kate, 184, 254
Picture of Dorian Grey (Wilde), 118
Piketty, Thomas, 101–2
Pilley, Greg, 177
plutocracy, 36
  kleptocratic, 100
Polanyi, Karl, 171
'Politics of Belonging' (Monbiot), 254
Pollan, Michael, 156
Polzer-Hoditz, Arthur, 79, 80
Polzer-Hoditz, Ludwig, 78, 79
post-formal education (Gidley), 207
poverty in USA, 184
power: humanity's relationship to, 34–43
Prague Spring, 249
Precariat Charter, The (Standing), 36
predatory capitalism, 113
Presencing Institute, 252
presidential election (US, 2016), 117–26
price of inequality, The (Stiglitz), 187
'principled negotiation' approach (Fisher and Ury), 228
Pring, Professor Richard, 196
privatization, 99, 100, 203–7 *passim*, 252
  and health marketization, 106–7
profit(s)
  aggressive pursuit of, 219
  category of, 246
  see also capitalism, neoliberalism, surplus value
property rights, 236
Pruitt, Scott, 130
psychodynamics of policy making, 206
public goods, 248
  see also commons
public policy network paradigm (UN), 8

purchase money, 216–19 *passim*

R
Ray, Paul, 159, 236
Rayner, Angela, 202
rebalancing society, 99–116
Redditch Co-op Homes, 179
Regan, Ronald, 252
regulation
  addiction to, 236
  excesses of, 247
  financial, 189
Reich, Robert, 186–7
reincarnation, 50–2
Reinventing Organizations (Laloux), 236
residue of unresolved statism (RUST), 8
responsibilities
  fear of, 245
  rights and, 231
Rifkin, Jeremy, 191
rights (life), 55, 248
  empathy and civil, 232
  human, 236
  International Federation for Human Rights, 230
  of organizations, 60
  primacy of, 239
  vs responsibilities, 231
  rights-based politics, 109
  Universal Declaration of Human Rights, 230, 236
  see also property rights
Robinson, Sir Ken, 207
Rodborough Common (Stroud), 172
Roosevelt, Franklin D., 188
Rowntree, Joseph, 175
  Charitable and Housing Trusts, 175
ruling ideology (Althusser), 195
Ruskin, John, 169, 174–5

S
Safe and Accurate Food Labelling Act (2015), 156
St Paul, 212
Sandel, Michael, 107
Sanders, Bernie, 111, 122, 244
Saunders, Glen, 18, 211–20, 251, 261

scale economies, 228
Schaefer, Christopher, 17, 44–58, 117–26, 182–93, 261
Schall, Dr, 85
Scharmer, Otto, 252
school starting age (England), 206
schooling system (England), 195
   in Germany, 241
   industrial factory paradigm, 208
   see also education, free schools, school starting age
Schroder, Tom, 52
Schulden (Graeber), 135
Scott, Andrew, 16–17, 34–43, 261
Scott, James C., 199, 203
Scott Cato, Dr Molly, 173
Seeing like a state (Scott), 199
Seidler, Ernst, 79–80
SEKEM (Egypt), 7, 114, 139–62, 245, 250–1, 254
   Development Foundation, 149, 152n
   Environmental Science Centre, 149
   Future of agriculture in Europe, 150
   Heliopolis University, 147, 150, 152n
   today, 150–1
   Vocational Training Centre, 149
Self, Will, 170–1
self-interest
   myth of, 72
   see also selfishness
selfishness
   triumph of, 120
   see also self-interest
selflessness, 50, 247
self-sufficiency, 247
Senge, Peter, 226
shadow
   Jung on the, 118
   transforming the, 122–5
   of the USA, 118–22
Shaping globalization (Perlas), 8
Shumann, Michael, 157
'Sleep of Prisoners, The' (Fry), 124
Smith, Adam, 241
social banking: *see* banks (social), Triodos
'social bot', 136
social change, 47
Social Darwinism, 188, 251

social ideals: emergence of, 25–7
social life, 45–8 *passim*
   essential features of, 48–9
   fundamental change in, 214
   liberty in, 226
   see also anti-social forces
social renewal, 252–3
social/societal threefolding: *see* threefold organization, threefold social order, threefolding
socialism: voluntary, 83, 92, 159
socialization of the economy, 89
socially programmed robots, 133
Socratic method, 225–6
'solidarity economy', 248
Solnit, Rebecca, 56–7, 252
soul
   consciousness-, 151
   mind-, 151
   qualities, 150–1
   sentient-, 151
   of society, 46
SPACE, The: *see* Stroud Performing Arts Centre
spirit
   of the Community (Steiner), 165
   of society, 46
spirit level, The (Wilkinson and Pickett), 254
Spock, Marjorie, 225
stages of development, 45–6
Stalinism, 237–8
Standing, Guy, 36
Standing Rock oil pipeline, 109
state (the), 47
   anti-state notions, 239
   capture of, 252
   hiving-off of assets, 204
   Ideological State Apparatus (Althusser), 195
   'nanny', 236
   new role for, 243
   seeing like a (Scott), 199, 204
   state–business duopoly, 103
   see also statism
statism, 26, 102, 113
   accountability practices, 207
statistics: manipulation of, 203
Steiner, Rudolf, 13–16 *passim*, 44, 59, 72, 165, 168–9, 171, 182–3, 187, 191–2, 230, 231, 241, 243, 250

anthroposophy of, 143, 150
Appeal to the German People..., 82
Basic Sociological Law, 28, 53, 239
on biodynamic farming, 177
on cultural renewal, 173
on education, 194–5
and the emergent economy, 157–8
Fundamental Social Law, 53–4, 182–93 *passim*
gift money, 32
ideas on land, 170, 179
as individualist anarchist, 239
on karmic connection, 51
on land trusteeship, 172
on money, 216–19 *passim*
Motto of the Social Ethic, 54
'new sympathies', 227, 229
as social activist, 9, 82
Spirit of the Community, 165
talks to workers, 88–92 *passim*
Threefold Commonwealth, 72
threefold image of society, 23–33 *passim*
threefold social order, 55, 199, 208n
threefolding and, 75–97, 131, 139, 253, 254
Toward social renewal, 10, 16, 55, 77, 82
vision for schools, 20–45, 205
wage system, 31
World Economy lectures, 212, 214–16 *passim*, 219
Steiner education: *see* Waldorf education
Stevenson, Dr Ian, 52
Stiglitz, Joseph, 187, 189–90, 251
Stockholm co-housing schemes, 179
stories, 250–6
Strawe, Christoph, 19, 235–49, 262
Stroud (Glos, UK), 173
academization protest, 197–8
see also Cashes Green CLT, Exchange (The), Fordhall Farm community buy-out, Mehta (JoJo), Minchinhampton Common, Painswick Inn, Rodborough Common, Stroud Brewery, Stroud Common Wealth, Stroud Performing Arts Centre, Stroud Town Council, 'Wynstones Conferences'
Stroud Brewery, 173
Stroud Common Wealth, 107, 173, 177, 178
Stroud Performing Arts Centre (SPACE), 174
Stroud Town Council, 172

Stuttgart Waldorf school, 93
sub-prime mortgage scam, 170
Sunways Farm, 155
supply chain management, 42
surplus value: creation of, 215
see also profit(s)
surveillance, 37
of US citizens, 121
Sustainability Flower, 139–40, 146
sustainable development, 139–52 *passim*
sustainable integrated area development (SIAD), 8
Sustainable Food Trade Association, 160
sympathetic economy, 227–9
sympathy, 30, 223–4, 229, 232
sympathetic economy, 227–9
Syria, 245
'systemic responsibility', 129
systems theory, 37

T
taxation
as forced gift money, 217
levels, 188–9
on the rich, 121
Tea Party Movement, 239, 244
teaching
re-professionalizing, 208
'for the test', 206
Temple Wilton Farm (NH), 155, 166n, 177
Tennyson, Ros, 111
Terre de Liens farm land trust, 179
terrorism, 37, 127
9/11 attack, 44
'third way', 237
Threefold Commonwealth (Steiner), 72
threefold human being, 26–7
threefold image of society (Steiner), 23–33 *passim*
threefold social order, 14–15, 55, 208n, 250
in education, 199
encounter in, 223–34
money and, 211–20
nine propositions for a, 44–58
Steiner's withdrawal from, 214
threefolding, 6–10 *passim*, 13, 25, 37, 55, 75–97

    passim, 114, 131, 139, 150, 173, 207, 235–50
        passim, 253, 254
            approach to schooling, 197
            argument against, 236
            between capitalism and socialism, 237
            economic side of, 86–90 *passim*
            in human history, 248–9
            implicit, 99–100
            integration with colour, 73–4
            land and, 168–9
            macro-level, 7
            Memoranda of 1917 (Steiner), 78–9
            of money itself, 214–19 *passim*
            National Health Service and, 65–6
            primary approach to, 67–74
            and rebalancing society, 99–116
            sidelining of, 236
            as utopian vision, 239
            at work in organizations, 59–66
Tillerson, Rex (Exxon), 102
Titmuss, Richard, 106
Tolstoy, Leo, 175
Toward social renewal (Steiner), 10, 16, 55, 77, 82, 87–9 *passim*,
Toynbee, Arnold, 46
trade: facilitating healthy, 160
tragedy of the commons (Ostrom), 172
    see also commons (the)
transhumanism, 238
Transition Towns, 111, 255
Triodos bank (Neths), 218, 220n, 251
    see also banking: social
tri-sectoral partnership, 112, 235
tri-sectoral society, 104
Trump, President Donald, 12, 102, 117–25 *passim*, 129–30, 133, 184, 188
trusteeship, 246
    see also trusts
trusts: *see* Biodynamic Land Trust, Bourneville Village Trust, Canal and Rivers Trust, Champlain Community Land Trust, Community Land Trust, Joseph Rowntree Charitable and Housing Trusts land trusteeship, National Trust, Terre de Liens farm land trust, trusteeship, Woodland Trust

U
Uber, 252
Udell, Edward, 17, 75–97, 262
United States, 47–8, 54, 243–4
    American Civil Liberties Union, 122
    American Dream, 125
    Citizens United (2010), 187
    Declaration of Independence, 119
    Defence Budget, 185
    Family Assistance Plan, 190
    the food movement in, 153–67 *passim*
    Great Depression in, 186
    guard labour spending in, 183, 185–6
    healthcare spending, 184
    hidden money in politics, 120
    inequalities in, 54, 183–93 *passim*
    New Deal, 188
    new economy in, 153
    poverty rate in, 184
    presidential election (2016), 117–26
    Presidents of the, 128
    prison population in, 185–6
    protectionist tendencies, 237
    selfish interests in, 245
    the shadow of, 118–22
    Tea Party Movement, 239
    undermining democracy in, 187
    wealth inequalities in, 184
Universal Declaration of Human Rights, 230
Ury, Bill, 228
USA: *see* United States

V
value chain approach, 162–4
Varoufakis, Yanis, 39
Versailles Treaty, 10, 86
voluntary associations, 109
voluntary 'socialism', 83, 92, 159
voting, 42

W
wage system (Steiner), 31
    Living Wage Movement, 54, 190
Wakefield City Academies Trust, 202
Waldorf education/schools, 207, 245

in SEKEM, 149
  Stuttgart school, 93
wealth inequality: *see* income/wealth inequality
Webster, Professor Charles, 106
Weleda, 93
Wells Fargo Bank, 118
What money can't buy (Sandel), 107
Where do we go from here? (M.L. King), 190–1
White Dog Café (Wicks), 110
Wicks, Judy, 110
Wilde, Oscar, 208n
Wilkinson, Richard, 184, 254
Wilshaw, Sir Michael, 201
Wilson, Woodrow, 81
  national self-determination, 10, 24
Winstanley, Gerard, 168
Woodhead, Chris, 196
Woodland Trust, 172
work in organizations, 59–66
World Economy lectures (Steiner), 212, 214–16
  passim, 219
World Social Forums, 237
  Porte Allegre, 110
Württemberg government, 82–3
'Wynstones Conferences', 220n

Y
Young of Dartington, Lord Michael, 196
youth unemployment, 129

Other Books by Hawthorn Press

Common Wealth
For a free, equal, mutual and sustainable society
Martin Large

Just when 'the market' nearly took over all areas of life, the credit, climate and democratic crunches came along, challenging us to rebuild a society that works well for all. *Common Wealth* asks, 'How can we build a more free, equal, mutual and sustainable society?'

We know that we don't want a 'market state'. This turns our public services into businesses, uses relentless surveillance to secure compliance, destroys the planet for corporate growth and widens inequality. However, tripolar society is emerging as an alternative, where civil society, government and business push back the market, and work in partnership for the common good.

'Only by sharing the value of our common resources more fairly, is humanity likely to be able to avoid the worldwide self-destruction towards which our present path of development is leading us. In his masterly new book Martin Large explores the changes this implies for the structures of business, government and civil society and the relationships between them.

He identifies land value taxation and a citizen's income as among the measures that will help to bring the changes about. Please read it if you care about the future of our species.'

James Robertson, a founder of the New Economics Foundation and author of *Transforming Economic Life*

'All around us we see evidence of the sort of life we create when we forget that all our wealth is common wealth. Let's celebrate a book which reminds us of that fact, and gives clear guidance on how to make it a reality in the modern world.'

Molly Scott Cato, MEP

'Brings us bang up to date and tackles difficult questions from the perspective of a man who has made new ideas work. In fact, he has inspired me to re-think much of what I do.'

Alastair Sawday, Foreword

'A spine tingling read which leaves you feeling like you have lost kilos of weight from the hope it injects into your heart that is forever seeking real and powerful collaboration'
　　　Councillor Skeena Rathor, Labour Party National Policy Forum Member

'It is truly a manifesto for our time.'　　　　　　Mary Tasker, *Resurgence*, Issue 262

'A rest from the insanity of the day – Common Wealth.'
　　　Richard Murphy, www.taxresearch.org.uk/Blog, February 15th, 2011

256 pages; 234 × 156mm; pages; 978-1-903458-98-3; hardback

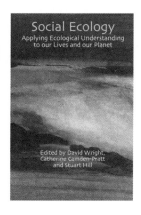

Social Ecology
Applying ecological understanding to our lives and our planet
Edited by David Wright, Catherine Camden-Pratt, Stuart Hill

Social Ecology addresses the burning question of how to apply ecological understanding to every aspect of our lives. The 27 contributors, all of whom have directly or indirectly contributed to the teaching of social ecology in Australia and beyond, share their experiences in this 'coming of age' anthology of keynote articles.

Social ecology provides a holistic framework for change, based on the interrelationships between the personal, social, environmental and 'spiritual'. It helps us understand how we got here, and how to realise more sustainable, caring futures. Educators and students from all disciplines will enrich their learning with insights and principles from social ecology.

'An excellent anthology giving a superb and exciting overview of the emerging and vitally important field of social ecology. We need to implement the ideas in this book as a matter of utmost urgency if we humans are to have a viable future on this planet.'
　　　　　　　　　　Dr Stephan Harding, Schumacher College, UK
　　　　　　　and author of *Animate Earth: Science, Intuition and Gaia*

336 pages; 234 × 156mm; 978-1-907359-11-8; paperback

Adam Curle
Radical Peacemaker
Tom Woodhouse and John Paul Lederach

Adam Curle's pioneering work as founding Professor of Peace Studies at Bradford University was far more significant in the peace studies field than is generally recognised. Even though his ideas were way ahead of his time, they have not been adequately taught and understood – partly because of the dominance of realist approaches to political science and partly because his writings are not now easily available. This book captures his core contributions in an accessible, edited form so that the breadth of his work can be introduced to a broader audience. It offers unique insights into the spiritual and external dimensions of making peace, and includes some striking personal poems from Adam himself.

'This book is both a tribute to the work of Adam Curle and testimony to his living legacy. It is also a timely reminder of the importance of personal integrity and an ethical world view, to better navigate contemporary challenges of conflict, violence and the turmoil of change.'
Judith Large, Senior Research Fellow, Conflict Analysis Research Centre (CARC), University of Kent, Canterbury, UK

262pp; 234 x 156mm; 978-1-907359-79-8; paperback

Confronting Conflict
A first-aid kit for handling conflict
Friedrich Glasl

Conflict costs! When tensions and differences are ignored they grow into conflicts, injuring relationships and organisations. So, how can we confront conflict successfully?

Dr Friedrich Glasl has worked with conflict resolution in companies, schools and communities for over 30 years, earning him and his techniques enormous respect. *Confronting Conflict* is authoritative and up to date, containing new examples, exercises, theory and techniques.

Confronting Conflict will be useful for managers, facilitators, management lecturers and professionals such as teachers and community workers, mediators and workers in dispute resolution.

192pp; 216 × 138mm; 978-1-869890-71-1; paperback

Ordering Books

If you have difficulties ordering Hawthorn Press books from a bookshop, you can order direct from our website www.hawthornpress.com or the following distributors:

UNITED KINGDOM
BookSource
50 Cambuslang Road,
Glasgow, G32 8NB
Tel: (0845) 370 0063
Email: orders@booksource.net

USA/NORTH AMERICA
Steiner Books
PO Box 960, Herndon,
VA 20172-0960, USA
Tel: (800) 856 8664
Email: service@steinerbooks.org
www.steinerbooks.org

Waldorf Books
Phil & Angela's Company, Inc.
1271 NE Hwy 99W #196, McMinnville,
Oregon 97128, USA
Tel: (503) 472-4610
Email: info@waldorfbooks.com
www.waldorfbooks.com

AUSTRALIA & NEW ZEALAND
Footprint Books Pty Ltd 4 /8 Jubilee Avenue,
Warriewood, NSW 2102, Australia
Tel: (02) 9997 3973
Email: info@footprint.com.au
www.footprint.com.au

www.hawthornpress.com

Today's advanced economies have reached a critical turning-point. Free, Mutual and Equal *shows a way ahead for rebalancing society, through a co-operative commonwealth economy based on 'voluntary socialism', with a rights-based state and a flourishing civil society – all working for the common good.*
David Drew Ph.D., MP, Shadow Minister for Rural Affairs, UK

Celebrates the growing diversity of ways to secure a pluralist commonwealth. Land reform, democratic ways to control money and co-operative ownership are exemplified as core foundations for building a new economy for the common good.
Pat Conaty, Common Futures, co-author of *The Resilience Imperative: Cooperative Transitions to a Steady-state Economy*

The world desperately needs new thinking and new narratives that transcend traditional disciplines and creatively overcome fixed polarisation. This collection of diverse essays shows how Rudolf Steiner's innovative three-fold thinking can be revisioned, 100 years on, to address the urgent issues now facing our planet, and the creative responses needed in politics, economics, education, ecology and culture. At the heart of all their thinking are the values of mutuality, collaboration and participation.
Peter Hawkins, Professor of Leadership, Henley Business School; author of *Leadership Team Coaching*

New Zealand has been an early adopter of both the best and the worst of social change and economic dogma. This book comes at a time when many here are waking up to the toxic effects of politics, economics and culture trespassing on each others' territory, and it offers pathways to a balanced society with inspirational examples, such as Sekem, on what it takes to get there.
Carolyn Hughes, Chair, The Land Trust NZ

Experts across the disciplines offer a timely introduction to the social threefolding concepts that will free the planet from the iron grip of market forces.
Frances Hutchinson, author of *The Politics of Money*, editor of *The Social Artist*